Forbidden

American

English

About the Author

Richard A. Spears, Ph.D., Associate Professor of Linguistics, Northwestern University. Specialist in lexicography; English language structure; phonetics; language standardization and codification; English as a second language; American culture.

Forbidden

American

English

Richard A. Spears

PASSPORT BOOKS
a division of *NTC Publishing Group*
Lincolnwood, Illinois USA

1993 Printing

Published by Passport Books, a division of NTC Publishing Group.
© 1990 by NTC Publishing Group, 4255 West Touhy Avenue,
Lincolnwood (Chicago), Illinois 60646-1975 U.S.A.
Manufactured in the United States of America.
Library of Congresss Catalog Card Number: 90-60250

2 3 4 5 6 7 8 9 TS 9 8 7 6 5 4 3

CONTENTS

TO THE USER

Why a Dictionary of This Type?

Within the last thirty years, the restrictions on the kinds of vocabulary, visual imagery, and subject matter that can be presented to the public have been reduced considerably. Films, television (especially cable television), the stage, print media, and even radio no longer avoid offending the most hypercritical segments of society. At the same time there are still major areas of American society where there are significant restrictions on the vocabulary that can be used in everyday social interactions. This dictionary has been prepared for persons who seek guidance in avoiding giving offense with potentially offensive vocabulary. Included among such persons are nonnative speakers within the U.S. and the foreign consumers of exported U.S. entertainment, especially films and television.

The Point of View Expressed in This Dictionary

American society has always been pluralistic. For that reason, it is not now, nor has it ever been, possible to make general and accurate statements about American tastes, values, and behavior. *Forbidden American English,* as the title indicates, presents a specialized vocabulary from the point of view of persons whose tastes and values cause them to avoid or renounce the use of these expressions. There are, of course, other points of view. One view might be that none of the expressions in this dictionary ought to be forbidden. Another view might consider the sexual expressions to be harmless and the racial epithets to be unspeakably vile. This dictionary does not seek to vindicate or eradicate any particular point of view. It is formulated in such a way as to provide guidance to persons, especially nonnative speakers, who are not familiar with the meanings of these expressions, and who wish to avoid the social consequences of offending people with this kind of vocabulary.

This dictionary does not argue for or against the use of forbidden vocabulary. It is a frank and straightforward resource for those who wish to learn about a very specialized kind of vocabulary. As pointed out frequently in the comments in the various entries, many of these expressions *will* hurt people deeply, provoke violence, or reflect negatively on the people who use them.

The Examples

The examples used in the dictionary are as realistic as it is possible to make them. Although it is intended that the examples *demonstrate* the offensiveness of some of the expressions, there is no intention of offending anyone in the process. Readers will note that two qualities, hostility and humor, are evident throughout the examples. From the point of view of the typical users of this vocabulary, the tone and style of the examples would be recognized as natural in the settings presented in the examples.

The Notes and Comments

The usage patterns of the various expressions are indicated by comments within each entry and, in some cases, by reference to a set of notes at the end of the book. Occasionally, examples appropriate to an entire class of words or meanings are presented only in the notes rather than at the individual entries. The notes apply to all the expressions having a particular meaning, whether the expressions are in this dictionary or not.

A thorough analysis of the use of this kind of vocabulary would have to account for many variables, such as point of view, setting, age of the speaker, sex of the speaker, age of the audience, sex of the audience, tone of voice, intent of the speaker, the audience's perception of the speaker's intent, etc. Most of these variables lie in the realm of the speech act itself and are not usually considered to be inherent to the expressions involved. It is, of course, possible to analyze and categorize taboo language, but it is not possible to make people use these expressions according to the analysis. In actual use, much of the effect of this vocabulary is dependent on performance variables, especially tone of voice.

The general and essential characteristics of this kind of language include (1) the exercise of total freedom, (2) spontaneous customizing, (3) shock, (4) transgression against social custom, and (5) innovation. It is hard to capture the patterns of usage for a kind of language that delights in breaking the rules. A dictionary of this type shows the *potential* uses of expressions as realized possibilities—not limits—on use. The notes and comments found here are designed only to provide the information needed to explain the notion of "forbidden" or "taboo" vocabulary. The aim is to enhance understanding rather than to promote use.

Who Uses This Vocabulary?

It should not be assumed that all Americans know and use all these expressions. In fact, there is virtually no one in the entire world who knows and uses every single expression listed in this dictionary. In the last three decades the communications media have brought these expressions into our living rooms and movie theaters. The "Free Speech" movement of the 1960s expanded both the users of, and audiences for, previously forbidden subjects and the forbidden vocabulary associated with them. Hardly anyone can escape from at least hearing some of these expressions.

The sexual patterns of the use of forbidden vocabulary have also been in flux. The free and constant use of "foul language" on the part of men in groups, such as in the military or in all-male work places, has long been regarded as typical. The use of such language in the presence of women (and children) was, and still is for a broad segment of the population, a strong social taboo. The historical pattern of the male use of forbidden expressions, and the female opposition to the use of forbidden expressions, has come under strong challenge in the last three decades. Most strikingly, the proponents of the "women's liberation" movements of the 1960s and '70s and, later, the feminists have adopted and adapted the typical male patterns of forbidden language use for their own purposes. It is still too early to predict how these conflicting sexual patterns of forbidden language use will be resolved, if, indeed, they ever will.

Young people also remain the creators and prime users of forbidden vocabulary. As many teachers, parents, and grandparents have learned, the use of forbidden vocabulary among the young is amazingly widespread.

The notes and comments in this dictionary attempt to show what the *typical* use patterns are for each entry. The statements about typical users really describe the kinds of people for whom the vocabulary items seem most appropriate—given the point of view of this dictionary. There is no notion that the phrase *typical of male-to-male talk* means that only males use the expression in question; it simply means that the expression is perceived as more typical of male-to-male use than any other use. The comments about typicality refer to perceived typical patterns; they are not limitations. One would expect that many of the expressions marked as *typical of male-to-male talk* are already in frequent use by females.

How Much Forbidden Vocabulary Exists?

At any time, there are thousands of expressions that some people—or even most people—would find offensive to some degree. New uses for expressions of this type can be made at will, and most such expressions have variations in form and meaning. This dictionary contains a sampling consisting either of high-frequency, widespread expressions or expressions that have worked their way into our consciousness by way of the communications media.

HOW TO USE THIS DICTIONARY

1. Expressions are entered in an alphabetical order that ignores hyphens, spaces, and other punctuations. Each expression is entered in its normal form and word order.

2. An entry head may have one or more alternate forms. The main entry head and its alternate forms are printed in **boldface type,** and the alternate forms are preceded by AND. Two or more alternate forms are separated by a comma. Words enclosed in parentheses in any entry head are optional. For example: **(poor) white trash** stands for **poor white trash** and **white trash.** When entry heads are referred to in the dictionary, they are printed in *slanted type*.

3. Some of the entry heads have more than one major sense. These meanings are numbered with boldface numerals. Numbered senses may also have additional forms that are shown in boldface type after the numeral. See, for example, **all-night trick.**

4. Alternate forms of the definitions are separated by semicolons, and most definitions are followed by comments or explanations in parentheses. See, for example, **barf.**

5. Each entry or sense has either two examples printed in *italics* or a reference to a note containing examples.

6. The entries or words within entries that are judged difficult to pronounce are provided with a phonetic transcription.

The transcription system is explained in the PRONUNCIA-
TION GUIDE that begins on page xiv.

7. Many of the examples utilize "eye-dialect" spelling to indicate that certain words are contracted or shortened in the
colloquial speech style of the examples. These words are
gimme "give me," *gonna* "going to," *kinda* "kind of," *lemme*
"let me," *oughtta* "ought to," *outa* "out of," *sorta* "sort of,"
wanna "want to," and *ya* "you."

8. Some entries refer to one or more notes. These notes begin at the back of the book on page 204.

9. The TERMS section explains the vocabulary of the ex-
planatory matter used in this dictionary. Neither convention-
ally used language nor simple grammatical terminology is
explained in this section. The TERMS section begins on page
xvi.

PRONUNCIATION GUIDE

Some expressions in this dictionary are followed by a phonetic transcription in the International Phonetic Alphabet (IPA) symbols. These expressions include words whose pronunciation is not predictable from their spellings, difficult or unfamiliar words, and words where the stress placement is contrastive or unique. The style of pronunciation reflected here is informal and tends to fit the register in which the expression would normally be used. The transcriptions distinguish between [a] and [ɔ] and between [w] and [ʍ] even though not all Americans do so. In strict IPA fashion, [j], rather than the [y] substitute, is used for the initial sound in "yellow." The most prominent syllable in a multisyllabic word is *preceded* by the stress mark, [ˈ]. There may be additional prominent or stressed syllables in compounds and phrases, but their weight and placement varies from speaker to speaker and utterance to utterance.

The use of spaces, hyphens, AND, or OR in phonetic transcriptions echoes the use of spaces, hyphens, AND, or OR in the preceding entry heads. The use of "..." in a transcription indicates that easy-to-pronounce words have been omitted from the transcription. Parentheses used in a transcription either correspond to parentheses in the preceding entry head or indicate optional elements in the transcription. For instance, in [ˈɑrtsi ˈkræf(t)si] "artsy-craftsy," the "t" may or may not be pronounced.

The following chart shows the American English values for each of the IPA symbols used in the phonetic transcriptions. To use the chart, first find the phonetic symbol whose value you want to determine. The two English words to the right of the symbol contain examples of the sound for which the phonetic symbol stands. The letters in boldface type indicate where the sound in question is found in the English word.

[ɑ] { stop / top }   [ɚ] { bird / turtle }   [m̩] { bottom / chasm }   [t] { top / pot }

[æ] { sat / track }   [f] { feel / if }   [n] { new / funny }   [tʃ] { cheese / pitcher }

[ɑʊ] { cow / now }   [g] { get / frog }   [n̩] { button / kitten }   [θ] { thin / faith }

[ɑɪ] { bite / my }   [h] { hat / who }   [ŋ] { bring / thing }   [u] { food / blue }

[b] { beet / bubble }   [i] { feet / leak }   [o] { coat / wrote }   [ʊ] { put / look }

[d] { dead / body }   [ɪ] { bit / hiss }   [ɔɪ] { spoil / boy }   [v] { save / van }

[ð̆] { that / those }   [j] { yellow / you }   [ɔ] { caught / yawn }   [w] { well / wind }

[dʒ] { jail / judge }   [k] { can / keep }   [p] { tip / pat }   [ʍ] { wheel / while }

[e] { date / sail }   [l] { lawn / yellow }   [r] { rat / berry }   [z] { fuzzy / zoo }

[ɛ] { get / set }   [l̩] { bottle / puddle }   [s] { sun / fast }   [ʒ] { pleasure / treasure }

[ə] { but / nut }   [m] { family / slam }   [ʃ] { fish / sure }   [ˈ] { ˈwater / hoˈtel }

TERMS

☐   (a box) marks the beginning of an example.

AND   indicates that an entry head has variant forms that are the same or almost the same in meaning as the entry head. One or more variant forms are preceded by AND.

colloquial   describes an expression that is usually considered appropriate when spoken but not when written, usually because of the meaning or intent of the expression.

common   describes an expression well-known to many people.

Compare to   means to consult the entry indicated and examine its form or meaning in relation to the entry head containing the "Compare to" instruction.

contrived   describes an ingenious expression created with forethought and imagination.

crude   as used here, describes an expression that embarrasses people, typically because it refers to either sexual matters or excrement.

derogatory   describes an expression that insults, mocks, or abuses someone or a class of people.

disguise   is an expression that means the same and sounds like another more offensive term.

elaboration   is an expression that is built on, or is an expansion of, another expression.

entry head   is the first word or phrase, in boldface, of an entry; the word or phrase that the definition explains.

euphemism   is a *euphemistic* expression. See the following.

euphemistic   describes an expression that is used as a substitute for a less acceptable expression.

eye-dialect   is a class of spelling variants that attempts to capture colloquial pronunciation or indicates that the person who uttered the words or phrases is illiterate. Sometimes incorrectly spelled *I-dialect*.

food-dirtying   describes an expression that is applied to an article of food to make it seem less appetizing or even revolting.

four-letter word   is one of a set of English words—so-called "dirty words"—that are spelled with four letters. They include *cunt, fart, fuck, shit, turd,* and sometimes *arse* [British] and *twat.* The term is sometimes used as a synonym for "dirty word."

general slang   is the body of widely known slang expressions that are not considered taboo or forbidden.

(I-dialect)   is a spelling error for *eye-dialect.*

informal   describes a very casual expression that is most likely to be spoken but not written.

jocular   describes an expression that is intended to be humorous.

juvenile   describes an expression typical of children's speech.

low   describes the uncultured or crude use of an expression or the users of such expressions.

military describes expressions that are, or were originally, used in the U.S. military services.

More at means that an additional, frequently used form of the entry head has its own separate entry. Consult the indicated entry for additional examples or explanation.

Pig Latin is a type of wordplay in which the first consonant of a word or syllable is shifted to the end of the word or syllable and followed by "ay", (phonetic [e]). For example: eep-kay our-yay outh-may ut-shay. ['ip-ke 'ɚ-je 'ɑʊθ-me 'ət-ʃe]. "Keep your mouth shut!"

provocative describes expressions that may bring on anger or violence.

See means to turn to the entry indicated.

See also means to consult the entry indicated for additional information or to find expressions similar in form or meaning to the entry head containing the "See also" instruction.

See under means to turn to the entry head indicated and look for the phrase you are seeking *within* the entry indicated.

slang describes an expression that is recognized as casual or playful. Such terms are not considered appropriate for formal writing.

standard English is the widely known and accepted style or register of English taught in schools.

taboo as used here, describes expressions that are completely forbidden under certain social circumstances. The consequences of breaking this taboo are limited to social scorn.

teens describes an expression used typically—but not exclusively —by teenagers.

term of address describes an expression that is used to address someone directly.

unrefined describes speakers who lack polite manners or who are crude and boisterous.

A

abso-fucking-lutely [ˈæbsoˈfəkɪŋˈlutli] absolutely. (An exclamation of agreement. Typical of male-to-male talk. Always low and unrefined. Typical of a widespread type of infixing where a taboo word is put into the middle of another word for emphasis. Taboo. See comment at note 32; see note 4 for caution.) □ *Do I want to go out for a beer? You're abso-fucking-lutely right!* □ *You are abso-fucking-lutely out of your mind.* □ *You bet! Abso-fucking-lutely!*

A.C-D.C. [ˈe ˈsi-ˈdi ˈsi] bisexual; alternating between male and female. (From the initials of *alternating current* and *direct current*. Usually refers to an electrical appliance that can operate on both currents. Partly euphemistic and jocular. Widely known and used by both sexes, especially as a euphemism. See also *swing, swing both ways, swinger.*) □ *Somebody said that Fred is A.C.-D.C.* □ *Those A.C.-D.C. types are driving away the straights.* □ *When Marge is turned on, she's A.C.-D.C. At least that's what they say.*

ace boon coon [ˈes ˈbun ˈkun] one's best and most dependable friend. (Chiefly black-to-black and male-to-male. Presumably a black friend. See *coon*. Provocative if used casually by non-blacks. See also *coon, waccoon*. See caution at note 1; see use as a slur at note 2.) □ *Where is my ace boon coon, Freddy?* □ *I like the guy, but he's not what you would call my ace boon coon.* □ *This white dude called Freddy his ace boon coon, and Freddy knocked him down.*

ace of spades ['es əv 'spedz] an American black; a very dark American black. (The name for the "one" of spades in card playing. The term alludes to the blackness of spades. Intended and perceived as derogatory when used by whites. Not widely known. Male use. Also a term of address. See also *spade*. From the expression "black as the ace of spades." See caution at note 1; see use as a slur at note 2.) □ *Freddy came in looking like the run-of-the-mill ace of spades, platform shoes, and the like.* □ *Who's that ace of spades coming around the corner?*

ag-fay ['ægfe] a male homosexual; a *fag*. (Intended and perceived as derogatory. Some euphemistic use. Typical of nonhomosexual male talk. Pig Latin for *fag*. Also a term of address. See note 5 for additional examples and caution.) □ *Who's that ag-fay just going out the door?* □ *Don't act like an ag-fay!*

A.H. ['e 'etʃ] an *asshole*; a really wretched person. (A euphemistic disguise. Also a term of address. See note 3 for additional examples.) □ *The guy acts like such an A.H. No wonder nobody likes him.* □ *Fred is an A.H. about things like that.* □ *Look here, you goddamn A.H.! Who the hell do you think you are?*

A-hole ['e-hol] an *asshole*, a very stupid or annoying person. (Usually refers to a male. Used informally by both sexes in avoidance of *asshole*. Also a term of address. See note 3 for additional examples.) □ *Tom can be an A-hole before he's had his coffee.* □ *This A-hole comes up to me and asks for a free oil change.*

alley cat ['æli kæt] **1.** a prostitute; a woman who is as promiscuous as a prostitute. (Stray cats or alley cats are notoriously sexually promiscuous. See also *cat house, cat house detail.* Partly euphemistic.) □ *I always told you she was an alley cat. You're the one who married her!* □ *He's running around with some alley cat he met on Fourth Street.* **2.** a lecherous man. (Like a tomcat.) □ *The guy's an alley cat. What do you expect him to do when he sees a good-looking dame?* □ *Bob flirts a lot, but he's no alley cat.*

alligator bait [ˈæləgetɚ ˈbet] an American black, especially a black child. (Intended and perceived as derogatory ridicule. Also a term of address. Implies that the best use for blacks is as bait to catch alligators. Typical of male and southern use. User is considered to be racially bigoted. See caution at note 1; see use as a slur at note 2.) □ *He's just alligator bait. Pay him no attention.* □ *Hey, alligator bait! Beat it!*

all-nighter See the following entry.

all-night trick 1. AND **all-nighter** a prostitute's customer who pays for one entire night. (Prostitute's jargon. *All-nighter* is currently more common as an entire night spent partying or studying. See *trick*.) □ *Marge is tied up with another all-night trick. Would Suzy be okay?* □ *The cops hauled in the hooker and her all-nighter.* **2.** an act or series of acts of prostitution lasting one entire night. (Prostitute's jargon.) □ *The guy asked for an all-nighter, and he got it.* □ *The john who asked for an all-night trick was a cop.*

alls-bay [ˈɔlz-be] **1.** testicles; *balls*. (Pig Latin for *balls*. Typical of male-to-male talk. Partly euphemistic.) □ *Pow, the football whopped him right in the alls-bay.* □ *Well, doc, you see, I got this itch, like—sorta like all over the alls-bay.* **2.** courage; *balls*. (Not necessarily for a male. Euphemistic.) □ *Man, he's really got alls-bay.* □ *She got more alls-bay than you!* **3.** nonsense. (Usually an exclamation: **Alls-bay!** Typical of male-to-male talk. Euphemistic.) □ *That's all I ever hear outa you, alls-bay—bullshit and alls-bay!* □ *The guy talks alls-bay. He's just a loudmouth.*

apeshit [ˈepʃɪt] **1.** excited; freaked out. (See also *go apeshit over someone or something.* See comment at note 32.) □ *He was really apeshit about that dame.* □ *Don't get so apeshit over nothing all the time.* **2.** drunk. (Acting as strangely or comically as an ape. See comment at note 32.) □ *The guy was really apeshit.* □ *How apeshit can you get on two beers?*

ass [æs] (See also the entries that follow and the list at the end of this entry.) **1.** the buttocks. (*Ass* in American English is usually assumed to refer to the buttocks and not to a donkey. See note 29 for additional examples.) □ *This big monster of a guy threatened to kick me in the ass if I didn't get out of the way.* □ *So, did you move or did you end up with a sore ass?* **2.** women considered as sexual gratification. (See notes 17 and 23 for examples.) **3.** the female sex organs. (Usually low male-to-male talk. See note 6; see note 12 for examples.) **4.** one's whole body; oneself. (Usually in phrases. See *gripe one's ass, save someone's ass, someone's ass is grass.*) □ *Your ass is really in trouble!* □ *Get your damn ass outa here!* **5.** pederasty; the male object of pederasty. □ *This A.C.-D.C. guy said he wanted some ass, but I'm not sure which kind—if it matters.* □ *There's all the ass you want on that island.* (See also *backassed, backasswards, bad-ass, bag ass (out of some place), bare-ass(ed), barrel ass (out of some place), bassackwards, bigass, bouquet of assholes, break one's ass (to do something), bust-ass, bust ass (out of some place), bust (one's) ass (to do something), candy-ass, candy-ass(ed), chew someone's ass out, cover one's ass, cut ass (out of some place), dead-ass, drag ass around, drag ass (out of some place), duck's ass, dumb-ass, fat-ass(ed), flat-ass, flat on one's ass, get a piece of ass, get one's ass in gear, get some ass, gripe one's ass, hairy-ass(ed), half-ass(ed), hard-ass(ed), haul ass (out of some place), have a wild hair up one's ass, have one's ass in a crack, have one's ass in a sling, horse's ass, hot-assed, hunk of ass, It's no skin off my ass., jive-ass, kick-ass, kick-ass on someone, kick in the ass, kick some ass (around), kiss-ass, Kiss my ass!, kiss someone's ass, know one's ass from a hole in the ground, lard ass, My ass!, on one's ass, pain in the ass, peddle ass, piece of ass, piss-ass, play grab-ass, put one's ass on the line, red-assed, save someone's ass, shag ass (out of some place), shit-ass, shit-ass luck, Shove it (up your ass)!, smartass, soft-ass(ed), someone's ass is grass, sorry-ass(ed), stupidass, suck-ass, tight-ass, tight-ass(ed), tired-ass(ed), tits and ass, wild-ass(ed), wise-ass, wise-ass(ed), work one's ass off, You bet your (sweet) ass!*)

ass-fuck AND **butt-fuck** (Taboo in all senses.) **1.** to commit pederasty. (See note 4 for caution and see note 31.) □ *Some creep came by and asked somebody to ass-fuck him.* □ *Is that what* *they do, butt-fuck each other?* **2.** an act of pederasty. (Low. See note 31.) □ *One of them said he'd pay as much as $60 for a butt-fuck.* □ *Can't you get a disease from just one ass-fuck?* **3.** someone who practices pederasty. □ *He looks like a choir-boy, but he's a butt-fuck from way back.* □ *Who's the ass-fuck I saw you with last night?* **4.** a disliked and annoying person. (Usually a male. See comment at note 32. Also a provocative term of address.) □ *Get outa here, butt-fuck!* □ *Who is that ass-fuck over there in the plaid pants?*

asshole ['æshol] **1.** the opening at the lower end of the large bowel; the anus. (See note 30 for examples; see also note 31.) **2.** a worthless and annoying person. (Intended as strongly derogatory. Also a term of address. Very common. See also *A.H., A-hole.* See comment at note 32; see note 3 for additional examples.) □ *Shut your goddamn mouth, you smelly asshole!* □ *Somebody get this asshole outa here before I bust in his face!*

ass-kisser AND **ass-licker** a flatterer; an apple polisher; someone who would do absolutely anything to please someone. (Rude and potentially provocative. See comment at note 32.) □ *Sally is such an ass-kisser. The teacher must have figured her out by now.* □ *Don't act like an ass-licker all the time. We're getting tired of it.*

ass-kissing AND **ass-licking** **1.** the act of fawning over and flattering people. □ *After his show of ass-kissing, Fred thought the judge would let him off with a light fine.* □ *Some people go a long way on nothing but ass-licking.* **2.** pertaining to the act of fawning over and flattering people. □ *Fred's few minutes in court was the ass-kissing event of the century!* □ *Shut your ass-licking mouth and start talking straight, or I'm gonna bust you one.*

ass-licker See *ass-kisser*.

ass-licking See *ass-kissing*.

ass-man 1. a male who is attracted by the female buttocks. (See note 6; see *ass,* sense 1.) □ *Did you see his eyes light up when she went by? There's an ass-man if I ever saw one.* □ *Fred says he's quite an ass-man, but I think he's just telling tales.* **2.** a male who is obsessed with copulation; a lecher. (See note 6; see *ass,* sense 2. Typical of male-to-male talk and joking.) □ *You're an ass-man, Wally. You're just a horny old ass-man.* □ *Why does Tom act like such an ass-man around the girls? They don't like that kind of stuff.*

ass-peddler AND **butt-peddler** a prostitute. (Typically concerned with female prostitution, but also in male prostitution. Low slang. Not in wide use.) □ *Wally is an ass-peddler. At least that's what somebody says.* □ *You can't move an inch through this city without being assaulted by one of these butt-peddlers!*

ass-wipe AND **butt-wipe 1.** a useless and annoying person. (Provocative and rude. Typical of male-to-male talk. Also a term of address. See comment at note 32; see note 3 for examples.) □ *Get outa here, you ass-wipe!* □ *Nobody but a goddamn fucking ass-wipe would do what you did!* **2.** toilet paper. (Typical of low male-to-male talk. See note 31.) □ *There's no goddamn ass-wipe left in here!* □ *I always carry my own butt-wipe, you jerk. I'll sell you some—nickel a sheet.*

aunt AND **auntie** [ænt AND 'ænti] an aged male homosexual. (See note 5 for additional examples and caution.) □ *He said he was up all night with his auntie, if that means anything to you.* □ *This old aunt was actually wearing false eyelashes!*

aunteater ['æntitɚ] a homosexual male. (A play on the animal [anteater] and *aunt.* See *aunt, eat.* See note 5 for additional examples and caution.) □ *Well, I guess you don't have to go to the zoo to see an aunteater. I didn't know this was that kind of bar!* □ *They say that Fred is a real aunteater. I knew he had no taste.*

B

backassed ['bækæst] pertaining to a manner that is backwards, awkward, or roundabout. (Old and widely known.) □ *That is a stupid, backassed way to polish a car!* □ *Of all the backassed schemes I've ever seen, this one is tops.*

backasswards AND **bassackwards** ['bæk'æswɚdz AND 'bæs'ækwɚdz] backwards; awkwardly; in a topsy-turvy manner. (A humorous play on *ass backwards*. Old and widely known. More jocular than offensive. Widely used by both sexes.) □ *You've got the lid on this thing backasswards.* □ *I tend to go about things bassackwards.*

bad-ass ['bædæs] **1.** a cruel male; a tough guy. (Typical of male-to-male talk. Perhaps with sarcasm. See comment at note 32.) □ *Wally is a real bad-ass. Don't make him mad, whatever you do.* □ *Don't be such a bad-ass, you jerk.* **2.** bad; wicked. (See comment at note 32. Typical of male-to-male talk.) □ *Man, he's in a real bad-ass mood today. Watch your step.* □ *I had one hell of a bad-ass day today, and I'm mad as hell.*

bad shit **1.** a bad event; bad luck; evil practices. (See comment at note 32. Used by either sex. Typical of drug culture talk.) □ *I had to put up with a lot of bad shit at my last job. Is this one gonna be the same?* □ *Man, you gotta get rid of all that bad shit that seems to follow you around.* **2.** bad drugs; adulterated drugs. (See comment at note 32. Compare to *good shit*. Drug culture.) □ *Where'd you get this bad shit, man?* □ *Freddy got hold of some bad shit, and he's really sick.*

bag ass (out of some place) AND **barrel ass (out of some place), bust ass (out of some place), cut ass (out of some place), drag ass (out of some place), haul ass (out of some place), shag ass (out of some place)** [ˈbæg æs..., AND ˈbɛrəl æs..., ˈbəst æs..., ˈkət æs..., ˈdræg æs..., ˈhɔl æs..., ˈʃæg æs...] to hurry away from some place; to get oneself out of a place in a hurry. (Typical of male-to-male talk, but widely known to both sexes. See comment at note 32.) □ *Man, I gotta bag ass outa this place but fast. I'm gone!* □ *I gotta shag ass, Fred. Catch you later.*

bald-headed hermit AND **bald-headed mouse, one-eyed pants mouse** [ˈbɔld-hɛdəd ˈhɚrmət AND ...ˈmɑʊs.] the penis. (Jocular and contrived. See note 8 for additional examples; see note 31.) □ *Tom quickly poked the old bald-headed hermit back into his pants, and pretended that nothing had happened.* □ *Somebody said something about the attack of the one-eyed pants mouse, and all the boys howled with laughter.*

bald-headed mouse See the previous entry.

ball [bɔl] **1.** to copulate [with] someone. (Used by either sex. Used without regard to the sex of the participants. Transitive and intransitive. See notes 13 and 14 for examples; see note 31.) **2.** a testicle. See *balls*.

ball-breaker AND **ball-buster** **1.** a difficult task; a difficult or trying situation requiring extremely hard work or effort. (Typical of male-to-male talk. Each sense suggests damage to the testicles. See *balls*.) □ *That whole construction job was a real ball-breaker.* □ *Oh, no! Not another goddamn ball-breaker of an afternoon! I can't take it.* **2.** a hard taskmaster; a hard-to-please boss. □ *Fred, why are you such a ball-breaker? The men aren't going to put up with this much longer.* □ *Tom gets a day's work for a day's pay out of his men, but he's no ball-breaker.* **3.** a female who is threatening to males. (See note 6. Typical of male-to-male talk.) □ *Marge is such a ball-breaker. Probably a bad home life.* □ *Mrs. Samuels has a terrible reputation as a ball-breaker. Wholly deserved, I might add.*

ball-buster   See the previous entry.

ball-busting   **1.** very difficult or challenging. (Each sense suggests damage to the testicles. See *balls*.) □ *Man, that was a real ball-busting job. I hope I never have to do that again.* □ *You are the worst ball-busting foreman I've ever worked for!* **2.** very obnoxious and threatening. (See note 6. Often applied to an obnoxious female by a male.) □ *Who is that ball-busting bitch?* □ *If you didn't come on so ball-busting, maybe you'd have some friends.* **3.** very industrious. □ *What a ball-busting guy. He works harder than all the rest of you put together.* □ *That's a real ball-busting crew working on that job.*

ball-face   an ugly and disgusting white person. (Originally black for a Caucasian. Also a rude and provocative term of address. See note 1; see comment at note 32, and see *balls*.) □ *Tell that ball-face to shut up and go home.* □ *Look, ball-face, get outa this car, right now!*

ball off   See *beat off*.

balloons   [bə'lunz] a woman's breasts, especially large ones. (Intended as jocular. Usually plural. See note 6; see note 7 for examples.)

balls   **1.** the testicles. (Common, informal, and slang term for the testicles. Partly euphemistic. Widely used by both sexes. See note 31. See also the entries below and *blue balls, break someone's balls, have a man by the balls, put one's balls on the line, put (some) balls on something.*) □ *I got some sort of itch on my balls.* □ *He got hit in the balls in the football game.* **2.** an exclamation of disbelief. (Usually an exclamation: **Balls!** See comment at note 32. Typical of male-to-male talk.) □ *Oh, balls! You never went to China. They wouldn't let you in!* □ *Out of gas! Balls! I just filled it up!* **3.** courage; bravado. (Usually refers to a male, but occasional use for females.) □ *The jerk may be stupid, but he's got balls.* □ *He doesn't have enough balls to do that.*

ball someone or something up to mess someone or something up; to put someone or something into a state of confusion. (A much milder version of *fuck someone or something up*. Widely known and used by both sexes. See intransitive version at *ball up*.) □ *Who balled up my garden?* □ *When you interrupted, you balled me up and I lost my place.*

ballsy ['bɔlzi] **1.** courageous; daring; foolhardy. (Usually said of a male.) □ *That guy is really ballsy!* □ *Who is that ballsy jerk climbing the side of the building?* **2.** aggressive; masculine. (See note 6. Said of a female, especially a masculine female.) □ *Who's that ballsy dame over there?* □ *You act too ballsy, Lillian. You put people off.*

ball up to mess up; to make a mess of things. (Widely known. Not connected to the meaning [testicle]. See transitive version at *ball someone or something up*. See also *fuck up*.) □ *I really balled up yesterday.* □ *Take your time at this. Go slow and you won't ball up.*

banana [bə'nænə] a person of East Asian [including Japanese] descent who acts [too much] like a Caucasian. (That is to say, yellow on the outside and white on the inside. Jocular and contrived. Based on *oreo*, a term used for blacks who are [black on the outside and white on the inside] like the Oreo™ cookie. See caution at note 1; see use as a slur at note 2.) □ *Chin-wu has become a real banana. Look how she dresses!* □ *Leave your eyes the way they are, Liani! You want to be just another banana?*

B. and D. ['bi n̩ 'di] bondage and discipline. (A sexual act involving tying or chaining up a person and administering discipline with a whip or something similar. See note 31. Widely known.) □ *They say Wally is into B. and D.* □ *There was an ad in the Sunday paper, of all places, about a party for people interested in B. and D.*

bang [bæŋ] **1.** to copulate [with] someone. (See *boom-boom*. Transitive and intransitive. See notes 13 and 14 for examples; see note 31. Partly euphemistic. Used by either sex, especially teens and college students.) **2.** an act of copulation. (See note 16 for examples; see note 31.)

bare-ass(ed) ['bɛr-æs(t)] with a naked posterior exposed; totally naked. (Compare to *butt-naked*. Widely known.) □ *He ran right through the room—totally bare-assed—looking scared as hell.* □ *He's got pictures of bare-ass women taped up all over his room.*

barf [barf] (All senses widely known and used by all sexes and all ages. Euphemistic and playful.) **1.** to vomit. (See note 31. Widely known and used, especially among teens and college students. See also *chuck up, earp, puke, pump ship.*) □ *Oh, God! I'm gonna barf!* □ *Don't you dare barf in my back seat! Stick your head outa the window.* **2.** vomit. (See note 31.) □ *My God! You got barf all over the car seat!* □ *Don't step in that barf! Looks like pizza.* **3.** an exclamation. (Usually an exclamation: **Barf!**) □ *Oh, barf! I forgot my keys.* □ *Barf! I just missed my bus.* **4.** junk; worthless matter. □ *I've got a whole lot of barf to straighten out before I can go. Just wait awhile.* □ *Just put that barf on the floor and have a seat. I can't seem to get this place cleaned up.*

barf out ['barf 'aut] to become very upset; to freak out; to psych out. (Somewhat dated, but still heard.) □ *Sally was so upset! I just knew she was going to barf out!* □ *I nearly barfed out when I heard he was coming.*

barf someone out to totally disgust someone. (Somewhat dated, but still heard.) □ *God! That kind of music just barfs me out! Who can stand all that slow stuff?* □ *Fred said that the party barfed him out and that he was going out to pound a beer.*

barrel ass (out of some place) See *bag ass (out of some place)*.

bassackwards See *backasswards*.

bastard ['bæstərd] **1.** a person of illegitimate birth. (Standard English. Considered by some as impolite, at best, except in historical references.) □ *I guess you could call Sue a bastard, although she's by no means a real bastard, if you know what I mean.* □ *When I learned I was a bastard, I couldn't help but think of all the times I have been called one.* **2.** an obnoxious and offensive person, often applied to a male. (Especially with *dirty.* Provocative. Also a term of address. See note 3 for additional examples.) □ *You goddamn, stupid bastard! What the hell do you think you are doing? Get your butt out of here—now!* □ *What a dirty bastard! Who does he think he is? God's gift to the human race?* □ *Tell the bastard to go to hell.*

bat-shit 1. the dung of the bat; bat guano. (Low or crude. See note 27 for examples; see note 31.) □ *The cave was full of bat-shit, so we came back out.* □ *They sold bat-shit for fertilizer. They made a living that way.* **2.** nonsense; lies and deception. (Intended as jocular. Patterned on *bullshit.*) □ *Don't give me that bat-shit! You're lying and you know it!* □ *That stupid jerk talks bat-shit and nothing more. Couldn't tell the truth if he had a mouth full of it.*

bazoo AND **wazoo** ['ba'zu AND 'wa'zu] **1.** the human mouth. (Not forbidden unless it is confused with sense 3 below.) □ *You want me to punch you in the wazoo?* □ *Shut up your goddamn big bazoo, or I will shut it for you!* □ *Look at the size of the wazoo in that dame!* **2.** the stomach or belly. □ *His great wazoo hung poised, out over his belt, like it might dive down to the floor and bounce off across the room.* □ *You want I should poke you in that fat bazoo of yours?* **3.** the anus. (Jocular and euphemistic. Many references to the anus are included in threats. See the examples. See note 30 for additional examples; see note 31.) □ *One more word like that and I'll give you a kick in the wazoo that you'll remember for a long time.* □ *How would you like this jammed up your bazoo, you son of a bitch?*

bazoom(s) [bə'zum(z)] a woman's breasts; the female bosom. (Intended as jocular. Either singular or plural. In the singular it is equal in meaning to standard English [bosom]. Typical of male-to-male talk and joking. A play on [bosom]. See notes 6 and 7 for additional examples.) □ *Who is the redhead with the yummy ba-*

zooms? □ *I don't know how it happened, but a whole bowl of jello went down this lady's, uh, bazoom, and we haven't the slightest idea what to do about it!*

bazoongies [bəˈzuŋgiz] a woman's breasts. (Intended as jocular. Usually plural. Typical of male-to-male joking. See notes 6 and 7 for additional examples.) □ *If you want to see some big bazoongies, go see* Under the Bed *at the Roxy Theater.* □ *Every time she moved forward, even just a little, her bazoongies tended to stay behind, for just a second. Oh, God!*

beach whistle [ˈbitʃ ʍɪsl̩] a tampon inserter washed up on a beach. (Jocular. New Jersey.) □ *Residents reported many instances of finding beach whistles on the Eastern seaboard last weekend.* □ *The number of beach whistles and used hypodermic syringes that wash up on public beaches is increasing by leaps and bounds.*

bean-eater AND **chili-eater** [ˈbin-itɚ AND ˈtʃɪli...] a Mexican; a Hispanic person. (Usually intended and perceived as derogatory. Also a term of address. See also *beaner.* See caution at note 1; see use as a slur at note 2.)

beaner [ˈbinɚ] a Mexican; a Hispanic person. (Usually intended and perceived as derogatory. Also a term of address. See also *bean-eater.* See caution at note 1; see use as a slur at note 2.)

bearded clam [ˈbɪrdəd ˈklæm] the female genitals; the vulva. (The shells of the clam are the *labia majora,* and the beard is the pubic hair. See also *munch the bearded clam.* Essentially jocular and not widely known. See notes 6 and 31; see note 12 for examples.)

beat off AND **ball off, jack off, jag off, jerk off, pull oneself off, toss off, wack off, wank off, whack off, whank off, whip off 1.** to masturbate. (Said of the male, but is occasionally applied to a female. See also the series of entries immediately following. See note 21 for additional examples; see note 31.) □ *They say if you beat off too much, you'll get pimples.* □ *The teacher* *caught him whanking off.* □ *During the movie, he snuck out and whacked off.* **2.** to waste time; to waste one's efforts; to do something inefficiently. (See note 31.) □ *Stop whacking off and get to work!* □ *The whole lot of them were jacking off rather than sticking to business.*

beat the dummy AND **beat the meat, beat one's meat, beat the pup, choke the chicken, pound one's meat, pull one's pud, pull one's wire, whip one's wire, whip the dummy, yank one's strap** [ˈbit ðə ˈmit AND . . .pəp, ˈtʃok ðə ˈtʃɪkn̩, ˈpaʊnd wənz ˈmit, ˈpʊl wənz ˈpəd, ˈpʊl wənz ˈwaɪr, ˈʌɪp. . ., . . .ðə ˈdəmi, ˈjæŋk wənz ˈstræp] to masturbate. (See note 19 for additional examples; see note 31.) □ *Are you going to sit around all day pulling your pud?* □ *The guy yanks his strap whenever he gets a chance.*

beat the meat AND **beat one's meat**   See the previous entry.

beat the pup   See *beat the dummy.*

beat the shit out of someone AND **kick the shit out of someone, knock the shit out of someone**   to beat someone very hard. (Most often as a threat rather than a deed. Typical of male-to-male talk.) □ *Shut up, or I'll beat the shit out of you!* □ *He knocked the shit out of the jerk. He'll never be back again.*

beaver   [ˈbivɚ] **1.** the female genitals. (Named for the pubic hair that, in some patterns, resembles the smooth fur of the beaver. Used in male-to-male talk and joking. Best known in the 1970s. See use in compound in the entries below. See note 12 for examples; see notes 6 and 31.) **2.** women considered as receptacles for the penis. (See notes 6 and 31; see examples at note 23.)

beaver-flick   [ˈbivɚ-flɪk] a film showing naked women. (See note 6.) □ *Did you see that beaver-flick over at the Roxy? I can't believe they can show that stuff.* □ *You can rent beaver-flicks at the corner video store.*

beaver-retriever [ˈbivɚ-rɪˈtrivɚ] a lecher. (Jocular and contrived. Typical of male-to-male talk. See *beaver*. See note 6.) □ *Wally's an old beaver-retriever. Can't pass up a good-looking piece of tail.* □ *What a beaver-retriever! A real woman-chaser.*

beaver shot [ˈbivɚ ʃat] a photograph of the genitals of a woman. (See notes 6 and 31.) □ *Billy carried around a beaver shot in his wallet for years before he found out what it was.* □ *Some kid had a pack of cards with a beaver shot on each one.*

bed-bunny [ˈbɛd ˈbəni] **1.** a young female who will copulate with any male. □ *Wally says he's looking for a nice warm bed-bunny.* □ *Sally's a bed-bunny. Anybody can tell you that.* **2.** a female who enjoys sex immensely. □ *I'm a real bed-bunny, and I'm lonely tonight.* □ *Wanda turned out to be a bed-bunny even though she had seemed sort of dull.*

beef [bif] **1.** to break wind; to release intestinal gas audibly through the anus. (See note 31.) □ *Okay, who beefed?* □ *Why are you all the time beefing? You sick?* **2.** an act of breaking wind. (Probably short for *beef-hearts.* See note 31.) □ *That was the worse smelling beef I ever smelled!* □ *Whose beef was that?*

beef-hearts audible releases of intestinal gas through the anus. (Rhyming slang for "farts." See note 31.) □ *All right! All right! Who's responsible for the beef-hearts?* □ *No more of these beef-hearts!*

begonias [bɪˈɡonjəz] a woman's breasts. (From the flower name. Usually plural. Intended as jocular. Typical of male-to-male joking. See note 6; see note 7 for additional examples.) □ *Look at them beautiful begonias!* □ *Now there's a fine set of begonias over there on the blond.*

bend down for someone **1.** to submit to someone sexually, especially for a male to submit to another male for pederasty. (See note 31.) □ *What does he expect me to do, bend down for him?* □ *This guy comes up and asks me how much money I want to bend down for him.* **2.** to submit to someone's domination, not necessarily sexual domination. □ *I won't bend down for you or for anyone else.* □ *If I am expected to bend down for everyone around here, I guess I'll get another job.*

bent See *kinky.*

bezongas [bɪˈzɔŋɡəz] a woman's breasts. (Intended as jocular. Usually plural. See notes 6 and 7 for additional examples.) □ *I've never seen so many definitely fine bezongas all in one place at the same time.* □ *Look at them bezongas, would ya!*

B.F.D. [ˈbi ˈɛf ˈdi] "Big fucking deal!"; "So what?" □ *So, you've got serious money problems. B.F.D.!* □ *B.F.D., we ain't none of us got it made!*

B-girl [ˈbi-ɡɚl] a woman who works in a bar persuading male customers to buy drinks. (She is usually provided with a nonalcoholic drink for which the customer pays. She may also engage in prostitution.) □ *Sally worked as a B-girl in Fourth Street bars for years.* □ *The cops hauled in a couple of B-girls, but had to let them go.*

bi [baɪ] **1.** a person who is bisexual. (See note 31.) □ *Is Molly a bi, or what?* □ *Some character, a bi I guess, came in in a big blonde wig and started pinching all the girls.* **2.** pertaining to someone or something bisexual. (See note 31.) □ *He walked in and asked if anybody objected to bi people.* □ *She called her clothes "bi clothes" because you couldn't tell which sex they were for.*

bigass [ˈbɪɡæs] **1.** a person with very large buttocks. □ *Who is that bigass over there in the corner?* □ *Some bigass came in and broke the chair when he sat down.* **2.** pertaining to someone who has very large buttocks. (See note 31.) □ *Tell that bigass jerk to get out!* □ *Look, here, you bigass mama, just move along!* **3.** pertaining to a person who is self-important, overbearing, or arrogant; pertaining to anything having to do with arrogance. (See comment at note 32.) □ *What is all this talk about some bigass executive coming in to buy this town?* □ *Take your bigass ideas and go back where you came from.*

big brown eyes a woman's breasts; a woman's nipples, especially if heavily pigmented. (This seemingly innocent phrase should be used with some caution in any circumstance. Usually plural. See notes 6 and 7 for additional examples.) □ *I wanna get a closer look at her big brown eyes.* □ *I bet she has beautiful big brown eyes.*

big shit **1.** an obnoxious person. (Provocative. See comment at note 32.) □ *You are just a big shit, Freddy!* □ *Tell that big shit to pull his stuff together and get out.* **2.** an important person. (See comment at note 32.) □ *You're not such a big shit!* □ *So, you think you're some sort of big shit or something.*

birdshit ['bɔ˞dʃɪt] **1.** bird dung. (Low. See note 27 for additional examples; see note 31.) □ *Look, I got birdshit on my jacket!* □ *There's birdshit on the windshield.* **2.** an obnoxious person. (See comment at note 32. Also a term of address.) □ *Some stupid birdshit just came in and started a fight with Chuck.* □ *Beat it, birdshit!* **3.** worthless. (Compare to *chicken shit*.) □ *Get your birdshit car off my lawn.* □ *That's the dumbest birdshit idea I've ever heard!*

bird-turd ['bɔ˞d-tɔ˞d] **1.** bird dung, especially if dried. (See note 27 for examples. Jocular, for the sake of the rhyme.) □ *There's a bird-turd on your shoe.* □ *Oh, shit, there's bird-turd smeared all over my windshield.* **2.** a worthless and obnoxious person. (See comment at note 32. Also a term of address.) □ *Shut up, you bird-turd.* □ *Hey, bird-turd! Why are you so ugly?* **3.** lousy; worthless. □ *I don't want this bird-turd job any longer. I quit!* □ *Get me out of this bird-turd place before I barf!*

bitch [bɪtʃ] **1.** an unpleasant or irritating female. (See note 6. Intended and perceived as derogatory. Very common and used by both sexes. Also a term of address.) □ *What a bitch! Why is she so mean?* □ *How can anyone be expected to deal with a bitch like that?* **2.** to complain. □ *Oh, stop bitching! I'm sick of hearing your noise.* □ *You should go to the front office and bitch about it if you don't like it.* **3.** a complaint. □ *I've got a bitch about this* *new foreman.* □ *You got a bitch about something, you tell it to me, you understand?*

bitch box [ˈbɪtʃ bɑks] a public address system loudspeaker. (Military. Because it is always nagging.) □ *I'm sick of listening to that bitch box day and night.* □ *Who smashed the bitch box outside of room 258?*

bitchen See *bitchin'.*

(bitchen-)twitchen [ˈbɪtʃn̩ˈtwɪtʃn̩] excellent. (California.) □ *This is a bitchen-twitchen way to boogie.* □ *She is like, twitchen!*

bitchin' AND **bitchen** [ˈbɪtʃn̩] **1.** excellent; great; classy. □ *This is a totally bitchin' pair of jeans!* □ *This is a way bitchen rally, my man!* **2.** "Terrific!" (Usually an exclamation: **Bitchin'!**) □ *Bitchen! Let's do it again!* □ *Four of them? Bitchen!*

bitch of a someone or something a very difficult or unpleasant person or thing. □ *Man, what a bitch of a day!* □ *This is a bitch of a math problem!*

bitch session a session of complaining; an informal gripe session. (See *bitch.*) □ *We had a little bitch session last night, Sarge, and there are some things we'd like to talk over with you.* □ *We were just having a bitch session. Come on in.*

bitch someone off to make someone very angry. (Compare to *piss someone off.*) □ *She really bitched me off.* □ *You know what bitches me off? Soggy French fries, that's what!*

bitch something up to mess something up; to ruin or spoil something. □ *Who bitched up my desk? It's really a mess.* □ *The rain really bitched up our picnic.*

bitchy [ˈbɪtʃi] irritable; complaining. (See note 6. Especially, but not necessarily said of a female. Widely known and in common use by both sexes.) □ *Why are you so bitchy today?* □ *She is really one bitchy bitch.*

bite the big one 1. to perform oral sex on a male. (The *big one* is the penis. See note 31.) □ *God, he wanted me to bite the big one!* □ *She looks like she would really like to bite the big one.* 2. to be annoying or useless. (A play on *suck* as in *It sucks!*. See *suck*.) □ *That last test really bit the big one.* □ *Your idea of a good time bites the big one as far as I'm concerned.*

bi-trade ['baɪ-tred] 1. the bisexual sex business. (See note 31.) □ *We went to a bar that was set up for the bi-trade.* □ *She's a hustler who caters to the bi-trade.* 2. persons seeking prostitutes of either sex. (See note 31.) □ *Wait till the bi-trade starts showing up about midnight. You never know what to do.* □ *She works with the bi-trade a lot. Says she meets higher types that way.*

blow [blo] to perform an act of oral sex on someone. (Originally and chiefly for males. See *blow job*. See note 31. Note also the general slang *blow someone or something off* which means to avoid dealing with someone or something and has no negative connotations.) □ *Tom was looking for some bone addict who would blow him for nothing.* □ *Why doesn't he blow himself, the twit?*

blow a fart to release a burst of intestinal gas through the anus. (Typical of male-to-male talk. See *fart*, and see note 31.) □ *Phewww! Who blew the fart?* □ *Man, I gotta blow a fart!*

blow job ['blo dʒab] an act of oral sex performed on the penis. (The name of a specific act that may be requested of a prostitute. Widely known. See *blow*, and see note 31.) □ *The hustler knew very well what the expression "blow job" meant.* □ *The dude swaggered in and yelled that he wanted a blow job.*

blue balls AND **hot-rocks** a painful condition of the testicles caused by unrelieved sexual need. (Typical of male-to-male talk. A male complaint. See *rocks, stones*, and see note 31.) □ *She always gives me hot-rocks.* □ *Oh, man. Do I ever have the blue balls! That movie was too much!*

B.M. [ˈbi ˈɛm] **1.** "bowel movement"; an act of defecation. (Mostly a euphemism used with children. See note 31.) □ *I got to have a B.M.* □ *If I don't have a B.M. soon, I'm gonna die.* **2.** a disgusting and annoying person. (Also a term of address. A humorous way of calling someone a *shit*.) □ *Get out of here, you stupid B.M.!* □ *You lousy B.M. Get outa my sight!*

bob [bɑb] to copulate [with] someone. (Refers to the motions of copulation. Transitive and intransitive. See notes 13 and 14 for examples; see note 31. Known to both sexes, used especially by teens and college students.) □ *Those two are bobbing every chance they get.* □ *Do you think he's bobbing her?*

boff [bɔf] to copulate [with] someone. (Transitive and intransitive. See notes 13 and 14 for examples; see note 31.)

bohunk [ˈbohəŋk] **1.** a resident of or an immigrant from an Eastern European country, such as Poland, Hungary, etc. (A nickname. Can be perceived as derogatory. See caution at note 1.) □ *The bohunks can really cook up some fine food.* □ *Some old bohunk down by the docks told me this great story.* **2.** an oafish person. (Usually refers to a male.) □ *Get outa here, you stupid bohunk!* □ *Tell that bohunk to get off his ass and get over here.* **3.** a term of endearment for a close friend or child. (Also a term of address.) □ *Come here, you little bohunk. Let me tuck in your shirt.* □ *Okay, you bohunks, come to dinner now.*

boink [bɔɪŋk] to copulate [with] someone. (Transitive and intransitive. See note 13 and 14 for examples; see note 31.)

bone See *boner.*

bone addict [ˈbon ædɪkt] a female who is obsessed with copulating with males. (Typical of male-to-male talk. See *bone* at *boner,* and see note 31.) □ *That silly bed-bunny is a bone addict for sure.* □ *The dame's a regular bone addict. You get tired of that fast.*

boner AND **bone** [ˈbonɚ AND bon] an erection of the penis. (Common male-to-male talk and joking. Potential confusion with the colloquial term "boner" meaning an error or a mistake. See note 9 for examples; see note 31.) □ *My God! I think I'm gonna get a boner, right here!* □ *He wanted to make it, but couldn't get a bone.*

bonk [boŋk] to copulate [with] someone. (Transitive and intransitive. Known and used by both sexes, especially teens and college students. See notes 13 and 14 for examples; see note 31.)

boob [bub] a woman's breast. (Usually plural: **boobs**. Very common and widely known. Used especially by women. See note 7 for additional examples; see note 31.) □ *Do you think my boobs will ever grow, Dr. Jones?* □ *There's a little sore right here on my boob.* □ *That dame's really got boobs!*

booby ['bubi] a woman's breast. (Usually plural: boobies. See note 7 for examples; see note 31.)

boodie See the following.

boody AND **boodie, bootie, booty** ['budi AND 'budi, 'buti, 'buti] **1.** the buttocks. (Primarily or originally black use. See note 29 for additional examples; see note 31.) □ *You just move your boody right outa here! We're busy.* □ *Freddy, you ain't got enough bootie to make a poor man a bowl of soup!* **2.** the female genitals; the vulva. (Primarily or originally black use. Widely known and used among the young, especially teens and college students. See note 12 for examples; see notes 6 and 31.) **3.** women considered as a receptacle for the penis. (See notes 6 and 31; see examples at note 23.) **4.** male sexual release through copulation with a female. (Usually with *some*. See notes 6 and 31; see note 17 for examples.)

booger ['bugɚ] a blob of nasal mucus, moist or dry. (Widely known. See note 31.) □ *Keep your boogers to yourself!* □ *Who got boogers all over my bedspread?*

boogie ['bugi OR 'bugi] **1.** to copulate; to have sex. (There are many other general slang senses, such as those having to do with dancing, partying, departing, etc. Intransitive. See note 14 for examples; see note 31.) **2.** an American black. (Derogatory. User is considered to be racially bigoted. See caution at note 1; see use as a slur at note 2.)

boom-boom ['bum-bum] copulation. (See *bang*. See note 17 for additional examples; see note 31.) □ *Come on, baby, how about a little boom-boom?* □ *All you want is boom-boom. Don't you ever eat?*

boomin(g) ['bumɪŋ OR 'bumɪn] having large buttocks. (Black.) □ *Who is that boomin' mama over there?* □ *Man, is that dude booming! All that meat and no potatoes!*

boosiasms ['buziæzm̩z] a woman's breasts. (Intended as jocular. Either singular or plural. In the singular it is equal in meaning to standard English "bosom." Perhaps akin to "enthusiasm." See notes 6 and 31; see note 7 for examples.)

bootie See *boody*.

booty See *boody*.

bop [bɑp] to copulate [with] someone. (Transitive and intransitive. Widely known and used by both sexes, especially teens and college students. See notes 13 and 14 for examples; see note 31.)

bottom ['bɑdm̩] **1.** the buttocks. (A common term, almost polite. See note 29 for examples; see note 31.) **2.** the female genitals. (Euphemistic. Definitely taboo in British English. More a female euphemism than a rude word in American English. See note 6 and 31; see note 12 for examples.)

bouquet of assholes [bo'ke əv 'æsholz] an annoying or disgusting person or thing. (Also a provocative and rude term of address.) □ *Don't pay any attention to him. He's just another one of the bouquet of assholes you find around here.* □ *Look here, you bouquet of assholes, shut up or get out!*

box [baks] **1.** the genitals of the male, especially as contained within a garment, such as underwear. (Usually in a homosexual context. See note 31.) □ *He said I had a nice box, but I wasn't carrying anything. I didn't like his looks either.* □ *God, did you see the box on him?* **2.** the genitals of a female; the vagina considered as a container for the penis. (Usually rude male-to-male talk. Not widely known. See notes 6 and 31; see note 12 for examples.)

box lunch ['baks 'ləntʃ] the genitals of a male as thought of in terms of oral sex. (See *box*, and see note 31.) □ *What I need is a good box lunch this afternoon.* □ *Sally said she was hungry for a box lunch.*

boy [bɔɪ] **1.** an American black male of any age. (Intended and perceived as strongly derogatory and demeaning. Also a term of address. An intentional denial of manhood. Deeply resented and provocative. Also a term of address. User is considered to be bigoted. See caution at note 1; see note 31.) □ *Look, boy, when I tell you to move, I mean move!* □ *Well, boy, it looks like your arthritis is punishing you for your misspent youth.* **2.** a young male of any race. (Usually intended and perceived as derogatory. Also a term of address. See note 3 for additional examples; see note 31.) □ *Hey, boy! Come here a minute.* □ *I say, boy, try to keep up with us.* **3.** any male of any age. (A term of endearment. Also a term of address. Especially with *my, old, good old*, etc.) □ *Hey, boy, it's good to see you.* □ *Well, my boy, it's time to go.* □ *He's a good old boy! You can trust him.* **4.** "Wow!"; an expression of surprise or amazement. (Usually an exclamation: **Oh, boy!** Use with caution to avoid confusion with senses 1 or 2. Universally known and used by both sexes and all ages.) □ *Oh, boy! Am I tired.* □ *We got trouble now. Oh, boy, do we ever!*

bra-buster ['bra-bəstɚ] **1.** a woman with large breasts. (Typical of male-to-male talking and joking. See notes 6 and 31.) □ *That mama is a real bra-buster.* □ *Let me get my hands on one of them bra-busters, and you'll see some action!* **2.** a very large breast. (Always in the plural, **bra-busters**. See notes 6 and 31; see note 7 for examples.)

break one's ass (to do something)   See *bust (one's) ass (to do something)*.

break someone's balls   to wreck or ruin someone; to overwork someone; to overwhelm someone. (Typically refers to a male. See also *break one's balls to do something* at *bust (one's) ass (to do something)*, and see note 31.) ☐ *If you cross me one more time, I'm gonna break your balls. You understand me?* ☐ *He'll do the work at my speed, or I'm gonna break his balls to get it done on time.*

bring someone off   to cause someone to have an orgasm through copulation or masturbation. (See note 31.) ☐ *She tried to bring him off, but he was too tired.* ☐ *He succeeded in bringing her off.*

bring someone on   to arouse someone sexually. (Also in general slang meaning to excite someone, without any sexual reference. See note 31.) ☐ *Look at her! She's doing her best to bring him on! Why are men so stupid?* ☐ *Are you trying to bring me on or something?*

broad   a woman. (Originally underworld slang. Intended as offensive or even jocular, but perceived as offensive by some women.) (See note 6. Probably from "broad in the beam," referring to the breadth of the female pelvis.) ☐ *When is that broad gonna show up?* ☐ *When are you broads gonna get yourselves ready so we can leave?*

brown   [braʊn] **1.** the anus. (Refers to the color of feces. See also *brown hole*. See note 30 for additional examples; see note 31.) ☐ *How would you like a swift kick right in your brown?* ☐ *Tom got cobbed right in the brown.* **2.** to perform anal intercourse on someone. (See note 31.) ☐ *These guys were browning when the coach came in. What a ruckus!* ☐ *Wally told the hustler he knew somebody who wanted to brown her.* **3.** a Mexican or Puerto Rican; a Hispanic person. (Intended as derogatory. Perceived as strongly derogatory. Refers to skin color only. See caution at note

1; see use as a slur at note 2.) **4.** a light Negro or black. (See caution at note 1; see use as a slur at note 2.)

brown hole   1. the anus. (See note 30 for examples; see note 31.) **2.** to poke someone in the anus; to *goose* someone. (See note 31.) □ *Freddy brown-holed Tom on the stairway, and they had quite a fight.* □ *Man, it hurts to get brown-holed!*

brownie   See the following entry.

brown-nose(r) AND **brownie**   a sycophant; someone who fawns over and flatters someone; an *ass-kisser.* (Such a person would go to any extreme to please someone. Refers to rubbing one's nose in the anus of another person.) □ *She is such a brown-noser! Who does she think she's got fooled?* □ *Some brown-nose came around to say how much he appreciated your efforts.*

B.S.   ['bi 'ɛs] **1.** *bullshit;* nonsense; deception. (Partly euphemistic.) □ *Don't feed me that B.S.! I know the score!* □ *All that guy talks is B.S.* **2.** to deceive or attempt to deceive someone with lies or flattery. □ *Don't try to B.S. me with your sweet talk!* □ *Fred is always B.S.-ing somebody about something.*

buck nigger   ['bək 'nɪgɚ] a young and strong black male. (Intended and perceived as strongly derogatory. User is considered to be racially bigoted. Provocative. See caution at note 1; see note 3 for examples; see use as a slur at note 2.)

Buddha head AND **buddhahead**   ['budəhɛd] someone of East Asian descent who wears a turban or other distinctive cloth headdress. (Intended as jocular and derogatory. Perceived as derogatory. See also *towelhead.* See caution at note 1; see use as a slur at note 2.) □ *Who's the Buddha head behind the counter? I never saw him before.* □ *This town is overrun with buddhaheads!*

bufu   ['bufu] **1.** a homosexual male. (From *butt* and *fuck,* referring to pederasty. See note 5 for examples and caution; see note 31.) **2.** having to do with male homosexuality; in the manner of a male homosexual. □ *We found ourselves in a bufu bar by accident.* □ *Cut out all this bufu nonsense and get down to business.*

bug-fucker ['bəg-fəkɚ] **1.** a male with a small penis. (Also a term of address. Used mostly as an epithet. Provocative. See note 31.) □ *Tell the little bug-fucker to pay the price if he wants some action. No, he doesn't get a discount, no matter what he's got!* □ *Don't worry, we aim to please even bug-fuckers like you.* **2.** a small penis. (Taboo. See note 4 for caution, note 8 for examples, and note 31.) □ *Well, a bug-fucker is better than no fucker at all.* □ *Someday this bug-fucker's gonna grow up. Just you wait!* **3.** an insignificant and worthless male. (Also a term of address. Provocative. See also *N.D.B.F.*, and see note 3 for examples.) □ *Listen to me, you stupid bug-fucker! Get your things and get outa here!* □ *You goddamn stupid bug-fucker!*

bug juice ['bəg-dʒus] **1.** any type of fruit flavored drink. (A food-dirtying term.) □ *How about another glass of that bug juice?* □ *Give the man another helping of bug juice.* **2.** soy sauce. (Because soy sauce is dark brown like the spittle of a grasshopper. A food-dirtying term.) □ *Do you always put bug juice on your rice?* □ *They use a lot of that bug juice in Chinese food, don't they?*

built like a brick shithouse [. . . 'brɪk 'ʃɪthɑus] **1.** pertaining to a very strong and well-built person. (Usually refers to a male. Refers to the sturdiness of an outhouse [outdoor toilet] built of brick rather than the traditional wooden outhouse.) □ *Chuck is built like a brick shithouse. The only fat on him is where his brain ought to be.* □ *Then this guy who's built like a brick shithouse comes in and asks me what I'm doing there.* **2.** pertaining to a beautiful and curvaceous woman. (Refers to the imagined curving and uneven walls of an outhouse built hastily and carelessly of brick. This sense is a misinterpretation of the first sense.) □ *Look at that dame! She's really built like a brick shithouse.* □ *Sally's not exactly built like a brick shithouse, but she's got what it takes.*

bull [bʊl] nonsense; lies. (A short form of *bullshit* with less negative impact.) □ *Oh, that's just bull! Don't believe any of it!* □ *Stop giving me all that bull!*

bull bitch ['bʊl 'bɪtʃ] a strong and masculine woman. (Intended and perceived as derogatory. Typical of male-to-male talk. See *bulldiker*.) □ *So, this bull bitch walks up to me and says, "Hey, buddy, got a match?"* □ *That bull bitch is a goddamn truck driver!*

bull-dagger See the following entry.

bulldiker AND **bull-dagger, bulldyker** ['bʊldɑɪkɚ AND 'bʊldægɚ, 'bʊldɑɪkɚ] a lesbian, especially if aggressive or masculine. (Intended and perceived as derogatory. Widely known, although more typical of male talk. See note 5 for additional examples and caution; see note 3 for examples.) □ *Some old bulldiker strutted in and ordered a beer and a chaser.* □ *I wonder how many times a day that bull-dagger shaves.*

bulldyker See the previous entry.

bullfuck ['bʊlfək] **1.** nonsense; lies. (Often an exclamation: **Bullfuck!** An intensified *bullshit*. Low. Typical of male-to-male talk. Taboo. See note 4 for caution, and see comment at note 32.) □ *That's just a lot of bullfuck!* □ *Bullfuck! That's a lie and you know it!* **2.** bull semen. (Rural and low. Little occasion for wider use. See note 31.) □ *Man, I really love potatoes and bullfuck.* □ *What Bessie wants is a little bullfuck.*

bullshit ['bʊlʃɪt] **1.** lies; deception; hype; nonsense. (Also an exclamation: Bullshit! Widely known and used by both sexes.) □ *That's just a lot of bullshit!* □ *Cut out the bullshit and start talking straight if you know what's good for you.* □ *I've heard enough of your bullshit.* **2.** to deceive someone verbally. (Transitive. Widely known and used by both sexes.) □ *Are you trying to bullshit me?* □ *You can't bullshit an old hand like Wally.* **3.** to tell lies; to hype and promote. (Intransitive. Widely known and used by both sexes.) □ *Are you still bullshitting? Why can't you tell* *the truth.* □ *Can't you stop bullshitting about how good you are?* **4.** false; deceptive. □ *I'm sick of those bullshit ads on TV.* □ *So, you got some bullshit degree from the university. So what?*

bullshit artist a person expert at lies, deception, and hype. (See *bullshit.* Widely known and used by both sexes.) □ *Wally is one of your classic bullshit artists. He'd rather lie than tell the truth.* □ *What can you expect from a bullshit artist? The truth?*

bullshitter ['bʊlʃɪtɚ] a person who tells lies constantly. (Not necessarily with any skill. See also *shitter.*) □ *Fred's no bullshitter. He tells it straight.* □ *Sally's a sweet girl, but a bullshitter at heart.*

bumps [bəmps] **1.** immature breasts. (Usually plural. See notes 6 and 31.) □ *When are these damn bumps gonna grow?* □ *God, those little bumps make me hot!* **2.** small breasts. (Usually plural. See note 6 and 31; see note 7 for examples.)

bunch-punch ['bəntʃ-pəntʃ] **1.** an act of serial copulation, with one female and a group of males. (See also *gang-bang.* See notes 6 and note 31.) □ *The hustler named Wanda specialized in bunch-punches.* □ *Sam always dreamed about being involved in a bunch-punch.* **2.** an act of group rape of a woman. (See notes 6 and 31.) □ *If that stupid bitch doesn't be careful about where she goes, she's gonna find out what a bunch-punch is.* □ *There was a bunch-punch in this neighborhood last night, and the night before, and the night before that. Where are the police?*

bunghole ['bəŋhol] the anus. (See *hole.* See note 30 for examples; see note 31.)

bunny fuck ['bəni fək] a quick act of copulation. (As with rabbits, which require only an instant to copulate. Taboo. See note 4 for caution; see note 16 for additional examples; see note 31.) □ *The hooker likes doing bunny fucks because she can handle more customers that way.* □ *He was always in a hurry. A bunny fuck and the late news was all he needed at night.*

buns the buttocks of either sex. (Has become a widely known and used term by women for attractive and well-formed male buttocks. Like *butt,* this term is heard often in public and on radio and television. See note 29 for additional examples.) □ *Look at the buns on that guy!* □ *Me and my girlfriend just love to go down to the beach and look for guys with cute buns.*

burrhead ['bɚhɛd] an American black. (Intended and perceived as derogatory, but not widely known. Compare to *velcro head.* See caution at note 1; see use as a slur at note 2.) □ *A couple of burrheads came into the bar and sat down.* □ *Them burrheads is hard workers.*

bush 1. the pubic hair. (Usually that of a female. See also *wool.* See note 24 for examples; see notes 6 and 31.) 2. women considered as a receptacle for the penis. (See notes 6 and 31; see examples at note 23.) 3. male sexual release through copulation with a female. (Usually with *some.* See notes 6 and 31; see note 17 for examples.)

bust-ass See *kick-ass.*

bust ass (out of some place) See *bag ass (out of some place).*

bust (one's) ass (to do something) AND **break one's balls (to do something), bust one's butt (to do something)** to work very hard to do something; to work very hard at something. (Widely known. Can refer to either sex.) □ *You get down there and bust your ass to get the job done right! You hear me?* □ *Come on, you guys! Let's bust ass! Get busy!* □ *I've been busting my butt at this job for 30 years and look where it's got me!*

bust one's nuts (to do something) [...nɔts...] to make every effort to accomplish something. (Usually said by a male.) □ *He busted his nuts to make her happy, and then she runs away with some other guy.* □ *After busting my nuts all day, I'm really tired.*

butch [butʃ] masculine, when applied to a homosexual person. (Widely known.) □ *He has become so butch lately. What's he* *been taking?* □ *That guy's not butch! He's wearing false eye-lashes!* □ *Her leather jacket is just too, too butch!*

butt [bət] the buttocks. (Has become the public word of choice for many people. It is universally used in school athletics at all levels. See note 29 for additional examples; see note 31. See also *duck-butt, kick in the butt, pain in the butt, work one's butt off.*) □ *Careful, or you'll fall on your butt!* □ *He slapped each player on the butt as he went by.* □ *She's got a nice butt on her.*

butter ['bətɚ] semen. (See also *duck-butter.* Partly euphemistic. See note 31.) □ *Is that butter on your pants leg, or what?* □ *About how much butter does a dog make?*

butterfly queen ['bətɚflaɪ kwin] a homosexual male who prefers mutual oral sex with another male. (See note 5 for examples and caution.)

butt-fuck See *ass-fuck.*

butthead ['bəthɛd] a stupid or obnoxious person of either sex. (Also a term of address. Quite popular and heard everywhere, including radio and television. See comment at note 32.) □ *Don't be such a butthead!* □ *Wally can be a butthead, but he's an okay guy.*

butthole ['bəthol] the anus. (See also *asshole.* See note 30 for examples; see note 31.)

butt naked ['bət 'nekɪd] totally nude. □ *And she came into the room butt naked and kissed all the old men, and then left.* □ *I was butt naked in the shower and couldn't get the phone.*

butt-peddler See *ass-peddler.*

butt-wipe See *ass-wipe.*

C

caca AND **kaka** ['kɑkɑ] dung; feces. (Often juvenile. See note 27 for additional examples; see note 31.) □ *The dog made caca on the front lawn.* □ *There's kaka on my shoe.*

cack [kæk] **1.** dung. (See note 27 for examples; see note 31.) **2.** to defecate. (See note 28 for additional examples; see note 31.) □ *Fred said he had to cack. He'll be back in a minute.* □ *Boy, do I need to cack!*

call-girl ['kɔl-gɚl] a woman who is "on call" as a prostitute. (Possibly refers to a prostitute who can be contacted by a telephone call. Widely known, verging on standard English.) □ *Sally worked as a call-girl for about a year before she got hooked on coke.* □ *The cops dragged in a whole flock of call-girls after the convention.*

call-house a brothel; a house of prostitution. (Where customers "pay a call" to get sex for pay. Somewhat euphemistic for "whore house." Widely known.) □ *She worked in a call-house as a receptionist, at least that's what she said.* □ *The cops closed down a call-house over on Fourth Street.*

can [kæn] **1.** the buttocks. (See note 29 for examples; see note 31.) **2.** a toilet; a restroom; an outhouse. □ *Restroom! Hell, I ain't tired! Where's the can?* □ *I'll be with you as soon as I use the can.* **3.** a woman's genital region. (See *bottom* and *cans*. Usually rude or low male-to-male talk. It is difficult to know when it refers to a woman's genitals, buttocks, or both. See notes 6 and 31; see note 12 for examples.)

candy-ass ['kændi-æs] a coward; a timid person. (Widely known. Used by both sexes. See comment at note 32. More at *candy-assed.*) □ *Sue is such a candy-ass when it comes to dealing with her children.* □ *Come on! Show some guts! Don't be a candy-ass!*

candy-ass(ed) ['kændi-æs(t)] timid; frightened; cowardly. (See comment at note 32. Widespread use.) □ *What a candy-assed twit you are!* □ *Who is the little candy-ass bastard hiding in the back room?*

can house a brothel; a house of prostitution. (See *can.* Typical of male-to-male talk.) □ *Well, these two guys went into this can house, and the madam says, "What can I do for you gentlemen?"* □ *The cops closed down a can house over on Fourth Street last week.*

cannibal ['kænəbl̩] someone who performs oral sex on the penis. (See *eat, man-eater,* and note 31.) □ *Old Sally is a regular cannibal. At least that's what Freddy says.* □ *He walked into the can house and asked for a cannibal.*

cans [kænz] a woman's breasts. (See also *can.* Usually plural. See notes 6 and 31; see note 7 for examples.)

Canuck [kə'nʊk] a French Canadian. (Considered provocative and derogatory by some French Canadians, despite a hockey team of the same name. Tone of voice and context are doubtless the sources of resentment. See use as a slur at note 2.)

cat house a brothel; a house of prostitution. (Widely known. Typical of male talk.) □ *All those old Western towns always had at least one cat house.* □ *How many cat houses do you suppose there are in this town?*

cat house detail the prostitution squad of a police department. (Jocular. Police use. See *pussy-posse.*) □ *He had worked on the cat house detail for a few months before he got transferred.* □

There are three dames working on the cat house detail. Don't ask me what they do.

cheese-eater See *fish-eater.*

cheezer ['tʃizɚ] a very bad smelling release of intestinal gas; a foul-smelling *fart*. (Typical of male-to-male talk and joking. See note 31.) □ *God, who let the cheezer?* □ *I saw what you ate for dinner. I guess it'll be cheezers again all night tonight.*

cherry ['tʃɛri] the hymen, the membrane that blocks the opening to the vagina. (See note 31.) □ *Man, I'm nearly sixteen, and I ain't never yet broke me no cherry.* □ *Look out, cherries of the world! I'm horny as hell tonight!*

chew someone's ass out ['tʃu...] to scold someone severely. (See comment at note 32.) □ *I was pretty sure he was going to chew my ass out, and he sure did.* □ *If you do that again, I won't chew your ass out. I'll bite off your goddamn nose and spit it in your ear!*

chichis ['tʃitʃiz] a woman's breasts. (Wartime. From Japanese. Usually plural. See notes 6 and 31; see note 7 for examples.)

chicken-choker ['tʃɪkn̩-tʃokɚ] a male masturbator. (See *choke the chicken.* Refers to the penis as the neck of a chicken. See note 22 for additional examples; see note 31.) □ *After seven months at sea as a first-class, registered, card-carrying chicken-choker, I arrived in port with no money.* □ *You chicken-chokers can reform! You just gotta take yourselves in hand!*

chicken-grabbing [...græbɪŋ] pertaining to a male who masturbates. (Refers to the penis as the neck of a chicken. See *chicken-choker, choke the chicken.* See note 31.) □ *Hey, you old chicken-grabbing dude! How's it going?* □ *Tell that chicken-grabbing jerk to hurry up.*

chicken queen a male homosexual who is sexually attracted to pubescent males. (See note 5 for examples and caution.)

chicken shit **1.** virtually nothing. (See comment at note 32.) □ *Fifty bucks! That's just chicken shit!* □ *I worked for him for three years, and he paid me chicken shit.* **2.** a cowardly person. (Derogatory and provocative. Also a term of address. Usually, but not necessarily, applied to males. See comment at note 32.) □ *You are such a chicken shit coward! Stand up and fight!* □ *That was a chicken shit thing to do.* **3.** worthless. (See comment at note 32.) □ *I don't want this chicken shit pizza! Get me one with pepperoni on it, not dead fish.* □ *I can't afford anything but a lousy chicken shit car, so I'd rather walk.*

chick(en) shit habit a weak or beginning addiction to a drug. (Drug culture. Originally applies to heroin. See comment at note 32.) □ *It always starts out with a chicken shit habit, then it grows.* □ *What do you mean, you're hurting? You just got a little chicken shit habit! Can't make you hurt very much!*

chili-eater See *bean-eater.*

Chinaman [ˈtʃɑɪnəmən] a Chinese male. (Formerly used in strong derogation. Still regarded by some as derogatory, though it is in wide use with no derogatory intent. See caution at note 1.) □ *See if the Chinaman will give us some help.* □ *No, he's not a Chinaman, he's Korean.*

chink [tʃɪŋk] a person of Chinese nationality or descent. (Intended and perceived as derogatory. User is considered to be racially bigoted. See caution at note 1; see use as a slur at note 2.)

chinky [ˈtʃɪŋki] pertaining to Chinese people or things. (From *chink.* Derogatory. See caution at note 1.) □ *Okay, I've had enough chinky food to last me for a week. Tomorrow we eat something else.* □ *My old aunt had a whole room full of chinky stuff, pots and vases, all that kind of stuff.*

chippy [ˈtʃɪpi] **1.** a young female, assumed to copulate freely. (Widely used by both sexes.) □ *Who is that chippy he's running around with now?* □ *That silly chippy will have a toss in the hay with anybody.* **2.** [for a man] to consort with young women, usually intending to have sex with them. □ *Tom is out chippying again. The guy never gets tired.* □ *He likes to chippy better than anything else.*

chippy around ['tʃɪpi ə'rɑʊnd] to play around sexually with someone, anyone, or everyone. □ *Don't try to chippy around with me!* □ *Come on, it was just a little chippying around.*

chippy-chaser ['tʃɪpi-tʃesɚ] a lecher; a man who chases after women hoping to have sex if he catches one. (Jocular.) □ *Max is a dirty old chippy-chaser.* □ *Fred used to be a chippy-chaser when he was younger.*

chippy-house ['tʃɪpi-hɑʊs] a brothel; a house of prostitution. □ *There's a bunch of chippy houses down by the docks.* □ *That place looks like a chippy house. Look at all those guys going in and out at all hours.*

chippy on someone to cheat on one's lover sexually. □ *She's been chippying on him, they say.* □ *You know I wouldn't chippy on you, Martha—I mean Sally.*

chism See *jism.*

chocolate 1. AND **chocolate drop** ['tʃɔklət AND ...drɑp] an American black. (Intended as mildly derogatory and perceived as derogatory. See note 1 for caution; see use as a slur at note 2.) **2.** Negroid; having to do with black Americans. (Intended as jocular and mildly derogatory. Perceived as derogatory and racially bigoted.) □ *I really like chocolate music.* □ *She's from one of the chocolate neighborhoods.*

choke the chicken See *beat the dummy.* (See also *chicken-choker.* The penis is compared to the neck of a chicken. See note 19 for examples; see note 31.)

chones [tʃonz] **1.** testicles. (From Spanish *cojones.* See note 31.) □ *You look at me that way again, and you will be saying goodbye to your chones.* □ *Just looking at her makes my chones ache.*

2. bravado. (See *balls, ballsy.*) □ *Man, has he got chones!* □ *Why are you always trying to prove that you have chones?*

Christ-killer ['kraɪst-kɪlɚ] a Jewish person. (Intended and perceived as derogatory. With reference to the betrayal and crucifixion of Jesus Christ. User is considered to be bigoted and antisemitic. See caution at notes 1; see note 3 for examples; see use as a slur at note 2.)

chuck up AND **upchuck** ['tʃək 'əp AND 'əptʃək] to vomit. (*Upchuck* is colloquial and euphemistic. See note 31.) □ *Outa my way! I'm gonna chuck up!* □ *Who upchucked over there?* □ *Somebody chucked up on the sidewalk over there.*

circle-jerk ['sɚkl̩-dʒɚk] **1.** a gathering of males performing mutual masturbation. (Partly jocular. See note 31.) □ *There were twelve boys involved in a circle jerk, and the principal caught them.* □ *They were sitting in a circle. They were either telling ghost stories or having a circle jerk.* **2.** a boring or time-wasting meeting. (From sense 1.) □ *That board meeting was the typical circle-jerk that it always is.* □ *I won't waste my time going to a circle-jerk like that again!*

clap [klæp] a case of gonorrhea. (Very old and still in use. See note 31.) □ *I think I got a case of the clap from him.* □ *He thinks he got the clap from her.*

cling like shit to a shovel AND **stick like shit to a shovel** [klɪŋ . . . 'ʃəvl̩] **1.** to stick or adhere [to someone or something] tightly. □ *That oily stuff sticks like shit to a shovel.* □ *That soap is too sticky. It sticks like shit to a shovel.* **2.** to be very dependent on someone; to follow someone around. (Often with an indirect object.) □ *She's so dependent. She clings to him like shit to a shovel.* □ *You stick to me like shit sticks to a shovel so you won't get lost again.*

clipped-dick ['klɪpt 'dɪk] a Jewish male. (Intended and perceived as derogatory. Not widely known. Refers to circumcision. User is considered to be bigoted and antisemitic. See caution at note 1; see note 3 for examples; see use as a slur at note 2.)

clit AND **clitty** [klɪt AND 'klɪti] the clitoris. (Widely known and used by both sexes. See notes 6 and 31.) □ *She says it hurts her clit to do that.* □ *Have I got a present for you and your clitty!*

clitty See the previous entry.

clod [klɑd] a stupid and oafish person. (Usually refers to a male. Old. Widely known.) □ *Don't be such a clod! Put on your tie, and let's go.* □ *What a clod! He can't even hold a fork right!*

closet queen AND **closet queer** a male homosexual who keeps his homosexuality secret from everyone. (See note 5 for examples and caution.)

closet queer See the previous entry.

cluck See *dumb cluck.*

cluster fuck ['kləstɚ fək] **1.** an act of group rape. (Taboo. See note 4 for caution; see note 31.) □ *My God, there was a cluster fuck right out there in the alley!* □ *Look at her! She's just asking for a cluster fuck.* **2.** any event as riotous as an act of group rape. (Taboo. See note 4 for caution; see note 31.) □ *This goddamn day has been one long cluster fuck!* □ *Let's finish up this glorified cluster fuck and go home.*

coals [kolz] a group of American blacks. (Intended and perceived as derogatory. See caution at note 1; see use as a slur ar note 2.)

cob [kɑb] **1.** a sharp poke or *goose* in the anus. (See note 31.) □ *Tom gave Fred a cob when he passed by.* □ *Ouch! That cob hurt!* **2.** to give someone a sharp poke in the anus. (See note 31.) □ *Tom cobbed Fred when he passed by.* □ *You stand a good chance of getting cobbed on that stairway.*

cock [kɑk] **1.** the penis. (Perhaps the current most popular word for penis in American English. See also *dick.* See note 8 for examples; see note 31.) **2.** the female genitals. (Usually considered southern. Known only sporadically elsewhere. The first sense is displacing this sense currently. Typical of rude male-to-male talk and joking. See note 12 for examples; see note 31.)

cock-block ['kɑk-blɑk] an act of one male interfering with another male's sexual activity. (Originally black.) □ *Man, you do a cock-block like that on me again, and your ass is grass!* □ *Sam is a master at the cock-block. It's his form of birth control.*

cock-cheese See *crotch-cheese.*

cock-happy pertaining to a woman who is always willing to copulate. (Typical of male-to-male talk and joking.) □ *Who is that cock-happy dame?* □ *If she's so cock-happy, why do you look so sad?*

cockhound See *cocksman.*

cock ring a ring that circles the penis tightly, maintaining a solid erection. (Usually in a homosexual context. See note 31.) □ *Wally found a cock ring on the floor in the movie theater.* □ *Sam says he uses a cock ring and life is much better for everybody.*

cocksman AND **cockhound** a lecher; a male who lives to serve his genitals. (Typical of male-to-male talk.) □ *Old Freddy is a real cocksman!* □ *Hi, Tom, you cockhound, you!*

cocksucker ['kɑksəkɚ] **1.** a male who performs fellatio (licking and sucking of the penis). (See *dick-sucker.* Also a provocative term of address. See note 31.) □ *I asked him what he did for a living, and he said he was a cocksucker. I guess he was a male whore or something.* □ *There is one question I've always wanted to ask a cocksucker, but I have never had the chance.* **2.** a low and despicable male; a male who is despicable enough to perform fellatio. (See *dick-sucker.* Also a term of address. See note 3 for examples; see note 31.) **3.** a male who performs oral sex on a woman. (In some parts of the southern U.S., cock refers to the female genitals. See note 31.) □ *Sally heard that Tom was a great cocksucker, and now she's putting the make on him.* □ *I don't care if he's a cocksucker, as long as he loves his mother.* **4.** an obsequious and flattering male; a male sycophant. (Also a term of address. See comment at note 32.) □ *Why doesn't that stupid cocksucker talk straight. He's always trying to butter somebody up.* □ *Don't be such a goddamn cocksucker!*

cocksucking despicable; contemptible. (Used for people or things. See comment at note 32. Provocative.) □ *Get your goddamn cocksucking foot outa my doorway!* □ *Shut up, you cocksucking jerk!*

cock-tease(r) See *prick-teaser.*

cock-wagon AND **sin-bin** [ˈkɑk-wægn̩ AND ˈsɪn-bɪn] a car or van used especially for teenage sexual activity; a nickname for a teenage boy's car or van. (Intended to be jocular. Used especially by teens and college students.) □ *I paid nearly $400 for that there cock-wagon, and I'm gonna enjoy it.* □ *Did you see Chuck's new sin-bin? It's got a sink in it!*

cojones [kəˈhoniz AND koˈhoniz] the testicles. (Spanish. Typical of male-to-male talk. See note 31.) □ *He kicked that old cat right in the cojones and sent it flying.* □ *I don't think you have any cojones at all!*

colder than hell very cold. (Common, colloquial English.) □ *It's colder than hell in here.* □ *Shut the door. It's getting colder than hell.*

come AND **cum** [kəm] **1.** to experience an orgasm. (Widely known and used. There is no other single word for this meaning. See note 31.) □ *He always comes right away.* □ *God, I thought she'd never cum.* **2.** semen. (This sense is less well known. Typical of male-to-male talk. See note 31.) □ *There's come on the cuff of his pants.* □ *Do you think cum is alive?*

come on to someone   to try to get someone to respond romantically or sexually. □ *She was just starting to come on to me when her parents came home.* □ *I was coming on to her, but she didn't even know I was there.*

come out of the closet   [... 'klɔzət] to appear publicly as a homosexual. (See *closet queen.* The phrase has many nonsexual metaphorical meanings. In wide use by both sexes.) □ *If he'd just come out of the closet, he'd be a lot better off.* □ *They say he came out of the closet when he was 8 years old.*

cooch   [kutʃ] **1.** the female genitals; the vulva. (An older term, not widely known. Primarily low male-to-male talk or joking. See notes 6 and 31; see note 12 for examples.) **2.** women considered as a receptacle for the penis. (Primarily low male-to-male talk or joking. See notes 6 and 31; see examples at note 23.) **3.** male sexual release through copulation with a female. (Primarily low male-to-male talk or joking. Usually with *some.* See notes 6 and 31; see note 17 for additional examples.) □ *Man, could I use some cooch!* □ *There's nothing like cooch to calm a man down and bring him to his senses.*

coon   [kun] an American black. (Intended and perceived as derogatory and provocative. Also a term of address. See also *ace boon coon.* From *raccoon.* Users are considered low and racially bigoted. See caution at note 1; see note 3 for examples; see use as a slur at note 2.)

coozey AND **coozie**   ['kuzi] **1.** the female genitals; the vulva. (Low male-to-male talk or vulgar joking. Not widely known. See notes 6 and 31; see note 12 for examples.) **2.** women considered as a receptacle for the penis. Low male-to-male talk or vulgar joking. (See notes 6 and 31; see examples at note 23.) **3.** male sexual release through copulation with a female. (Usually with *some.* Low male-to-male talk or vulgar joking. See notes 6 and 31; see note 17 for examples.)

cop a cherry   ['kɑp ə 'tʃɛri] to break a woman's hymen. (See *cherry.* See note 31.) □ *Here I am twenty-six years old, I never* *even copped a cherry!* □ *I always thought that copping a cherry would be the greatest thing in the world.*

cop a feel to casually or seemingly accidentally manage to feel someone's private parts or the buttocks. (Usually refers to a male feeling a woman's breast(s). *Cop* means to grab or take. See also *feel someone up.* See note 31.) □ *As she passed by, he reached down to cop a feel.* □ *She darted a hand over to cop a feel as he turned the corner. He damn near wrecked the car.*

cornhole ['kornhol] **1.** the anus. (Typical of low male talk. See note 30 for examples; see note 31.) **2.** a sharp poke or *goose* in the anus. (See note 31.) □ *Tod gave some guy a cornhole because he looked like Freddy.* □ *They delivered a painful cornhole to the bully and then ran off.* **3.** to poke someone in the anus. (Typical of low male talk.) □ *Let's sneak up and cornhole that guy!* □ *Tod cornholed some guy because he thought the guy was Freddy.*

cover one's ass AND **cover one's tail** to protect oneself; to act in advance to protect one's interests. (Not normally used literally. See comment at note 32. Widely known and used by both sexes.) □ *The first rule in politics is to cover your ass.* □ *I put this clause in to cover my tail. We can take it out if you want.*

cover one's tail See the previous entry.

cowshit ['kauʃɪt] **1.** the dung of the cow. (See note 27.) □ *I want you to start out by cleaning up that cowshit in the barn.* □ *Don't step in that cowshit.* **2.** nonsense; *bullshit.* (Not as common as *bullshit*, or even *horseshit*. Typical of male-to-male talk. See note 31.) □ *I've heard enough of your stupid cowshit!* □ *He stood right in front of the judge and told some cowshit about how I was the one that did it.*

crabs [kræbz] lice, especially lice in the genital region. (Because of their shape.) □ *Stop scratching your crabs and take a bath.* □ *Man, I think I have the crabs!*

crabwalk [ˈkræbwɔk] the area between the anus and the genitals where lice could travel back and forth. (Based on the form of a verb meaning to walk sideways, in the manner of a crab. Not widely known. See note 31.) □ *Man, do I have an itch in the crabwalk!* □ *She said she needed some action in the crabwalk, whatever that means.*

crack [kræk] **1.** the gap between the buttocks; the natal fold. (Used when no other term is known. See note 31.) □ *You can take your old summons and stick it up your crack!* □ *You wanna get kicked in the crack?* **2.** the gap between the lips of the vulva. (Low. Typical of low male talk. See notes 6 and 31.) □ *I think she wants something in her crack.* □ *Stick it up your crack, lady!* **3.** women considered as the object of copulation and male sexual release. (Usually with *some*. See notes 6 and 31; and see note 17 for examples.)

cradle-custard [ˈkredl̩-kəstɚd] a baby's feces. (Jocular euphemism. See note 31.) □ *What'll I do with this diaper full of cradle-custard?* □ *Well, I think I smell a new batch of cradle-custard.*

crank [kræŋk] the penis. (Jocular. See *yank someone's crank.* See note 8 for examples.)

crap [kræp] **1.** dung; feces. (Often used as a milder replacement for *shit*. See, for example, *crap-house* at *shit-house*. See note 27 for examples; see note 31. See the following entries and *Holy dog crap!, shoot the crap, take a crap.*) **2.** nonsense. (See *B.S.*) □ *What a lot of stupid crap! I don't believe it!* □ *Stop talking crap and get serious!* **3.** junk; shoddy merchandise. □ *Send this crap back. I won't pay for it!* □ *This thing is just crap! It hasn't worked right since I bought it.*

crap-house See *shit-house.*

crap-list See *shit-list.*

crapola [kræpˈolə] **1.** dung. (From *crap*. See note 27 for examples; see note 31.) **2.** nonsense; *bullshit*. □ *That's just crapola! I* *don't believe a word of it!* □ *You're full of the old crapola! You don't know what you're talking about.*

crapped (out) ['kræpt (aʊt)] dead; finished. (From dice, not from the other senses of *crap*.) □ *After a serious encounter with a rattlesnake, my two dogs were crapped by dawn.* □ *The whole army was crapped out by dawn.*

crapper ['kræpɚ] **1.** a toilet; an outhouse. □ *Man, I gotta go! Where's the crapper around here?* □ *The crapper's out back.* **2.** someone who tells lies or exaggerates; a *bullshitter.* □ *She's such a crapper. You can't believe a word she says.* □ *That crapper on television says it's gonna rain again today.*

crappy ['kræpi] **1.** messed up with dung; dungy. (See note 31.) □ *And you stay out of that crappy barnyard!* □ *Clean off your crappy shoes before you go in there!* **2.** lousy. (See *crap*.) □ *This has been a real crappy day for me.* □ *What a crappy thing to do!*

crater-face AND **pizza-face** ['kredɚ-fes AND 'pitsə...] a person with acne or many acne scars. (Intended as jocular, perceived as cruel. Also a term of address. *Pizza-face* refers to the messy and disorderly look of a pizza.) □ *I gotta get some kind of medicine for these pimples. I'm getting to be a regular crater-face.* □ *Hey, pizza-face! Want some chocolate?*

crawl [krɔl] to copulate [with] a woman. (Transitive. See notes 6 and 31; see note 13 for examples.)

cream [krim] **1.** semen. (See notes 6 and 31.) □ *His father found some cream in the john and went into a purple rage.* □ *Some of them swallow the cream, they say.* **2.** vaginal secretions. (See notes 6 and 31.) □ *Ah, I just love that cream!* □ *Now, that ought to bring on the cream!* **3.** to copulate [with] someone, usually a female. (Typical of low male-to-male talk and joking. Frequently in the passive. See note 31.) □ *He acted like he wanted to cream her.* □ *She went out and got herself creamed.* □ *She looks like she wants to get creamed.*

creamed foreskins ['krimd 'forskɪnz] creamed chipped beef on toast. (The same as *S.O.S.* A food-dirtying term. Military.) □ *Oh, boy! It's creamed foreskins again tonight!* □ *That stuff they call creamed foreskins is not so bad if you close your eyes.*

cream (in) one's pants AND **cream one's jeans** [for a male] to ejaculate in his pants from excessive sexual excitement. (Typical of male-to-male talk and joking. See note 31.) □ *God, when I saw her I nearly creamed in my pants.* □ *The kid creamed his jeans in that movie.*

crock (of shit) ['krɑk...] **1.** a mass of lies and deception worth no more than dung. (Widely known and used by both sexes.) □ *That's nothing but a crock of shit! I don't believe a word of it.* □ *What a crock! Nothing but lies!* **2.** a person who tells lies. □ *He's just a crock of shit. He never tells the truth.* □ *Don't pay any attention to that crock.* **3.** a braggart. □ *He's such a crock. He makes everything he has done sound ten times better than it really is.* □ *Listen to that crock talk about himself!*

crotch-cheese AND **cock-cheese** ['krɑtʃ-tʃiz AND 'kɑk-tʃiz] smegma; any nasty, smelly substance—real or imagined—that accumulates around the genitals, especially in athletes. (See also *toe jam.* Typical of male-to-male talk and joking, but known and used by both sexes. See note 31.) □ *Man, this stuff is vile. It smells like crotch-cheese.* □ *When I think of Simon, I can only think of cock-cheese.*

crotch-cobra ['krɑtʃ-kobrə] the penis. (Jocular and contrived. See note 31; see note 8 for examples.)

crotch rot a severe fungal itch, perhaps with a rash, in the crotch; any skin disease of the crotch or vaginal area. (Jocular. Compare to *jock itch.* See note 31.) □ *Man, do I have a case of crotch rot.* □ *I asked the doctor what to do for crotch rot, and he says to scratch it.*

crud [krəd] **1.** any nasty substance. (An old form of the word *curd.* See note 31.) □ *There's some crud on your left shoe.* □ *I* *got some sort of crud on my new pants.* **2.** junk; stuff; personal possessions. □ *Get your crud outa my way, will you!* □ *Pack all this crud up and send it back to the manufacturer.*

Crud you! ['krəd 'ju] "Go to hell!" (A disguise for *Fuck you!*) □ *Crud you, you creep!* □ *Well, crud you, you mungshit!*

crystals ['krɪstəlz] the testicles. (From "crystal balls." See note 31.) □ *He got hit right in the crystals. It was real embarrassing, as well as painful.* □ *Man, every time I see her, my crystals ache.*

cum See *come*.

cum freak ['kəm frik] a female who loves copulation. (Typical of male-to-male talk. See note 31.) □ *What I am looking for is a blond cum freak who earns enough to support us both.* □ *She is a real, true cum freak!*

cunt [kənt] **1.** the female genitals; the vulva. (One of the English "four-letter words." It is widely known and considered very vulgar. Typical of low and rude talk and joking. A very offensive word to women and refined men. See also *unt-cay*. *Unt-cay* can be substituted in all examples below. See notes 6 and 31; see note 12 for examples. See the following entries and *decunt, get some cunt*.) **2.** women considered as nothing more than a receptacle for the penis; a wretched and despised woman. (See notes 6 and 31; see examples at note 23.) **3.** male sexual release through copulation with a female. (Usually with *some*. See notes 6 and 31; see note 17 for examples.) **4.** a wretched and disgusting male. (Also a term of address. See notes 6 and 31; see comment at note 32.) □ *What a cunt that guy is!* □ *Don't act like such a cunt, you twit!*

cunt cap ['kənt kæp] the two-pointed military hat. (Military. See note 6; see comment at note 32.) □ *Get that cunt cap off your head in here!* □ *He lost his cunt cap overboard.*

cunt fart AND **pussy fart** ['kənt fɑrt AND 'pʊsi...] a vaginal "fart," the sudden release of air—from the vagina—trapped on insertion of the penis during copulation. (See also *kweef*. Many people are surprised to learn that there is a name for this phenomenon. See notes 6 and 31.) □ *He heard a little cunt fart and started laughing so hard, he had to stop.* □ *Did I hear a cunt fart, or what?*

cunt hair the female pubic hair. (See notes 6 and 31; see note 24 for examples.) □ *Who's the one who keeps itching her cunt hair?* □ *I like pictures that show less cunt hair.*

cunt-hooks AND **shit-hooks** the fingers; the hands. (Typical of low male-to-male talk. See note 6; see comment at note 32.) □ *Get your cunt-hooks off my car!* □ *Put your shit-hooks around those oars and row!*

cunt hound a lecher. (Typical of low male-to-male talk and joking. See note 6; see comment at note 32.) □ *Tod is such a cunt hound. All he thinks about is dames.* □ *All right, cunt hounds, take a look at this next picture!*

cunt juice AND **vagina juice** [ˈkənt dʒus AND vəˈdʒaɪnə...] vaginal secretions. (Low male-to-male talk and joking. See also *cream.* See notes 6 and 31; see comment at note 32.) □ *Man, without cunt juice, it's pure hell.* □ *Nothing like vagina juice to make life easier.*

cunt-rag a perineal pad or sanitary napkin. (Typical of low male-to-male talk. See notes 6 and 31; see comment at note 32.) □ *She's in the can tending to her cunt-rag.* □ *I gotta stop and get a box of cunt-rags for my ho.*

cunt-sucker [ˈkənt-səkɚ] **1.** someone who practices oral sex on a female; usually, but not necessarily a lesbian. (Typical of low male-to-male talk and joking. See notes 6 and 31.) □ *There were a couple of cunt-suckers holding hands in the corner.* □ *The guy's a cunt-sucker and a dick-sucker, both.* **2.** a wretched and disgusting person. (Compare to *cocksucker.* Typical of low male-to-male talk and joking. See note 6; see comment at note 32.) □ *You goddamn cunt-sucker! Get out of my sight!* □ *I ought to punch that cunt-sucker in the mouth!*

cunt-teaser [ˈkənt-tizɚ] a male who stimulates a woman sexually and then will not copulate. (Compare to *prick-teaser.* Low, typical of male-to-male talk. See notes 6 and 31.) □ *He's a woman hater and a cunt-teaser.* □ *He's a strange sort of cunt-teaser. It's not that he won't; he can't.*

cunt-wagon See *pimpmobile.*

curse a woman's monthly menstrual period; menstruation. (Always with *the.* Widely known to both sexes. Typically used by females. See notes 6 and 31.) □ *I am so sick of the curse!* □ *The curse has struck again!*

cut a fart AND **cut one, let a fart, let one** to release intestinal gas through the anus. (See *fart.* Typical of low and juvenile male talk and joking. See note 31.) □ *Fred cut a fart right in the middle of English class, and nobody moved a muscle.* □ *Somebody cut one. Who did it?* □ *Wally let one, and everybody howled.*

cut ass (out of some place) See *bag ass (out of some place).*

cut-cock [ˈkət-kak] a Jewish male. (Intended and perceived as derogatory. Refers to circumcision. Not widely known. See note 3 for examples; see use as a slur at note 2.)

cut one See *cut a fart.*

cut the cheese [... ˈtʃiz] to release bad-smelling intestinal gas through the anus. (Refers to the foul smell of some cheese. See also *cut a fart.* Widely known. Typical of low talk, especially teens and college students. See note 31.)

D

Dago ['dego] an Italian male. (Intended and perceived as strongly derogatory and provocative. Also a term of address. Originally a term for a Spaniard. From *Diego*. User is considered to be bigoted. See caution at note 1; see examples at note 3; see use as a slur at note 2.)

Dammit all! ['dæmɪt ɔl] a curse; an expression of anger or pain. (Universally known. Objected to by some.) □ *Dammit all! I locked my keys in the car.* □ *Dammit all! I missed my favorite television program.*

Damn(ation)! [dæm(neʃn̩)] a curse; an expression of anger, pain, or disappointment. (Universally known. Objected to by some.) □ *Oh, damn! We're late!* □ *Damnation! I hit my finger!*

damn(ed) cursed; bad; detestable. (Universally known. Objected to by some.) □ *This damned old car is a pain in the ass.* □ *What a damn jerk you are.* □ *Yes, I'm mad! I'm damn mad!* □ *Get your damned junk out of here!*

damn(ed) sight better much better. (See *damned*.) □ *Okay, now. That's a damned sight better!* □ *This one is not a damn sight better than the old one.*

damn(ed) well very well. (See *damned*.) □ *You know damned well what I'm talking about.* □ *You're damn well right!*

Damn it!   a curse; a common expression of anger or pain. (Universally known. Objected to by some. See *Dammit all!*.) □ *Oh, damn it! I'm late!* □ *I hit my finger, damn it!*

Damn it to hell!   a curse meaning condemn something to hell. (Widely known. Objected to by some.) □ *Damn it to hell, I mean it!* □ *Oh, damn it to hell, go ahead and do it!*

Damn the war!   a curse made milder by condemning something that everyone already condemns. □ *Oh, damn the war! I'm late!* □ *Damn the war! He did it again!*

dark meat   a black woman considered sexually. (Compare to *white meat*. Usually with *some*. See note 6; see caution at note 1; see examples at note 23.) □ *I wanna get my hands on some of that dark meat.* □ *Do you like dark meat or white meat?*

darky AND **darkie**   ['dɑrki] an American black. (Once mild and polite. Now derogatory and provocative. User may be considered racially bigoted. See caution at note 1; see use as a slur at note 2.) □ *The darkies were humming softly in the moonlight.* □ *Has the darkie showed up yet?*

day the eagle shits   [... 'ig]...] payday. (Military. See comment at note 32. Refers to the eagle that represents the U.S.) □ *Tomorrow is the day the eagle shits, and do I ever need it.* □ *I can't wait till the day the eagle shits. I need cash now!*

dead-ass   ['dɛd-æs] **1.** stupid and useless. (Usually refers to a male. See comment at note 32.) □ *Poor old Max is such a dead-ass jerk.* □ *What a dead-ass idea that was!* **2.** a useless and worthless oaf, usually a male. (Also a term of address. See comment at note 32,) □ *Get out, you dead-ass!* □ *Hey, dead-ass, what's new?*

dead whore   ['dɛd 'hor] a very easy college course. ("As easy as copulating with a dead whore." Collegiate.) □ *I had a light load last semester, three dead whores and calculus.* □ *That course is nothing but a dead whore. No work at all.*

decunt [diˈkənt] to remove the penis from the vagina. (Compare to *cunt*. See notes 6 and 31.) □ *He hollered through the door that he'd be there as soon as he decunted.* □ *Okay, you creep, decunt and pay up!*

diarrhea of the mouth [daɪəˈriə...] an imaginary medical condition that is supposed to account for someone talking too much. (Jocular. Widely known and used by both sexes.) □ *Sorry, every now and then I get diarrhea of the mouth.* □ *She's really afflicted with diarrhea of the mouth.*

dick [dɪk] **1.** the penis. (Currently a very popular and well-known word for the penis. See also *cock*. See note 8 for examples; see note 31. See the following entries and *clipped-dick, donkey dick, needle dick, pencil dick, whiskey dick*.) **2.** to copulate [with] a woman. (Transitive and intransitive. See notes 13 and 14 for additional examples; see note 31.) □ *He vowed he would dick her before dawn.* □ *They dicked till the sun came up.* □ *Hell, she's never been dicked. I don't care what she says!* □ *If you think I'm going out with a guy who only wants to get me dicked, you're crazy.* **3.** to cheat or deceive someone. (Low. Known and used by both sexes.) □ *You're dicking me again! How dumb do you think I am?* □ *That salesman dicked me for ten extra bucks.* □ *Man, I really got dicked at that store! Those creeps are crooks.* □ *If you don't wanna get dicked, go to a good store where you can trust the dude selling you stuff.*

dick around to waste time; to goof off. (See note 31.) □ *Stop dicking around and get to work!* □ *She's always dicking around when she should be working.*

dick for [ˈdɪk for] a person dumb enough to ask "What's a *dick* for?" (Jocular and contrived. Teens and college student use.) □ *The guy's a real dick for.* □ *You bums are all dick fors. Straighten out or get out!*

dickhead [ˈdɪkhɛd] **1.** a stupid male. (Possibly also for a female. Also a term of address. See note 31. See note 15 for additional examples.) □ *You feeble dickhead! Let me do it!* □ *See if you can* *get that dickhead to do it right this time.* **2.** the head of the penis. (See note 31.) □ *You gave me a pain in the dickhead. I think I got something from you.* □ *If you like your dickhead attached, you had better do just exactly as you are told.*

dick-sucker **1.** a male who performs fellatio (licking and sucking of the penis). (Also a term of address. Not as well known as *cock-sucker.* See note 31.) □ *They say he's a dick-sucker, but who would really know?* □ *This dick-sucker came up and wanted to know my sign.* **2.** a low and despicable male; a male who is despicable enough to perform fellatio. (Also a term of address. See *cocksucker.* See note 31; see note 3 for examples; see comment at note 32.) □ *You slimy dick-sucker. I'll get you for this.* □ *I had no idea you were such a sneaky dick-sucker.*

dicky-licker ['dɪki-lɪkɚ] someone who performs oral sex on the penis, usually a homosexual male. (See note 31.) □ *One of the dicky-lickers started staring at me.* □ *Can you imagine a whole roomful of dicky-lickers, licking?*

diddle ['dɪdl̩] **1.** to feel someone sexually. (See also *cop a feel, feel someone up.* See note 31.) □ *He was trying to diddle her, and she was trying to watch the movie.* □ *She moved her hand over, like she was going to diddle him, then she jabbed him in the crystals.* **2.** to masturbate oneself. (See note 21 for examples; see note 31.) **3.** to masturbate someone else. (Transitive. See note 20 for examples; see note 31.) **4.** to cheat someone. □ *The shop owner diddled me out of ten bucks.* □ *They will diddle you if you don't watch out.*

diddly-shit AND **doodly-shit** ['dɪdli-ʃɪt AND 'dudli...] **1.** anything at all. (Usually in the negative. See comment at note 32; see the examples which follow.) □ *I don't give a diddly-shit what you do!* □ *This thing ain't worth diddly-shit.* □ *You ain't worth doodly-shit!* **2.** virtually worthless; useless. (See comment at note 32.) □ *I'm gonna take this diddly-shit watch back to the store and get my money back.* □ *What am I gonna do with this doodly-shit car?*

dike AND **dyke** [dɑɪk] a lesbian; a *bulldiker.* (Usually intended and perceived as derogatory. Also a term of address. Potentially provocative. See note 5 for examples and caution; see note 3 for additional examples.) □ *Tell the dike to get back on her bike and get outa here.* □ *I guess she was a dike. She looked mean enough.*

dikey AND **dykey** ['dɑɪki] in the manner of a lesbian; pertaining to lesbians. (See *dike, dyke.*) □ *She walks kinda dikey, doesn't she?* □ *This place is a little too dikey for me. I'm leaving.*

dildo ['dɪldo] **1.** a substitute for a penis used by a woman to simulate real copulation. (See note 31.) □ *She had a dildo with a vibrator and heater in it.* □ *They sell dildos by mail, and there are shops that have them, but not around here.* **2.** a stupid and worthless male. (See note 15 for examples.)

ding-dong ['dɪŋ-dɔŋ] **1.** the penis. (See note 8 for examples; see note 31.) **2.** a stupid person of either sex. (General slang. Easy to confuse with senses 1 and 3.) □ *You silly ding-dong! Try again.* □ *Come on, you ding-dongs! Settle down.* **3.** damned. (A euphemism.) □ *Get your ding-dong junk outa my way!* □ *I have to go to a ding-dong concert tonight.*

dinge AND **dinghe** ['dɪndʒ] an American black. (Derogatory and provocative, but somewhat out of date. See caution at note 1; see use as a slur at note 2.)

dinge queen a homosexual male who prefers sex with black males. (See also *dinge.* See note 5 for examples and caution.)

dinghe See *dinge.*

dingle ['dɪŋgl̩] the penis. (Jocular and juvenile. See note 8 for additional examples; see note 31.) □ *Come on, Billy. Shake your dingle and put it away.* □ *It's so damn cold my dingle's gone!*

dingleberry ['dɪŋgl̩bɛri] **1.** a blob of fecal matter clinging to the hairs around the anus. (See note 31.) □ *Is there no permanent cure for the heartbreak of dingleberries?* □ *There's nothing* *worse than dingleberries.* **2.** a stupid-acting person of either sex. □ *You are such a dumb dingleberry! Wise up!* □ *If you're gonna act like a dingleberry, I'm gonna leave.*

dingle-dangle ['dɪŋgl̩-dæŋgl̩] the penis. (Jocular and juvenile. See note 8 for examples; see note 31.)

dingus AND **dingy** ['dɪŋgəs AND 'dɪŋi OR 'dɪŋgi] the penis; the male "thing." (See note 8 for examples; see note 31.)

dingy See the previous entry.

dink [dɪŋk] **1.** A person of East Asian [including Japanese] nationality or descent; originally a person of Chinese nationality or descent. (Rhymes with *chink.* Much use during the Vietnam War for the Vietnamese. Intended and perceived as derogatory. See caution at note 1; see use as a slur at note 2.) **2.** an American black. (Intended and perceived as derogatory. See caution at note 1; see use as a slur at note 2.) **3.** the penis, especially a small one. (See note 8 for additional examples; see note 31.) □ *God, Fred, you really got a dink. Is it full grown yet?* □ *What a dink! Does it work?*

dipshit ['dɪpʃɪt] **1.** an obnoxious person. (Usually refers to a male. See comment at note 32.) □ *Look, dipshit, I'm in a hurry.* □ *Here comes another dipshit looking for trouble.* **2.** pertaining to someone or something obnoxious, stupid, or offensive. (See comment at note 32.) □ *Here's another one of his dipshit ideas.* □ *Throw this dipshit book in the trash.*

dipstick ['dɪpstɪk] **1.** the penis. (See *put lipstick on his dipstick.* From the name of the metal stick used to measure the amount of oil in an automobile engine. See note 8 for examples; see note 31.) **2.** a stupid and obnoxious male; a *dipshit.* (Also a term of address. Partly euphemistic for *dipshit.* See note 15 for examples.) □ *The guy means well, but he's still a dipstick.* □ *Well, dipstick, what're you gonna do for an encore?*

dirt-chute AND **slop-chute** [ˈdɪrt-ʃut AND ˈslɑp-ʃut] the anus; the rectum. (See note 30 for examples; see note 31.)

dive a muff [ˈdɑɪv ə ˈməf] to perform oral sex on a woman. (The *muff* represents the pubic hair. See also *muff-diver,* and see note 31.) □ *Marge asked me if I knew how to dive a muff, and I said no.* □ *Tod likes to dive a muff every now and then. So he says.*

diver See *muff-diver.*

do [du] to copulate [with] someone. (Transitive. See note 13 for additional examples; see note 31.) □ *She wanted to do him, but he went to sleep first.* □ *He did Martha, then he did Sue, then he did Gloria.*

do a grind [... ˈgrɑɪnd] to perform an act of copulation. (See *grind.* Said of a male or female. See note 31.) □ *He kept saying he had to do a grind or he was going to die.* □ *She wanted to do a grind and then go back to work, but things didn't work out.*

do a number on someone to cheat or betray someone; to do something bad to someone. (Widely known and used. See also the following entry.) □ *They really did a number on me in that store.* □ *You wouldn't try to do a number on me, would you?*

do a number on something **1.** to urinate or defecate on something. (See *number one, number two.* See note 31.) □ *The puppy did a number on the carpet.* □ *Billy did a number on the bathroom floor.* **2.** to damage or ruin something; to destroy something. (Widely known, general slang.) □ *The truck really did a number on my car.* □ *The teacher did a number on the class by having a surprise test.*

dodads [ˈdudædz] the testicles. (From a general slang term for "gadgets." See note 31.) □ *Bob got hit right in the dodads.* □ *She makes my dodads ache!*

dogess [ˈdɔgəs] a vile tempered woman; a *bitch.* (See note 6. Euphemistic.) □ *You don't have to be such a dogess about it!* □

Here comes the dogess now. Pretend we were talking about something else.

dog-fashion See *dog-ways.*

dog-log ['dɔg-lɔg] a rodlike lump of dog's feces. (Jocular euphemism. See note 31.) □ *Don't step on the dog-logs on the sidewalk.* □ *Please go out and clean up the dog-logs on the lawn.*

dog-style See *dog-ways.*

dog('s) vomit ['dɔgz vɑmɪt] any disgusting and gooey mass of food. (A food-dirtying term.) □ *I'm not gonna eat this dog's vomit.* □ *Well, it looks like dog vomit again tonight.*

dog-ways AND **dog-fashion, dog-style** copulation in the manner of dogs, that is, with the male approaching from the rear. (Typically found in dirty jokes. See note 31.) □ *Have you ever done it dog-ways?* □ *They did it dog-style, so they could both watch television.* □ *The doctor recommended they try it dog-fashion. Not in so many words, of course.*

dohickies ['duhɪkiz] the testicles. (A general slang term for "gadgets." See note 31.) □ *I got an itch on my dohickies.* □ *Wear this strap thing so you don't knock the hell out of your dohickies when you jump.*

dong [dɔŋ] the penis. (Perhaps compared to the clapper in a bell or the bell-shaped *head.* Very well known and used by both sexes. See note 8 for examples; see note 31.)

donkey dick ['dɔŋki dɪk] a sausage; a sausage as large as a donkey's penis. (A food-dirtying term. Compare to *horse cock.*) □ *Hey, chum, pass me the donkey dick, would ya?* □ *Whack me off a chunk of that donkey dick and give me some more potatoes.*

doodle ['dudl̩] **1.** the penis. (Juvenile. Humorous when used by adults. See note 8 for additional examples; see note 31.) □ *Put your doodle away, Jimmy, and flush the toilet.* □ *Nobody wants* *to look at your doodle, Billy.* **2.** feces, especially a baby's feces. (Juvenile. See *doo-doo*. See note 31.) □ *Billy's got doodle in his diapers.* □ *There's dog doodle on my shoe.* **3.** to defecate. (See *doo-doo*. See note 28 for additional examples; see note 31.) □ *I gotta doodle!* □ *The dog doodled on the back porch.*

doodly-shit See *diddly-shit*.

doo-doo ['du-du] **1.** dung; fecal material. (Juvenile or jocular. See note 27 for examples; see note 31.) **2.** to defecate. (Juvenile. See note 28 for examples; see note 31.)

do one's damnedest to try as hard as one can. □ *I did my damnedest, but it still didn't work out.* □ *Get in there and do your damnedest!*

dork [dork] **1.** the penis. (See note 8 for examples; see note 31.) **2.** a stupid and worthless male. (And lately also for a female. Widespread. Also a term of address. See note 15 for additional examples.) □ *You silly dork! Don't do that!* □ *Sally can be a dork at times, but she is basically good.*

dorky ['dorki] tacky, stupid, or awkward. (From *dork*. Widespread.) □ *I don't want any of this dorky food!* □ *What a dorky-looking hat!*

dothead ['dɑthɛd] an [East] Indian person who wears a red dot on the forehead. (Intended as jocular. Perceived as derogatory. See caution at note 1; see use as a slur at note 2.)

do the story with someone to copulate with someone; to have sex with someone. (Euphemistic. See also note 13 for related examples; see note 31.) □ *Well, she ended up doing the story with him, and now she's got twins.* □ *Tom and Sally did the story and never saw one another again.*

double-barreled slingshot ['dəbḷ-bɛrəld 'slɪŋʃɔt] a brassiere. (Jocular. See note 31.) □ *She needs a bigger double-barreled* *slingshot.* □ *Did you see the size of that double-barreled sling-shot hanging on that clothesline?*

double-damn a damn; an elaboration of *damn.* □ *I don't give a double-damn what you think!* □ *It's not worth a damn, and it's sure not worth a double-damn!*

douche-bag [ˈduʃ-bæg] **1.** a wretched and disgusting person. (Usually refers to a male. From the name of a device used to flush out the vagina.) □ *You stupid douche-bag! Go find yourself some other shoulder to cry on.* □ *Don't be a douche-bag. Pick up your things and go home, Chuck.* **2.** an ugly girl or woman. (See note 6.) □ *She is such a douche-bag!* □ *Look at that face! What a douche-bag!*

drag ass around to go around looking very sad and depressed. (Widely known. The verb "drag" is not usually in the past tense in this construction. See comment at note 32.) □ *Why do you drag ass around all the time, Tom?* □ *I'm so upset, I can only drag ass around. I can't get anything done.*

drag ass (out of some place) See *bag ass (out of some place).*

drag, in wearing women's clothing, said of a male. (Though this is viewed as a homosexual practice, this expression refers to any such cross-dressing by any male, such as for a play or a costume party.) □ *He showed up at her party in drag.* □ *He looks pretty good in drag.*

drag queen a male homosexual who gets pleasure from dressing in female clothing and pretending to be a woman in public. (See note 5 for examples and caution.)

drive the porcelain bus to vomit into a toilet. (The rim of the toilet bowl represents the steering wheel of the "bus." Compare to *ride the porcelain train.*) □ *Tom's in the john driving the porcelain bus.* □ *I think I gotta go drive the procelain bus!*

drop one's load AND **dump one's load** to defecate. (See also *dump.* See note 28 for examples.)

dry fuck AND **dry hump** **1.** to rub one's genitals against someone without penetrating. (Also done with layers of clothing between the participants. Taboo. See note 4 for caution; see note 31.) □ *They were dry fucking when the maid came in.* □ *Have you tried dry humping?* **2.** an act of rubbing one's genitals against someone without actual sexual penetration. (Taboo. See note 4 for caution; see note 31.) □ *He wasn't even in the mood for a dry fuck.* □ *No, not even a dry hump.*

dry hump See the previous entry.

duck-butt **1.** a very large pair of buttocks. (Cruel. See note 31.) □ *Who's the mama over there with the economy-size duck-butt?* □ *What an enormous duck-butt!* **2.** a person with very large buttocks. (Cruel. See also *booming.* Also a term of address. See note 31.) □ *Hey, duck-butt! Get it moving!* □ *That chair will hold anybody but a real duck-butt.*

duck-butter any nasty substance with the approximate consistency of liquid duck droppings, such as semen, mucus, etc. (See also *butter.* See note 31.) □ *God, clean up that duck-butter before somebody sees it!* □ *What is that damn duck-butter on the counter?*

duck's ass the name of a haircut popular in the 1950s and still seen occasionally. (The haircut was called a "ducktail" cut. The side hair is long and combed to the back of the head where it looks like the rear end of a duck where it meets.) □ *He showed up in a duck's ass, and most people thought it was something entirely new.* □ *Who's the dude in the greasy duck's ass?*

dugs [dəgz] a woman's breasts, especially if aged or withered. (Unflattering at best. Typically plural. See note 7 for examples; see notes 6 and 31.) □ *Her dugs made not even the slightest rise in her tight jersey.* □ *Not much in the dugs department, but okay otherwise.*

dumb-ass AND **stupid-ass** stupid; dumb. (The terms are elaborations of "stupid" and "dumb." Typical of male-to-male talk. See comment at note 32.) □ *That was a real dumb-ass thing to do.* □ *What a stupid-ass remark!* **2.** a stupid person. (Also a term of address. Typical of male-to-male talk. See comment at note 32.) □ *Hey, stupid-ass. Where're ya going?* □ *Don't be such a dumb-ass! You know what I mean!*

dumb cluck AND **cluck, kluck** ['dəm 'klək] a very stupid person; a person as stupid as a chicken. (Widely known and used by both sexes for either sex.) □ *What a dumb cluck!* □ *Don't be a cluck! Try again!*

dumbshit ['dəmʃɪt] **1.** a very stupid person. (Also a term of address. See comment at note 32.) □ *He's a dumbshit. He can't do any better than that.* □ *I can't get the job done with a crew of dumbshits.* **2.** stupid; dumb. (See also *dumb-ass.* See comment at note 32.) □ *What a dumbshit idea!* □ *That was really a dumb-shit thing to do.*

dummy ['dəmi] the penis. (See *beat the dummy.* See note 8 for examples; see note 31.)

dump [dəmp] **1.** to defecate. (See note 28 for examples; see note 31.) **2.** an act of defecation. □ *We stopped while John took a dump.* □ *I haven't had a dump in days.*

dump one's load See *drop one's load.*

dump on someone **1.** to scold someone severely. (Widely known and used by both sexes. Literally, to dump dung on someone.) □ *She really dumped on me when I broke her crystal vase.* □ *Please, don't dump on me. I've had a hard day.* **2.** to place a large burden of guilt or grief on someone; to give someone all of one's troubles. □ *Don't dump on me! I got my own troubles!* □ *She had had a bad day, so she dumped on me for about an hour.*

Dutchman AND **Dutchie** ['dətʃmən AND 'dətʃi] a German. (From *Deutsch.* A nickname, sometimes for an individual. Not usually derogatory. See caution at note 1.) □ *This Dutchman came in and ordered a pitcher of beer.* □ *I was surrounded by Dutchies, and I didn't know what to do, so I took a train to France.*

dyke See *dike.*

dykey See *dikey.*

E

earp AND **urp** [ɚp] **1.** to vomit. (See note 31.) □ *She went over by the bushes and earped and earped.* □ *I think I'm gonna urp.* **2.** vomit. (See note 31.) □ *God, there's earp right there on the sidewalk.* □ *Don't step in that urp.*

easy make a woman who can be copulated [with] without much trouble. (Can also be said of a man.) □ *She's got a reputation as an easy make.* □ *He thought she was an easy make, but was he surprised!*

eat to perform oral sex on someone. (See *cannibal.* See note 31.) □ *She said she wanted to eat me!* □ *They ate each other, time and time again.*

eat at the Y to perform oral sex on a woman. (Not widely known. See note 31. This "Y" refers to the crotch.) □ *Tod says he likes to eat at the Y.* □ *Hey, sailor, you wanna eat at the Y?*

Eat me! an expression meaning roughly "suck my genitals." (Rude and provocative. See note 31.) □ *Eat me, you creep!* □ *Shut up, you fart! Eat me!*

Eat shit! "Drop dead!" (Rude and provocative. See note 31.) □ *Eat shit, mother-fucker!* □ *Oh, go eat shit!*

effing AND **F-ing** ['ɛfɪŋ] "fucking." □ *What an effing stupid idea!* □ *Of all the F-ing stupid things to do!*

effing around AND **F-ing around** ['ɛf-ɪŋ ə'rɑʊnd] "fucking around"; "messing around." (See *fuck around.* Taboo. See note 4 for caution.) □ *They were F-ing around with the switch, and turned it on accidently.* □ *Stop effing around and get to work.*

eggplant ['ɛgplænt] an American black. (Intended and perceived as derogatory. From the dark color of the eggplant. See note 2 for examples.)

Esso-B ['ɛs'o-'bi] a *son of a bitch.* (A spelling disguise.) □ *What a stupid Esso-B.* □ *What does that Esso-B think she's doing?*

eyetie See the following entry.

eytie AND **eyetie, itie** ['ɑɪtɑɪ] a person of Italian nationality or descent. (Primarily a nickname. From *Italian.* Potentially derogatory. Wartime. See caution at note 1.) □ *The eyties live mostly down in the city.* □ *I really like that itie food.*

F

fag See *faggot.*

fag-bag AND **fag-hag** ['fæg-bæg AND 'fæg-hæg]   a woman who prefers the company of homosexual males. □ *Sally is a fag-bag, but she can still get along with Bob.* □ *There were some gays and a few fag-hags there.*

fag-busting See *gay-bashing.*

fag-factory   a place where male homosexuals gather. (See *fag.* Intended as jocular. Not widely known.) □ *He played saxophone in a fag-factory on the east side of town.* □ *They met in a fag-factory and have been happy together for years.*

faggot AND **fag** ['fægət AND fæg] a male homosexual. (Intended and perceived as strongly derogatory. Also a term of address. Deeply resented. *Fag* is also a harmless slang term for a cigarette. *Faggot* is a standard English term for a stick of firewood. See note 5 for examples and caution; see note 3 for examples.)

fag-hag See *fag-bag.*

fag-joint   a place where homosexual males gather; a bar patronized primarily by male homosexuals. (Widely known.) □ *You ever been to a fag-joint?* □ *He worked for a while in a fag-joint over on Maple Street.*

fag-mag a magazine that caters to the sexual interests of male homosexuals. □ *He's got his picture in all the fag-mags.* □ *Fag-mags are pretty expensive.*

fairy ['fɛri] a male homosexual. (Intended and perceived as derogatory. Also a term of address. Deeply resented. See note 5 for examples and caution; see note 3 for examples as a verbal weapon.)

falsies ['fɔlsiz] artificial breasts; stuffing for making the breasts appear larger and more shapely. (Old and universally known. The term is used by both sexes.) □ *I don't care if she is wearing falsies. She's got a beautiful smile.* □ *This bra had falsies built into it.*

family jewels the testicles. (Jocular and euphemistic. They are necessary to produce a family. See note 31.) □ *Hey, careful of the family jewels.* □ *He got hit in the family jewels, but he survived.*

fart [fɑrt] **1.** to release intestinal gas through the anus. (One of the English "four-letter words." Intransitive. Universally known, but frowned on by many people nonetheless. "Break wind" is the preferred expression. See note 31. See the following entries and *blow a fart, cunt fart, cut a fart, fiddle-fart, let a fart, monkey-fart, pussy fart, scared fartless.*) □ *Okay, who farted?* □ *I think I'm gonna fart.* **2.** the sound or odor of the release of intestinal gas. (See comments at sense 1.) □ *I heard a fart. Who did it?* □ *Who made that smelly fart?* **3.** a stupid, despicable, and annoying person. (Usually a male, especially with *old.* Also a term of address. See comment at note 32.) □ *You old fart! You are a real pain!* □ *The guy's nothing but a fart. Just forget him.*

fart around to waste time; to do something ineffectually or inefficiently. (See comments at *fart.* See comment at note 32.) □ *Stop farting around and get to work!* □ *He spent four years farting around at college and still can't hold a job.*

fart hole a wretched and worthless person; an *asshole.* (Also a term of address. See comment at note 32.) □ *Stop acting like such a fart hole!* □ *Come on, fart hole! Get moving!*

farting-spell See *pissing-spell.*

fart off to waste time; to goof off. (See comment at note 32.) □ *Why are you farting off when there's work to be done?* □ *She specializes in farting off. What a lazy chick.*

farts fine arts. (Jocular. A blend of two words, *fine* and *arts.* See comment at note 32.) □ *I'm taking art to fulfill the farts requirement.* □ *Farts is dull, but it's better than underwater basket-weaving.*

fart sack one's bed. (Military. Apparently a place where one can break wind at will. See comment at note 32.) □ *I can't seem to get enough time in the fart sack.* □ *Come on! Get out of the fart sack and get moving!*

fast-fuck (Taboo in all senses.) **1.** a rapid act of copulation. (See note 4 for caution; see note 16 for examples; see note 31.) **2.** a male who ejaculates soon after beginning to copulate. (See note 31.) □ *Fred's a fast-fuck, but he has a nice smile.* □ *The hustlers like the fast-fucks. They can make more money that way.* **3.** someone who agrees to copulate without much persuasion. (See note 31.) □ *Sally is a fast-fuck. A real bed-bunny.* □ *He's a fast-fuck, but all men are.*

fat-ass(ed) ['fæt-æs(t)] having large buttocks. (See also *booming.*) □ *Get your fat-ass self outa my car!* □ *Who is that fat-assed dame over there?*

father-fucker ['faðɚ-fəkɚ] a male who copulates anally with other males; a male homosexual. (The opposite of *mother-fucker.* Taboo. See note 4 for caution; see note 5 for examples and caution; see note 31.)

fay See *ofay.*

F.B. See *fuck bunny.*

feel hairy to feel sexually aroused; to feel *horny;* to need some *hair.* (Typically said of the male about sexual need for the female. See note 31.) □ *Man, do I feel hairy! Time to get it on and get it off.* □ *I tend to feel hairy about once a month.*

feel someone up to feel someone sexually. (Usually a woman. Often referred to as petting. See also *cop a feel.* See notes 6 and 31.) □ *He tried to feel her up, but she wasn't that drunk.* □ *She felt him up and kissed him passionately.*

fiddle-fart See *monkey-fart.*

F-ing See *effing.*

finger-fuck ['fɪŋgɚ fək] **1.** to perform a type of simulated copulation where a finger is substituted for the penis. (Taboo. See note 4 for caution. All senses are typical of male-to-male talk and joking. See notes 6 and 31.) □ *He is a master at finger-fucking.* □ *They did nothing but finger-fuck for three months.* **2.** [for a female] to masturbate. (Transitive and intransitive. Taboo. See notes 6 and 31; see note 4 for caution; see note 20 for examples.) **3.** AND **finger-job** an act of simulated copulation where a finger is substituted for the penis. (Taboo. See notes 6 and 31; see note 4 for caution.) □ *She was a lezzie, but she didn't even do finger-jobs.* □ *No, a finger-fuck doesn't sound very interesting.* **4.** AND **finger-job** an act of female masturbation. (Taboo. See notes 6 and 31; see note 4 for caution; see note 18 for examples.)

finger-job See the previous entry.

finger, the the sign of the upraised middle finger; the *digitus impudicus.* (See *finger wave.* Universally known and used by both sexes.) □ *Did I see you give her the finger?* □ *The governor gave the finger to a heckler.*

finger wave the sign of the upraised middle finger; the *digitus impudicus.* (See *finger, the.*) □ *She gave him the finger wave and ran out of the room.* □ *A finger wave like that can get you into a lot of trouble.*

fink [fɪŋk] **1.** an informer; someone who betrays people to the authorities. (Ultimately from the name of a private surveillance firm, "Pinkerton." Also a term of address.) □ *The guy's a fink. He'll tell the cops.* □ *The lousy fink squealed on me!* **2.** a rotten and distrusted person. (Also a term of address.) □ *You stupid fink! What a dumb thing to do.* □ *What can you expect from a fink like that?*

fink on someone to inform on someone; to betray someone. (See comments at *fink*.) □ *Sam finked on me.* □ *If you fink on me, I'll get even with you.*

fish-eater AND **cheese-eater, mackerel-snapper** a Roman Catholic. (Refers to the eating of meat substitutes on Fridays, especially when it was required. Intended and perceived as jocular and mildly derogatory.) □ *My mother married a cheese-eater.* □ *The fish-eaters crowd the fish market on Fridays.*

fist-fuck [ˈfɪst-fək] **1.** to perform a type of anal copulation by inserting the fist into the anus. (A homosexual activity. Taboo. See note 4 for caution; see note 31.) □ *These two guys were fist-fucking and creating a horrible racket.* □ *He asked him to fist-fuck his friend.* **2.** to masturbate. (Taboo. Transitive and intransitive. See notes 20 and 21 for examples; see note 4 for caution; see note 31.)

flame [for a male homosexual] to project himself blatantly and obviously. □ *Who is that guy who is flaming all over the place?* □ *Roland is always flaming, just in case nobody knows.*

flamer See the following entry.

flaming queen AND **flamer** [ˈflemɪŋ ˈkwin AND ˈflemɚ] a blatantly obvious homosexual male. (See note 5 for examples and caution.)

flash [flæʃ] to expose the genitals or breasts to someone. (See *flasher*. See note 31.) □ *The guy flashed and scared all of us.* □

He was flashing when the cops went by, and that was the end of him.

flasher   a male exhibitionist; a male who derives release from sexually based tension by exposing his penis to women. (Widely known and used by both sexes. See note 31.) □ *The cops hauled in a couple of flashers from the public library.* □ *Some drunken flasher walked down Michigan Avenue.*

flat-ass   absolutely; totally. (From a general slang term *flat-out*. See comment at note 32.) □ *She opened it up as flat-ass fast as it would go.* □ *You flat-ass wrecked that car of yours.*

flatbacker   ['flætbækɚ] a prostitute. (Refers to her usual working position.) □ *I won't take the word of some low-down flatbacker.* □ *The flatbackers were prowling the streets all night long.*

flat-chested   with little or no female breast development. (Said of a female. Widely known and used by both sexes. See notes 6 and 31.) □ *I wish I wasn't so flat-chested!* □ *She's the flat-chested one over there by the punch bowl.*

flat-fuck   See *tummy-fuck.*

flat on one's ass AND **on one's ass**   **1.** fallen on one's buttocks. □ *She tripped over the chair and was flat on her ass in no time.* □ *Here I am on my ass and nobody will offer me a hand to get up.* **2.** totally broke and without any funds. (See comment at note 32.) □ *I'm on my ass and I need a few bucks to tide me over.* □ *He's flat on his ass. Let's foreclose on his house.*

flesh peddler   ['flɛʃ pɛdlɚ] **1.** one who sells one's body or sexual services. □ *Sally has turned into a regular flesh peddler.* □ *The flesh peddlers crowded around his car, shouting out descriptions of their "wares."* **2.** a procurer; a *pimp.* □ *The lousy flesh peddlers swarmed all over the street.* □ *She fell in with a notorious flesh peddler who beat her almost every day.*

flip someone the bird to show someone the sign of the upraised middle finger; to give someone the *digitus impudicus*. (See *finger wave, the finger.*) □ *He flipped the teacher the bird and ran from the room.* □ *The pitcher flipped the bird at the umpire and got thrown out of the game.*

flopper-stopper ['flapɚ-stapɚ] a brassiere. (Jocular. See notes 6 and 31.) □ *I wouldn't dream of appearing in public without a flopper-stopper.* □ *Get your flopper-stopper on and let's go.*

flute(r) AND **piccolo-player** a person who performs male oral sex; the penis; a fellator. (Considering the erect penis to be the musical instrument to which the mouth is applied. See note 31.) □ *Harvey is a fluter and has quite a following among his crowd.* □ *He's a piccolo-player, but he also likes other things.*

flying-fuck **1.** an imaginary act of copulation where the male leaps or dives onto and into the female. (Jocular and taboo. See note 4 for caution; see note 16 for examples; see note 31.) □ *The movie showed some jerk allegedly performing a flying-fuck, just for laughs.* □ *A flying-fuck would probably kill one or two people.* **2.** AND **French-fried-fuck** something totally worthless. (See *I don't give a flying-fuck.* Taboo. See note 31; see note 4 for caution; see comment at note 32.) □ *This thing isn't worth a flying-fuck!* □ *I wouldn't give you a French-fried-fuck for all the crummy cars like that in the world.*

fomp [famp] to fool around sexually. (Known to both sexes. College use. See note 31.) □ *They were just fomping. They weren't doing it or anything!* □ *Have you heard who fomped whom on the soap operas?*

foot queen ['fʊt kwin] a male homosexual who is sexually stimulated by human feet. (See note 5 for examples and caution.)

fork [fɔrk] to copulate; to *fuck.* (A euphemism and disguise. Transitive and intransitive. See notes 13 and 14 for examples; see note 31.)

Fork you! "Fuck you!" (A euphemism and disguise. See note 31.) □ *You stupid pest! Fork you!* □ *Fork you, buster!*

for the heck of it   See the following entry.

for the hell of it AND **for the heck of it**   for no good reason at all. (The version with "heck" is milder.) □ *I just did it for the hell of it.* □ *Why don't you drop by for the heck of it some night?*

free-fucking   [ˈfri-fəkɪŋ] having to do with a person who will copulate with little or no persuasion. (Taboo. See note 4 for caution; see note 31.) □ *She's a free-fucking little bitch and everybody knows it.* □ *I think this free-fucking generation is going straight to hell.*

French   [frɛntʃ] **1.** an act of oral sex. (See note 31.) □ *He asked for a French, but she gave him something better.* □ *How much is a French at a cathouse like that?* **2.** referring to oral sex. (See note 31.) □ *He tried some French stuff on her, and she nearly killed him.* □ *They advertise a few French specialties.* **3.** to perform oral sex. (See note 31.) □ *He wanted her to French him.* □ *He Frenched her, and did some other things too.* **4.** to kiss someone using the tongue; to French kiss. (Transitive or intransitive. See the examples.) □ *We were French kissing when the teacher came in.* □ *I wouldn't French kiss her on a bet!*

Frencher   [ˈfrɛntʃɚ] someone who performs oral sex. (See note 31.) □ *Most flatbackers are Frenchers and will do anything else you want too.* □ *Tod says he is a Frencher, but I doubt it.*

French-fried-fuck   See *flying-fuck.*

fricking   [ˈfrɪkɪŋ] lousy; damn; *fucking.* (A euphemism for *fucking.* See note 31.) □ *What a fricking mess you've made of this!* □ *Get the fricking hell out of here!*

friend   a woman's monthly menstrual period; menstruation. (Euphemistic. Typically female-to-female talk. See examples. See notes 6 and 32.) □ *Her little friend has come to visit her.* □ *Her friend is no friend of mine.*

frig [frɪg] **1.** to copulate [with] someone. (Transitive and intransitive. From an old word meaning "to rub." See notes 13 and 14 for examples; see note 31. More at *frigging.*) **2.** to ruin something. □ *Somebody frigged my rear bumper.* □ *Stop frigging my stereo!*

frigging [ˈfrɪgɪŋ] damn; damnable. (A euphemism for *fucking.* See note 31.) □ *Get your frigging feet off my chair!* □ *I'm tired of this frigging job! I quit!*

frig oneself to masturbate [oneself]. (From an old word meaning to rub. See *frig.* See note 19 for examples; see note 31.)

Fritz [frɪts] a male of German descent or nationality; a German soldier. (A nickname. Also a term of address. See caution at note 1.) □ *Do you think Fritz will start any trouble while we're here?* □ *Ask Fritz for some more beer.*

frog AND **frog-eater, froggie** [frɔg AND ˈfrɔg-itɚ, ˈfrɔgi] a person of French nationality or descent; a French soldier. (Wartime. More jocular than derogatory. See caution at note 1.) □ *I think the frogs really know how to cook.* □ *The problem with the frogs is that their language is so strange.*

frog-eater See the previous entry.

froggie See *frog.*

frog's eyes [ˈfrɔgz aɪz] tapioca pudding. (A food-dirtying term.) □ *How would you like to have another big scoop of frog's eyes?* □ *Clyde lifted up his bowl of frog's eyes, and said, "Here's looking at you!"*

fruit AND **fruiter** [frut AND ˈfrutɚ] a male homosexual. (Usually intended and always perceived as derogatory. Also a term of address. See note 5 for examples and caution; see note 3 for examples.) □ *I walked in and the place was full of fruits!* □ *Harvey was the kind of fruiter that made you sit up and take notice.*

fruitcake ['frutkek] **1.** a silly-acting person. (Also a term of address. May be derived from the phrase "Nutty as a fruitcake," meaning very silly or crazy. Often used with caution to avoid confusion with sense 2.) □ *You can be such a silly fruitcake sometimes.* □ *Some fruitcake put salt in the sugar bowl.* **2.** a male homosexual. (An elaboration of *fruit*. Usually intended and perceived as derogatory. Also a term of address. See note 5 for examples and caution; see note 3 for examples.)

fruiter See *fruit.*

fruity ['fruti] **1.** silly-acting. (See comment at *fruitcake.*) □ *He's a fruity guy. Always silly and weird.* □ *Why are you acting so fruity? Not get enough sleep?* **2.** in the style or manner of a male homosexual. □ *The entertainers were sort of fruity, but other than that, the show was okay.* □ *The place was decorated with lots of fruity swags and plush, but it was comfortable.*

fuck [fək] (Taboo in all senses.) **1.** to copulate [with] someone. (Transitive and intransitive. One of the English "four-letter words." See note 4 for caution; see notes 6 and 31; see notes 13 and 14 for examples.) **2.** an act of copulation. (See notes 6 and 31; see note 16 for examples.) **3.** a person with whom one can copulate. (See notes 6 and 31.) □ *Man, he's a good fuck if I ever saw one.* □ *She's okay as a friend, but as a fuck, I've had better.* **4.** semen. (Not widely known or used. See notes 6 and 31.) □ *Clean up that fuck before somebody sees it!* □ *God, there's fuck running down my pants leg!* **5.** an exclamation of anger or exasperation. (Usually **(Oh,) fuck!** See note 6 and 32.) □ *Fuck! The hell you do!* □ *Oh, fuck! I'm outa beer.*

fuckable ['fəkəbl] (Taboo in all senses.) **1.** readily agreeable to copulation. (See note 4 for caution; see notes 6 and 31.) □ *About midnight, she got sorta fuckable, and then she fell asleep.* □ *Okay, sweetie. When you feel fuckable, call me.* **2.** highly desirable for copulation. (See notes 6 and 31.) □ *Isn't he about the* *most fuckable hunk you've ever seen?* □ *She's so fuckable, then she's so cold.* **3.** suitable or acceptable for copulation. (See notes 6 and 31.) □ *Is she fuckable or is she still on the rag?* □ *She is the most fuckable looking chick I have ever seen!*

Fuck a dog! See the following entry.

Fuck a duck! AND **Fuck a dog!** "Oh, hell!," an expression of anger or distress. (Taboo. See note 4 for caution; see comment at note 32.) □ *Fuck a duck! I won't do it!* □ *Fuck a dog! You're outa your mind.*

fuck around to waste time; to mess around. (Taboo. See note 4 for caution; see comment at note 32.) □ *Stop fucking around and get busy!* □ *She's always fucking around when she should be minding the store.*

fuck around with someone AND **fuck someone around** to harass or intimidate someone; to give someone a hard time. (Taboo. See note 4 for caution; see comment at note 32.) □ *Don't fuck around with me all the time! Give me a break.* □ *You fuck me around too much. I'm quitting!*

fuck around with something to fiddle or toy with someone or something. (Taboo. See note 4 for caution; see comment at note 32.) □ *Please, don't fuck around with my stuff.* □ *It's just a little radio. Don't fuck around with it.*

fuckathon ['fəkəθɑn] serial copulation or sexual activity; an orgy. (Taboo. See notes 6 and 31; see note 4 for caution.) □ *It was no honeymoon. It was a first-class fuckathon!* □ *What started out as a double date ended up as a fuckathon.*

fuck-brained [fək-brend] (Taboo in both senses.) **1.** stupid; mindless. (See note 4 for caution; see comment at note 32.) □ *What a stupid, fuck-brained idea!* □ *I don't know why I'm stuck in this fuck-brained job.* **2.** obsessed with sex. (See note 31; see comment at note 32.) □ *All he thinks about is dames. He is to-*

tally fuck-brained. □ *He was so fuck-brained when we got into port, he ran off with the first hooker he saw.*

fuck bunny AND **F.B.** ['fək bəni AND 'ɛf 'bi] someone who just loves to copulate. (Usually a female. Taboo. See notes 6 and 31; see note 4 for caution.) □ *She's a real fuck bunny, isn't she?* □ *Sally is sort of an F.B. I hope she doesn't catch some horrible disease.*

fucked out ['fəkt 'aut] (Taboo in both senses.) **1.** exhausted from copulation. (Typical of low male-to-male talk. See note 4 for caution.) □ *They went at it until they were both fucked out.* □ *Poor old Chuck is fucked out just from looking at girlie magazines.* **2.** totally exhausted from doing anything. (As exhausted as if one had been copulating excessively. Typical of low male-to-male talk. See comment at note 32.) □ *God, I'm really fucked out!* □ *Some fucked-out dude was lying on the floor, and another was collapsed on the chair.*

fucked up ['fəkt 'əp] messed up; confused; ruined. (Said of people or things. Widely known. Typical of male-to-male talk. Taboo. See note 4 for caution; see comment at note 32.) □ *Man, are you fucked up! You need a vacation.* □ *This whole project is so fucked up, it'll take months to straighten out.*

fucker ['fəkɚ] (Taboo in all senses.) **1.** a male who copulates frequently or well. (Low male-to-male talk and joking. See note 4 for caution; see note 31.) □ *That guy is a real fucker if I ever saw one.* □ *Tod thinks he's a big fucker. I think he's a big faker.* **2.** any male. (A rude but usually positive nickname. Low male-to-male talk and joking.) □ *Tell that Goddamn fucker to get the hell out of here!* □ *Hey, Bill, you old fucker! How's it going?* **3.** the penis; the erect penis. (See notes 6 and 31; see notes 8 and 9 for examples.) **4.** a female who is known to agree to copulate readily. (Low male-to-male talk and joking. See notes 6 and 31.) □ *She's a real fucker.* □ *I'm out to find me a real first-class fucker tonight.*

fuckery AND **fuck-house** [ˈfəkɚi AND ˈfək-hɑʊs] a brothel; a house of prostitution. (Taboo. Typical of male-to-male talk or joking. See note 4 for caution.) □ *This street is just one fuckery after another.* □ *That one on the right is the oldest fuck-house in town.*

fuck-film a film where any kind of copulation, including homo-sexual and animal copulation, is depicted in great detail. (Taboo. See note 4 for caution; see note 31.) □ *The boys wanted to go to a fuck-film, but they were stopped at the door.* □ *The cops broke into a place where they were showing a fuck-film and arrested the owner.*

fuck-freak someone who is obsessed with copulation. (Contrived for the sake of the alliteration. Teens and college student use, and male joking. Taboo. See note 4 for caution; see note 31.) □ *She is a hot little fuck-freak, and she'll wear out any dude that takes her on.* □ *She's just another fuck-freak. A real F.B.*

fuckhead [ˈfəkhɛd] a stupid and obnoxious person. (Taboo. Also a provocative term of address. Low male-to-male talk. See note 4 for caution; see examples at note 3; see comment at note 32.) □ *Don't be such a fuckhead! Go back there and stand up for your-self!* □ *All right, fuckhead, get your stuff and get moving!*

fuckheaded [ˈfəkhɛdəd] stupid; senseless. (See *fuck*. Taboo. Typ-ical of low male-to-male talk. See note 4 for caution; see com-ment at note 32.)

fuck-hole the vagina. (Compare to *pee-hole*. Taboo. See note 4 for caution. Low and rude word, used only in the lowest levels of male-to-male talk and joking. Not heard often. See notes 6 and 31; see note 12 for examples.)

fuck-house See *fuckery*.

fucking [ˈfəkɪŋ] damnable; lousy; cursed. (From *fuck*. See also *fricking*. Taboo. Typical of male-to-male talk. A frequently heard adjective in all-male situations, and heard more often from females. See note 4 for caution; see comment at note 32.) □ *Get that fucking idiot out of here!* □ *Somebody had better clean up this fucking mess.*

fucking machine [...mə'ʃin] (Taboo in both senses.) **1.** an imaginary machine that will simulate sexual intercourse for either sex with great success. (Jocular and contrived. The subject of a number of limericks. See note 4 for caution; see note 31.) □ *What I need is a fucking machine—something that works all month long.* □ *Fred thought he had invented a fucking machine, but he didn't.* **2.** someone who is uniquely proficient or insatiable at sexual intercourse. (A reinterpretation of the first sense. See note 31.) □ *My God! The dude's nothing but a fucking machine!* □ *You think of yourself only as some sort of a fucking machine! You're not even human!*

fucking-rubber [... 'rəbɚ] a condom. (See *rubber.* Taboo. Typical of male talk. See note 4 for caution; see note 31.) □ *You got a fucking-rubber I can use?* □ *I found a fucking-rubber machine in the john.*

Fuck it! "To hell with it!"; "Forget it!" (Taboo. See note 4 for caution; see note 31.) □ *Your idea is stupid. Fuck it! Try something else.* □ *You don't need your silly hat! Fuck it! Let's go!*

Fuck it (all)! "Damn!" an expression of anger and despair. (See also *If that don't fuck all!* Taboo. Typical of male-to-male talk. See note 4 for caution; see comment at note 32.) □ *Oh, fuck it all! I don't care what you do!* □ *Fuck it all! I broke my toe!*

fuck like a bunny [... 'bəni] to copulate rapidly, frequently, easily, or all three. (Taboo. See note 4 for caution; see note 13 for related examples; see note 31.) □ *He can fuck like a bunny. If you're in a hurry, that's great.* □ *She fucks like a bunny. Fast and frequently.*

Fuck me gently! [... 'dʒɛntli] "Do not do too much damage to me!" referring to copulation or any other activity. (Occasional low use by both sexes. See comment at note 32.) □ *Fuck me gen-*

tly, man! I've had a bad day. □ *How much are you going to charge for fixing my car? Fuck me gently, I'm short of cash.*

fuck off   (Taboo in all senses.) **1.** to masturbate. (Intransitive. See note 4 for caution; see note 21 for examples; see note 31.) **2.** to waste time. (Typical of male-to-male talk. See note 31.) □ *Stop fucking off and get to work.* □ *He'd rather fuck off than do an honest day's work.* **3.** to go away; to get out of a place; to beat it. (Usually an angry command: **Fuck off!** Typical of male-to-male talk. See comment at note 32.) □ *Oh, fuck off! Get out!* □ *I told him to fuck off, but he still keeps hanging around.*

fuck one's fist   [. . . fɪst] to masturbate. (Compare to *fist-fuck*. Taboo. See note 4 for caution; see note 19 for examples; see note 31.)

fuck-shit   a truly wretched and obnoxious person. (See both *fuck* and *shit* for similar meanings. Based on the shock values of the two terms combined. Taboo. See note 4 for caution; see note 3 for examples; see comment at note 32.)

fuck someone around   See *fuck around with someone.*

fuck someone or something up AND **fuck up someone or something**   to mess someone or something up; to damage or ruin someone or something. (Compare to *ball someone or something up, screw someone or something up.* Widely known by both sexes. Typical of male-to-male talk, but increasingly female in certain settings. Taboo. See note 4 for caution; see comment at note 32.) □ *Please don't fuck my stereo up.* □ *You fuck up everything you get your hands on!*

fuck someone over AND **fuck over someone**   to give someone a very hard time; to abuse someone physically or mentally. (Typical of male-to-male talk, but also teens and college student use. Taboo. See note 4 for caution; see comment at note 32.) □ *The big guys fucked him over for a while and then let him go.* □ *The cops fucked us over for a couple of hours and then put us in the lockup.*

fuck someone's mind (up) to confuse or disorient someone; [for a drug] to affect or destroy someone's mind. (Typical of male-to-male talk, but also teens and college students, especially in drug culture use. Taboo. See note 4 for caution; see comment at note 32.) □ *She's really fucked your mind up. I'd stay away from her if I were you.* □ *I don't know what this stuff is, but it really fucked my mind.*

fuck up to mess up; to fail. (See also the following entries. Typical of male talk, but also teens and college students. Increasing female use in certain settings. Taboo. See note 4 for caution; see comment at note 32.) □ *Don't fuck up this time or you're fired.* □ *You can count on him to fuck up.*

fuck-up (Taboo in both senses.) **1.** a mess; a hopeless hodgepodge. (See *fuck someone or something up.* Typical of male talk, but also with teens and college students. Increasing female use in certain settings. See note 4 for caution; see comment at note 32.) □ *When you went home yesterday, you left behind a first-class fuck-up. Now you can clean it up.* □ *Who's responsible for this fuck-up?* **2.** someone who does everything wrong; someone who messes everything up. (See note 3 for examples; see comment at note 32.)

fuck with someone or something (Taboo in both senses.) **1.** to meddle with someone or something. (Typical of male talk, but also teens and college students. Increasing female use in certain settings. See note 4 for caution; see comment at note 32.) **2.** to cause trouble for someone or something; to threaten someone or something. (Typical of low or aggressive male talk, but also with teens and college students. Increasing female use in certain settings. See comment at note 32.) □ *Don't fuck with me if you know what's good for you!* □ *You fuck with me one more time and you're a dead man.*

Fuck you! "Go to hell!" a very insulting curse. (Very provocative. Originally limited to male-to-male talk, now much use at all levels of society by either sex. Despite its power, very often in jest. See examples. Taboo. See note 4 for caution; see comment at note 32.) □ *Fuck you, you shit!* □ *Fuck you, if that's what you think.*

fugly ['fəgli] "fucking ugly," very ugly indeed. (Sometimes defined more softly as "fat and ugly." Mostly teens and college student use.) □ *God, she's fugly!* □ *Have you every seen such a fugly car?*

full of it See the following entry.

full of shit AND **full of it** full of lies; stupid. (Said of a person. The phrase *full of it* is euphemistic. See comment at note 32.) □ *You're full of shit, you liar!* □ *Don't pay any attention to her. She's full of it.*

fur-pie See *hair-pie*.

F-word ['ɛf-wɚd] the word *fuck*. (A euphemism that can be used to refer to the word alone without reference to the various meanings of the word.) □ *They said the F-word seven times in the movie we saw last night.* □ *What's so bad about the F-word?*

G

gang-bang AND **gang-shag** ['gæŋ-bæŋ AND 'gæŋ-ʃæg] **1.** an act of serial copulation, with one female and a group of males. (Widely known and used by both sexes. See notes 6 and 31.) □ *It was nothing but a gang-bang, and a drunken one at that.* □ *Old Sally used to like a good gang-shag every now and then.* **2.** group rape of a woman. (Widely known, but used with caution in this sense. See notes 6 and 31.) □ *There was another gang-bang in the park last week.* □ *The cops are gonna crush the creeps that did that gang-shag.* **3.** to perform an act of serial copulation, as in senses 1 or 2. (Intransitive. See notes 6 and 31; see note 14 for examples.) **4.** to perform an act of serial copulation, as in senses 1 or 2, on a woman. (Transitive. See notes 6 and 31; see note 13 for examples.)

gang-shag See the previous entry.

garbanzos [gɑr'bɑnzəz] a woman's breasts. (Based on the garbanzo bean, the chick pea. Usually plural. See notes 6 and 31; see note 7 for examples.)

gash [gæʃ] the female genitals; the vulva. (Primarily low male-to-male talk and joking. Not widely used, but readily understood. See notes 6 and 31; see note 12 for examples.)

gay [ge] **1.** a homosexual, now almost always a male. (Considered the term of choice by homosexuals, but sometimes used derogatorily by others. See note 5 for examples and caution.) □ *This gay asked me for a ride, so I gave him a lift.* □ *One of the gays was a guy from work, so we went over and said hello to him and* *his friend.* **2.** homosexual. (Considered the term of choice by homosexuals, but used derogatorily by others.) □ *Have you ever been in a gay bar?* □ *She spent her evenings studying gay language in the downtown bars.* **3.** stupid; undesirable. (A general expression derived from the first two senses.) □ *You won't find me wearing a gay shirt like that.* □ *That is about the gayest idea I've ever seen.*

gay-bashing AND **fag-busting** harassing or attacking male homosexuals; deriding male homosexuals. (See *gay.*) □ *The cop was hauled up before a review board for gay-bashing.* □ *Some creep who enjoys fag-busting caused a lot of trouble in a gay bar on Tenth Street.*

geechie ['gitʃi] a native girl or woman of the Pacific basin. (Wartime. See notes 1 and 6.) □ *I wanna shack up with a geechie.* □ *You keep your hands off my geechie, you hear?*

geek [gik] **1.** any strange, eccentric, or peculiar person. (Usually seen in specific applications, such as to a *nerd* or to various enemy peoples of the Far East during wartime. One of the oldest uses is to refer to a carnival side-show performer who bites the heads off live chickens. See also *gook.*) □ *Oh, dad, you're such a geek!* □ *Who is that geek over there with the long hair?* **2.** a person, soldier, or civilian of an East Asian country, especially in wartime. (Usually of derogatory intent. See caution at note 1; see use as a slur at note 2.)

george [dʒordʒ] **1.** to copulate [with] a woman. (Transitive and intransitive. See notes 6 and 31; see notes 13 and 14 for examples.) **2.** to defecate. (See note 28 for examples; see note 31.)

Gerry AND **Jerry** ['dʒɛri] a German soldier; a person of German nationality or descent; the average German, especially a German soldier. (A wartime nickname. Potentially derogatory. See caution at note 1.) □ *The Gerries are moving out, leaving us to clean up the mess.* □ *The Jerries left some pretty nice buildings standing in this one little French town.*

get a hold of oneself to masturbate. (Refers to a male, talking about himself. Jocular. See note 19 for examples.)

Get any? See note at *Getting any?*

get a piece of ass See *get some ass.*

get down 1. to begin doing something. (Not forbidden, but can be confused with sense 2.) □ *Come on, man, get down. We got a lot of ground to cover.* □ *Let's get down. There's tons of stuff to do!* 2. to copulate. (Both senses were originally black. Intransitive. See note 14 for examples; see note 31.)

get fixed up (with someone) 1. to have a date set up with someone. (Not forbidden, but can be confused with sense 2.) □ *My cousin wants to get fixed up with a date for Friday night. Can you help?* □ *I've got a friend who wants to get fixed up, too.* 2. to be provided with a sex partner. (Widely known and used by both sexes.) □ *Bellboy, can you get me fixed up with somebody tonight?* □ *I'll see if I can get you fixed up, sir. The hotel frowns on that, however.*

get horizontal [...horɪ'zɑntl̩] to go to bed and have sex. (See *get down.* See note 31.) □ *Hey, baby, let's get horizontal!* □ *He couldn't wait to get horizontal with her.*

get in to insert the penis; [for a male] to succeed in copulating with a female. (Typical of low male-to-male talk. See note 31.) □ *He wanted nothing more than to get in, but that was just not going to be.* □ *Hey, Fred. Did ya get in?*

get in(to) her pants to manage to copulate with a certain female; to seduce a female. (See note 13 for related examples; see note 31. Can also occur in a male version.)

get it in to manage to insert the penis; to succeed in copulating with a female. (Typical of male-to-male talk and joking. See note 31.) □ *He sat there talking for an hour with her, but all he could* *think of was getting it in.* □ *He tried to get it in, but the tension was too much.*

get it off AND **get off** to copulate; to have an orgasm; [for a male] to ejaculate. (See note 31.) □ *Man, I really need to get it off. Really soon!* □ *She got off once then two more times after that.*

get it on **1.** to get an erection; to become sexually aroused. (Widespread and used by both sexes when this subject is discussed. Used in the lyrics of rock songs, but difficult to distinguish from the general slang meaning "to begin to do something." See note 10 for examples; see note 31.) **2.** to copulate. (Also in general slang use meaning to begin to do anything. See note 13 for related examples; see note 31.) □ *Come on, babe, let's get it on!* □ *I wouldn't get it on with you for the whole world!*

get it up to get an erection of the penis. (Widely known and used by both sexes when this subject is discussed. More explicit and less ambiguous than *get it on*. See note 10 for additional examples; see note 31.) □ *He's so drunk all the time, he can hardly get it up.* □ *Sure, Tom. When you get it up, just give me a call. I'll be right over.*

get off See *get it off.*

get one's ashes hauled [... 'æʃəz 'hɔld] to have sex and ejaculate. (Said of the male. Typical of male-to-male talk and joking. See note 31.) □ *Man, if I don't get my ashes hauled pretty soon, I'm gonna be one sorry-ass bastard.* □ *My friend here wants to get his ashes hauled. Can you fix him up?*

get one's ass in gear [... gir] to get organized and ready to do something; to reform; to change or improve one's ways. (Widely known and used by both sexes.) □ *Come on, get your ass in gear and let's get moving.* □ *You'll never get anywhere in life if you don't get your ass in gear.*

get one's bowels in an uproar [... 'bɑwlz... 'əpror] to get overly excited. (Usually in the negative. Widely known and used by both sexes. Jocular.) □ *Now, now, don't get your bowels in an uproar. Everything will be all right.* □ *If I keep getting my bowels in an uproar, I'll go crazy.*

get one's knob polished [... 'nɑb 'pɑlɪʃt] to copulate or otherwise have sex. (Refers to a male. The knob is the head of the penis. Jocular. Not in wide use. See note 31.) □ *The kid's out in back, getting his knob polished.* □ *Man, if you want to get your knob polished, just let me know. I got girls; I got girls you wouldn't believe.*

get one's nuts off See the following entry.

get one's rocks off AND **get one's nuts off** [for a male] to copulate or ejaculate. (Typical of male-to-male talk and joking. See note 31.) □ *If he doesn't get his rocks off soon, he'll get violent, he says.* □ *He went into town to get his nuts off.*

get one's shit together **1.** to get oneself organized; to get one's act together. (See note 32.) □ *I gotta get my shit together and study for the test tomorrow.* □ *If you would get your shit together, you might manage to make it.* **2.** to assemble one's belongings. (See note 32.) □ *Get your shit together and get out of here!* □ *Hurry up and get your shit together so we can get going.*

get some action to find a sexual partner copulate. (Typically and originally refers to a male finding a female. Also slang for finding many types of activity, such as gambling, drinking, drugs, or even a basketball game. Widely known and used by either sex. See note 31.) □ *If I don't get some action pretty soon, I'm going to explode.* □ *I wanna get some action. What's doing around here?*

get some ass AND **get a piece of ass, get some cunt** [for a male] to succeed in getting a female to copulate with him. (See *ass, cunt, piece of ass.* Typical of male-to-male talk and joking. See notes 6 and 31.) □ *He went into town to get some cunt, he said.* □ *Hey, Tom, you wanna go get some ass?*

get some cunt   See the previous entry.

Get the hell out (of here)!   a rude demand that someone get out of or leave a place. □ *All right! That's it! Get the hell out of here!* □ *I've had enough! Get the hell out!*

Getting any?   "Have you been having any sexual activity?" (An inquiry or greeting between some males. The related **Get any?** makes a similar inquiry about having sexual activity during a specific period of time, as on a date. Usually regarded as quaint and somewhat backwards. See notes 6 and 31.) □ *Hey, Tom! Getting any?* □ *Get any, old pal?*

ghost turd   ['gost tɚd] a wad of lint as found under beds, etc. (Jocular. Something insubstantial left behind by a ghost. See note 32.) □ *Good grief! Look at the ghost turds under this bed!* □ *That's not a ghost turd, it's a dead mouse!*

G.I.B.   See *good in bed.*

gimp   [gɪmp] a crippled person; a person with a limp. (Low. Impolite and offensive.) □ *Fred knocked over a gimp on the way down the street.* □ *They fixed all the buses so the gimps can get on and off.*

gink   [gɪŋk] **1.** a Vietnamese person. (From the Vietnamese war. Also a term of address. See caution at note 1; see use as a slur at note 2.) **2.** a stupid person. (Also a term of address.) □ *Stop acting like such a gink!* □ *Why would a gink like that come into a saloon like this?*

Ginny AND **Ginzo**   ['gɪni AND 'gɪnzo] a person of Italian nationality or descent. (From *Guinea.* Mostly forgotten. See caution at note 1.) □ *His pal from Naples, yeah, the Ginny, can sure cook up a storm.* □ *My cousin's wife is a Ginzo, and she knows all those good recipes.*

Ginzo   See the previous entry.

G.I. shits ['dʒi 'aɪ 'ʃɪts] diarrhea. (From either *G.I.* "government issue" or "gastrointestinal." See note 31.) □ *Man, have I got a case of the G.I. shits!* □ *Go see if the pecker-checker has something for the G.I. shits.*

gism See *jism.*

give a flying-fuck See *I don't give a flying-fuck.*

give a fuck (about someone or something) See the following entry.

give a shit (about someone or something) AND **give a fuck (about someone or something)** to care about someone or something. (Often negative. See notes 4 and 32.) □ *If you think I give a shit about you or anyone else, you're full of shit.* □ *I don't give a fuck what you do!* □ *No, I don't give a shit.*

give head to perform oral sex on someone. (Widely known and in low use by either sex. Compare to *serve head.* See note 31.) □ *Does she give head?* □ *Sally is a pro at giving head. She makes her living at it.*

give someone hell **1.** to scold someone severely. □ *Give him hell, Fred!* □ *Please don't give me hell. I wasn't even there!* **2.** to put up a good fight against someone. □ *Hit him again, Tom! Give him hell!* □ *Give them hell! Don't let them get away with that.*

gizzum See *jism.*

go to urinate or defecate. (See notes 26 and 28 for examples; see note 31.)

go all the way to proceed with sexual activity all the way to copulation. (Euphemistic. Universally known and used by either sex. See note 31.) □ *Did they go all the way?* □ *I wouldn't go all the way with anybody like that.*

go apeshit over someone or something [...'epʃɪt...] to get very excited about someone or something. (Widely known. See comment at note 32.) □ *She really went apeshit over the ice cream.* □ *I could go apeshit over a hunk like that.*

Godamighty! ['gɑdəmɑɪti] an exclamation of surprise. (See caution at note 11.) □ *Godamighty! What did you do to cause that?* □ *What have you done? Godamighty!*

God-awful ['gɑd 'ɔfl̩] really awful; terrible. (See caution at note 11.) □ *Have you seen the God-awful decorations in that dining room?* □ *What a God-awful day!*

Goddamn (it)! ['gɑd 'dæm (ɪt)] an expression of anger or pain. (See caution at note 11.) □ *Goddamn it! Watch where you're going.* □ *Goddamn! What a mess!*

go down on someone to perform oral sex on someone. (In any combination of sexes. See note 31.) □ *She was just gonna go down on him when the camera panned over to the window.* □ *He wanted her to go down on him.*

Go fuck yourself! "Go to hell!"; "Get out of here!" (A rude and angry rebuke. Typical of low male talk. Taboo. See note 4 for caution; see comment at note 32.) □ *Go fuck yourself, you creep!* □ *You worthless mungshit. Go fuck yourself!*

golden shower ['goldn̩ 'ʃaʊɚ] a stream of urine. (In a homosexual context. See note 31.) □ *He is always on the lookout for a golden shower.* □ *What do you suppose he likes about a golden shower?*

good in bed AND **G.I.B.** able to copulate well or satisfactorily. (Used by either sex. See note 31.) □ *They say she's good in bed.* □ *He smokes, and he has bad breath, but he's G.I.B.*

good shit good drugs; good marijuana; good heroin. (Drug culture. Compare to *bad shit*. See comment at note 32.) □ *I'm look-*

ing for some good shit, man. □ *Man, this is good shit! Where'd you get it?*

gook AND **geek, gooner** [guk AND gik, gunɚ] **1.** a strange or weird person. (Also a term of address.) □ *Who's the gook in the plaid pants?* □ *Don't be a gooner, Max. Try to act civil.* **2.** a person, soldier, or civilian of an East Asian country, especially in wartime. (Usually of derogatory intent. See caution at note 1; see use as a slur at note 2.)

gooner See the previous entry.

goose [gus] **1.** to poke someone in the anus, sometimes hard enough to penetrate to some depth. (See note 31.) □ *Tom goosed Tod and that started a great fight.* □ *Don't go around goosing people!* **2.** a sharp poke in the anus. (See note 31.) □ *Tom gave him a sharp goose that made him wince.* □ *Mrs. Frederick accidently goosed Sally with her umbrella.*

go tits up to die; to go to ruin; to fall apart. (A play on "go belly up" which has the same meaning. Refers to an animal like a goldfish which turns belly up when it dies. Intended as jocular.) □ *Her firm went tits up after the stock market crash.* □ *My goldfish went tits up because I overfed it.*

go to bed with someone to copulate [with] someone. (Compare to *sleep with someone.* The act may or may not include actually going to bed. Widely known and used as a euphemism by both sexes. See note 31.) □ *Did Sam really go to bed with Sue, or is that just idle gossip?* □ *She went to bed with him a number of times.*

Go to hell! "Drop dead!"; "Go away!" □ *Go to hell, you little creep!* □ *Go to hell! I won't do it.*

goulash ['gulaʃ] a person of Hungarian nationality or descent. (A nickname. Intended and perceived as mildly derogatory. See caution at note 1; see use as a slur at note 2.) □ *Hey, you're an all-right guy for a goulash.* □ *Those goulashes sure can cook!*

goy [gɔɪ] a non-Jew; a gentile. (Can be intended as derogatory, but not usually perceived as such. See caution at note 1; see use as a slur at note 2.) □ *What can you expect from a goy?* □ *Even a goy knows better than that!*

gray [gre] a white American; a Caucasian. (Black use. Originally derogatory. Not widely known. See caution at note 1; see use as a slur at note 2.)

greaser ['grizɚ AND 'grisɚ] a person of Mexican nationality or descent; a Hispanic person. (See also *oiler.* User is considered to be bigoted. See caution at note 1; see use as a slur at note 2.) □ *Well, what do you greasers think about the new highway?* □ *If you ever call me a greaser again, I bash in your face!*

greek [grik] [for a male] to perform anal copulation on a male. □ *This guy greeked his friend and then cut his throat.* □ *The prisoner complained to the warden that he had been greeked against his will.*

Greek way, the male-to-male anal copulation. (With reference to the homosexuality practiced in ancient Greece.) □ *He said he prefers it the Greek way, whatever that means.* □ *His kind all like it the Greek way.*

grind [graɪnd] **1.** an act of genital copulation. (See *do a grind.* See note 31.) □ *Man, do I need a grind.* □ *I know just where you can get a grind that'll drive you out of your mind.* **2.** to copulate. (Intransitive. See note 14 for examples; see note 31.)

gringo ['grɪŋgo] a North American. (Used in Mexico and the U.S. as a nickname for a North American male. Probably from the [European] Spanish term for a Greek. Can be intended as derogatory, but not always perceived as such. Also a term of address. See caution at note 1; see use as a slur at note 2.) □ *The gringos bring a lot of money, but nothing else of value.* □ *Here come the gringos with their fat butts and fat wallets.*

gripe one's ass AND **gripes one's butt** to annoy someone; to bother or irritate someone. (Used by both sexes. See comment at note 32.) □ *You really gripe my ass when you act like that!* □ *That kind of thing really gripes my butt.*

groid [grɔɪd] racially black; Negroid. (Intended as jocular. College-age use. See caution at note 1.) □ *The guy was sort of groid and carried a briefcase.* □ *She had a groid nose and tits that took your breath away!*

ground ape ['grɑʊnd ep] an American black. (Intended and perceived as derogatory and demeaning. User is considered to be racially bigoted. See caution at note 1; see note 3 for examples; see use as a slur at note 2.)

group-grope ['grup-grop] a sex orgy; a gathering where a lot of sexual fondling goes on. (Jocular. Widely known. See note 31.) □ *There was a group-grope going on in the back seat.* □ *When somebody yelled "group-grope," the dorm monitor burst into the room.*

grunt [grənt] **1.** to defecate. (From the sounds vocalized when straining at the stool. See note 28 for examples; see note 31.) **2.** dung. (See note 27 for examples; see note 31.)

Guinea ['gɪni] a person of Italian nationality or descent. (Intended and perceived as derogatory. Mostly forgotten. See *Ginny.* See caution at note 1; see use as a slur at note 2.)

H

hair-pie AND **fur-pie** ['hɛər-paɪ AND 'fɚ-paɪ] the female genital region, especially the pubic hair, with reference to oral sex. (See *eat.* Typical of low male-to-male talk. See notes 6 and 31.) □ *He said he had hair-pie for dinner, whatever that means.* □ *He's out looking for fur-pie.*

hairy-ass(ed) ['hɛəri-æs(t)] strong and virile. (Widely known. Typical of male-to-male talk.) □ *He's a big, hairy-assed kinda guy.* □ *I don't want to make it with some smelly, hairy-ass jerk!*

half-ass(ed) ['hæf-æs(t)] clumsy; awkward and ineffectual. □ *She only made a half-ass try at passing the test.* □ *That was a half-assed remark to make on such an important occasion.*

halfbreed **1.** a person of mixed blood. (Usually Amerindian and Caucasian. Intended and perceived as derogatory, especially when used as an epithet. User is considered to be racially bigoted. See caution at note 1; see use as a slur at note 2.) **2.** pertaining to a person of mixed blood. (Intended and perceived as derogatory. See caution at note 1.) □ *I don't want no halfbreed kids running around my block.* □ *There was some old rickety house there, a halfbreed house it was.*

half-pissed ['hæf-'pɪst] nearly drunk. (See comment at note 32. See also *pissed.*) □ *Man, she's half-pissed. Look at her!* □ *Tod drank until he was half-pissed, and then drank the same amount to finish the job.*

hammer ['hæmɚ] the penis; the erect penis. (See notes 8 and 9 for examples; see note 31.)

hand job an act of masturbation performed on someone else. (An act which might be requested of a prostitute. See note 18 for examples; see note 31.)

handkerchief-head See *towel-head.*

hard erect. (Said of the penis or of a male with an erection. Essentially standard English. See note 31.) □ *He felt himself beginning to get hard.* □ *He was hard as a rock and had been for some time.*

hard-ass(ed) ['hɑrd-æs(t)] stern and unforgiving; cruel. (Usually refers to a tough male.) □ *He is such a hard-ass bastard, I wouldn't expect any help from him.* □ *He can be so hard-assed at times.*

hard-nosed ['hɑrd-'nozd] erect, said of the penis. (A play on an expression meaning stern or cruel. See note 31.) □ *Well, he was sort of hard-nosed, if you know what I mean.* □ *He began to get sort of hard-nosed and I began to move toward the door.*

hard off ['hɑrd ɔf] a dull and sexless male. (The opposite of *hard on.* In use by both sexes, especially by teens and college students.) □ *Wally is a silly hard off. He seems asleep half the time.* □ *Do you really think I'm going to go out on a date with a hard off like Jim?*

hard-on ['hɑrd-ɔn] an erection of the penis. (The basic slang term for an erection. Widely known and used by both sexes. See note 9 for examples; see note 31.) □ *He must have had his last hard-on years ago.* □ *Oh, God! I think I'm getting a hard-on!*

hard-up ['hɑrd-'əp] in serious need of sexual release. (Usually said of a male. Also in general slang or colloquial meaning in serious need of something.) □ *Old Chuck is really hard-up.* □ *When he gets hard-up, he's a little rough with the women.*

haul ass (out of some place)   See *bag ass (out of some place)*.

have a bone on   to have an erection. (Also with *got*. See *bone* at *boner*. Typical of male-to-male talk. See note 10 for examples; see note 31.) □ *Hey, Tom, you got a bone on?* □ *Look, friend, you can't do anything with me till you get a bone on. Get it up or get out. I got other customers waiting.*

have a hard-on   to have an erect penis. (The most common colloquial expression for this state. See *hard-on*. Widely known and used by both sexes. See note 10 for examples; see note 31.) □ *I had a hard-on through the whole movie.* □ *If you have one of those things—a hard-on—you'll just have to say goodnight and go home!*

have a hard-on for someone   to wish to do someone physical damage; to seek revenge on someone. (The aggressor and victim are usually males.) □ *The punk thinks he has a hard-on for Mr. Big.* □ *Max had a hard-on for Bruno. He was going to kill him if the chance came up.*

have a man by the balls   to have dominated a man; to have a man in a position where he has little choice but to do what one says. □ *She's really got him by the balls. He will go along with whatever she wants.* □ *What could I do? They had me by the balls!*

have a shit-fit   [. . . 'ʃɪt-fɪt] to have a fit; to throw a temper tantrum. (See *shit-fit*. See comment at note 32.) □ *If I'm not home on time, my father'll have a shit-fit.* □ *Come on! Don't have a shit-fit! It's nothing.*

have a wild hair up one's ass   [. . . wɑɪld hɛər . . .] **1.** to act in a hyperactive and energetic manner. (Widely known and used by both sexes.) □ *She has a wild hair up her ass about something. I don't know what.* □ *I'm sorry I was so rude. I guess I had a wild hair up my ass or something.* **2.** to be obsessed with some strange or off-beat idea. (Widely known and used by both sexes.) □ *You're acting like you've got a wild hair up your ass. Calm down.*

□ *He had a wild hair up his ass in the middle of the night and got this really weird idea for a new product.*

have hot pants (for someone) AND **have the hots (for someone)** to be sexually aroused over someone in particular; to lust after someone. (Used by both sexes. Also with *got* as in the examples. See note 31.) □ *She really has hot pants for him.* □ *She's really got the hots for him.* □ *He gets the hots for any chick he spends an hour with.*

have it both ways to be bisexual; to desire to copulate with males or females. (From an idiom that is roughly the equivalent of "have one's cake and eat it, too." See note 31.) □ *Tod has it both ways.* □ *People who have it both ways are seldom lonely.*

have lead in one's pencil [. . . ˈlɛd . . . ˈpɛn(t)sl̩] **1.** to be vigorous and active. (Widely known phrase. Not taboo.) □ *If he had lead in his pencil, he'd be able to run the whole race.* □ *Your problem, Tom, is that you should have more lead in your pencil. You just don't have the stamina.* **2.** to have an erection of the penis. (See note 10 for examples; see note 31.)

have one's ass in a crack to be in an awkward position. (Widely known. See comment at note 32.) □ *You gotta try to help me out. I really have my ass in a crack.* □ *I really have my ass in a crack at work. I'm in a real mess with the boss.*

have one's ass in a sling to be in a bad humor about something. (Not literal. See comment at note 32.) □ *Why does she have her ass in a sling? Is it something I did?* □ *Yes, I've got my ass in a sling, but so would you if you had been through what I've just been through!*

have shit for brains [. . . brenz] to be exceedingly stupid. (Also with *got*. See comment at note 32.) □ *You poor dumb jerk! You really got shit for brains!* □ *You have shit for brains if you think you can get away with it.*

have someone by the short hairs   to have someone in an awkward position; to have dominated someone. (This refers to the shorter pubic hairs. Sometime euphemized to "neck hairs.") □ *They've got me by the short hairs. There's nothing I can do.* □ *The prof had the whole class by the short hairs and made life miserable for all of us.*

have the hots (for someone)   See *have hot pants (for someone).*

have the rag on   [for a woman] to have her monthly menstrual period. (See note 31.) □ *She has the rag on again. Look out!* □ *She's so bitchy when she has the rag on.*

head   the end or head of the penis. (Compare to *give head.* See note 31.) □ *He noticed that his pecker had a little red sore on its head.* □ *She says she does something real special to the head.*

head-cheese   ['hɛd-tʃiz] a foul-smelling substance that collects around the prepuce of the male; smegma. (A reinterpretation of the name of a type of sausage. See *head.* Typical of low male-to-male joking. See note 31.) □ *You gotta wash to get rid of the head-cheese.* □ *Can you imagine anything worse than a whole bunch of head-cheese?*

headfucker   ['hɛdfəkɚ] a person, situation, or a drug that confuses someone or disorients someone mentally. (Typical of drug culture talk. Taboo. See note 4 for caution; see comment at note 32.) □ *This day was a real headfucker!* □ *Why did you have to lay this headfucker on me?*

head-job   an act of oral sex performed on the penis. (See note 31.) □ *The hooker asked him if he wanted a head-job.* □ *He wanted a head-job, but would settle for almost anything.*

headlights   ['hɛdlaɪts] a woman's breasts. (Intended as jocular. Usually plural. See notes 6 and 31; see note 7 for examples.)

Hebe   See the following entry.

Heeb AND **Hebe, Heebie** [ˈhib(i)] a Jewish person. (Usually intended and always perceived as derogatory. From *Hebrew.* User is considered to be bigoted and antisemitic. See caution at note 1; see use as a slur at note 2.)

Heinie [ˈhɑɪni] a German soldier; a person of German nationality or descent. (From the personal name "Heinz." Usually with derogatory intent. Wartime. See caution at note 1.) □ *The Heinies can cook up some pretty good grub.* □ *Some Heinie came over and tried to start a fight.*

Hell! a curse expressing anger or exasperation. (Universally known and used.) □ *Hell, I can't help it!* □ *Oh, hell, I'm late again!*

hellacious [hɛˈleʃəs] overwhelming; extreme; really awful. (Partly jocular.) □ *What a hellacious day!* □ *She gave me a hellacious time.*

hell and half of Georgia a tremendous amount of space. (Folksy. See examples.) □ *The blanket was so big it covered hell and half of Georgia.* □ *I had to cross hell and half of Georgia to get here, but I made it.*

hellhole [ˈhɛlhol] a very hot place; a troublesome place. (Widely known colloquial English.) □ *Let me out of this hellhole! I'm burning up!* □ *The auditorium was a regular hellhole and somebody even fainted.*

hell of a mess a very serious mess or problem; a very complex problem. (Universally known and used. Also with "one" as in the examples. Widely known and used by both sexes.) □ *This place is one hell of a mess.* □ *What a hell of a mess you've made.*

hell of a note AND **helluva note** [ˈhɛl əv ə ˈnot] a bad thing to hear about; bad news. (Folksy.) □ *Damn! That's a hell of a note! Can anything be done to help?* □ *What a helluva note! My girl just told me to drop dead.*

hell on wheels a person or thing who moves or functions very fast and aggressively. (Widely known, but a little out of date.) □ *Gary is hell on wheels when it comes to math.* □ *The quarterback was hell on wheels.*

hell-raiser ['hɛl-rezɚ] **1.** a person who acts wild and rowdy. (Old and widely known.) □ *Clyde is a real hell-raiser.* □ *All the hell-raisers were rounded up and put in jail.* **2.** a party where people act wild. (Widely known.) □ *Wasn't that a fine hell-raiser last Saturday night?* □ *What started out as a nice, peaceful party ended up being a hell-raiser.* **3.** anything boisterous; anything that will create noise or havoc, such as fireworks, loud orchestra music, etc. □ *Then the orchestra played that old hell-raiser, the "1812 Overture."* □ *The finale to the fireworks display was the biggest hell-raiser ever.*

Hell's bells (and buckets of blood)! ['hɛlz 'bɛlz n̩ 'bəkəts əv 'bləd] an expression of distress or anger. (An elaboration of *hell*. Widely known exclamation. See comment at note 32.) □ *Oh, hell's bells! I'll never be able to get this right!* □ *Hell's bells and buckets of blood! Your hair's a mess!*

Hell's fire and damnation! AND **Hell-fire and damnation!, Shit-fire and damnation!** [. . .dæm'neʃn̩] an expression of distress and anger. (Widely known exclamation.) □ *Hell's fire and damnation! It's twins!* □ *Oh, hell-fire and damnation! I won't do it!*

hell to pay See *There will be hell to pay.*

helluva a non-standard respelling of "hell of a." (See *hell of a note.*) □ *That's a helluva thing to do!* □ *What a helluva thing to say!*

helluva note See *hell of a note.*

herp See *herpie.*

herped up ['hɚpt 'əp] infected with herpies. (Typical of teens and college students.) □ *Sam got himself herped up and is taking* *some strange medicine.* □ *Stay away from him unless you want to get herped up.*

herpie AND **herp** ['hɚp(i)] someone who is infected with herpies. (Typical of teens and college student talk.) □ *How would you like to find out you've been going out with a herp?* □ *If you want to end up a herpie for the rest of your life, go ahead.*

hide the sausage [. . . 'sɔsədʒ] a name for an act of copulation. (Jocular avoidance. Known and used by both sexes. See note 31.) □ *Then he said he wanted to play hide the sausage.* □ *The last time we played hide the sausage, I knew where it was all the time.*

high-yellow an American black with a light, somewhat yellowish skin color. (Not necessarily derogatory. See caution at note 1; see use as a slur at note 2.)

ho [ho] **1.** a whore; a prostitute. (Black. Southern black pronunciation.) □ *She's just a ho.* □ *The whole neighborhood is full of hos.* **2.** a girlfriend. (Primarily black. Usually jocular. See note 6.) □ *Me and my ho is going out.* □ *My ho and me broke up.*

hole the vagina. (Primarily low and juvenile male-to-male talk and joking. See notes 6 and 31; see note 12 for examples.)

Holy dog crap! See the following entry.

Holy dog shit! AND **Holy dog crap!** a meaningless exclamation of surprise or anger. (The second version is somewhat less shocking. Typical of low male use. See comment at note 32.) □ *Holy dog shit! I won the lottery!* □ *Don't call me any of your family names! Holy dog crap, you creep!*

Holy fuck! a strong exclamation of surprise or anger. (Typical of low male talk. Taboo. See note 4 for caution; see comment at note 32.) □ *Holy fuck! Did you see that guy make the touchdown?* □ *Holy fuck! She's dead!*

Holy God! AND **Holy Christ!** an exclamation of surprise or anger. (Widely known and used by both sexes. See caution at note 11.) □ *Holy God! Look at them knockers!* □ *I'm 20 minutes late. Holy Christ!*

Holy Kerist! ['holi kɚ'ɑɪst AND 'holi ki'rɑɪst] an exclamation of surprise or anger. (Both eye-dialect and a spelling distortion. See *Holy Christ!* at *Holy God!* Widely known and used by both sexes. See caution at note 11.) □ *What a pair of garbanzos! Holy Kerist!* □ *Holy Kerist! He struck him out!*

Holy shit! an exclamation of surprise or anger. (Typical of male-to-male talk. See comment at note 32.) □ *Holy shit! I'm not your servant!* □ *What a wreck! Holy shit!*

homo ['homo] a homosexual. (Usually a male. Intended and perceived as derogatory. Resented. See note 5 for examples and caution; see note 3 for examples.)

honey fuck ['həni 'fək] a gentle and loving act of sexual intercourse. (Not widely known. Taboo. See note 4 for caution; see note 31.) □ *How about a little honey fuck, babe?* □ *I told him I'd prefer a honey fuck to a bunny fuck any day.*

honkers ['hɔŋkɚz] a woman's breasts. (Jocular. Usually plural. See *hooters.* See note 7 for examples. Typical of male-to-male talk and joking. See notes 6 and 13.)

honkie See **honky.**

honky AND **honkie** ['hɔŋki] a Caucasian. (This is a [black] southern pronunciation of *hunky*, although the original meaning of *hunky* has been broadened considerably. Usually intended, but not always perceived, as derogatory. Also a term of address. See also *hunky.* See caution at note 1.) □ *She's been dating some honky from the west side.* □ *The honkies don't come down here much.*

hooker ['hʊkɚ] a prostitute. (Usually a female, but of either sex. This has to do with "hooking" men into a situation where they can be exploited sexually or robbed. It has nothing to do with a certain "General Hooker." Widely known and used by both sexes.) □ *She's a model by day and a hooker by night.* □ *This neighborhood has a few hookers who hang around on the street corners.*

hooknose ['hʊknoz] a Jewish person. (Intended and perceived as strongly derogatory. User is considered to be bigoted and antisemitic. See caution at note 1; see examples at note 2.)

hooters ['hutɚz] a woman's breasts. (Jocular. Typically plural. See *honkers.* Typical of male-to-male talk and joking. See notes 6 and 31; see note 7 for examples.)

hoover ['huvɚ] to perform oral sex on the penis. (From the name of the vacuum cleaner manufacturer, in reference to suction. See note 31.) □ *Man, would I like to hoover you!* □ *She hoovered him twice and then left.*

horny ['horni] sexually aroused; in need of sexual release. (Refers to the horns of the goat, not a car horn. The goat is a symbol of lust. See note 31.) □ *God, I'm horny! I need a piece of something.* □ *He said he was so horny he could honk. What did he mean?*

horse cock a large sausage. (A food-dirtying term. Military. Compare to *donkey dick.*) □ *Whack me off a piece of that horse cock, would ya, Clyde?* □ *Oh, not horse cock again tonight!*

horse's ass an obnoxious person. (Rude. Also a term of address. See comment at note 32.) □ *Tell that horse's ass to shut up and get out.* □ *I don't know why I married that horse's ass!*

horseshit ['horsʃɪt] **1.** the dung of the horse. (See note 27 for examples; see note 31.) **2.** nonsense; *bullshit.* □ *I've heard enough of your horseshit!* □ *That's just a lot of horseshit!*

hose 1. the penis. (See note 8 for examples; see note 31.) 2. to copulate [with] a woman. (Transitive and intransitive. See notes 6 and 31; see notes 13 and 14 for examples.) 3. to cheat or deceive someone. □ *Don't try to hose me! I'm onto you!* □ *He's just hosing you! Ignore him.*

hose monster a sexually active woman; a nymphomaniac. (See *hose.* See note 31.) □ *God, she's just the kind of hose monster you dream about.* □ *Sally is no hose monster, but she doesn't put up much of a fight either.*

hot-assed ['hɑt-æst] sexually aroused. (Usually said of a woman. See note 31.) □ *Man, was she ever getting hot-assed!* □ *I was with this hot-assed dame who kept rubbing against me.*

Hotdamn! ['hɑt'dæm] "Damn!" (Probably a euphemism for *Goddamn!* Further elaborated or minced into **Hot dam, said the beaver when his house burned down!**) □ *Hotdamn! I got my raise!* □ *Hotdamn! I've just got time to get there!*

hot-rocks See *blue balls.*

hot shit a male who thinks he is the greatest person alive; a conceited male. (Probably also used for females. Used with or without *a.*) □ *You're not such a hot shit!* □ *The jerk thinks he is real hot shit.*

hot to trot sexually aroused, said of a female; eager to neck with someone. (For the sake of the rhyme. From a more general expression meaning "eager to dance." See note 31.) □ *She is really hot to trot.* □ *That whole sorority is hot to trot.*

house nigger a servile black. (Refers to a class of black slaves assigned to the master's house rather than the field. Intended and perceived as strongly derogatory. Considerable black-to-black derogatory use. User is considered to be racially bigoted. See caution at note 1; see use as a slur at note 2.) □ *Don't you go acting like no house nigger around me, James Brown!* □ *You can't ex-*

pect the mayor and his pack of house niggers to know or care about anything except lining his pockets.

How('re) they hanging?   an inquiry calling for a report of the state of a male's testicles. (Usually low male-to-male. See *Getting any?* See note 31.) □ *How they hanging, Fred?* □ *You're looking okay. How're they hanging?*

hum job   [ˈhəm dʒab] a sexual act involving holding the penis in the mouth while humming. (As might be requested from a prostitute. See note 31.) □ *He asked for a hum job, so she gave him a lullaby.* □ *The hooker wanted $30 for a hum job.*

hump   [həmp] **1.** to copulate [with] someone. (Transitive and intransitive. All senses from the male arching of the back in copulation, as in *fornicate*. See notes 13 and 14 for examples; see note 31.) **2.** an act of copulation. (See note 16 for examples; see note 31.) **3.** a person who will copulate without much persuasion. (Not widely known. See note 31.) □ *He's okay as a hump, but he can't dance.* □ *She's just a hump. They're not hard to find these days.*

humpy   [ˈhəmpi] sexually aroused; *horny.* (See *hump.* See note 31.) □ *I'm so humpy, I could screw a cow.* □ *She gets humpy when she watches those movies.*

Hun   [hən] a German soldier; a person of German nationality or descent. (A wartime nickname. See caution at note 1; see use as a slur at note 2.)

hung   See *well-hung.*

hung like a bull   having large testicles or genitals in general, like a bull. (Said of a male. Typical of male-to-male talk and joking. See note 31.) □ *Old Chuck is hung like a bull, but he don't care much for women.* □ *Well, he's not exactly hung like a bull, or anything else for that matter.*

hunkie   See *hunky.*

hunk of ass See *piece of ass.*

hunk of tail See *piece of ass.*

hunky AND **hunkie** ['həŋki] a person of Hungarian nationality or descent. (See also *honky.* See caution at note 1; see use as a slur at note 2.)

hustle ['həsl̩] **1.** to make a living as a prostitute. □ *She hustles about 18 hours a day.* □ *You think I like hustling for a living?* **2.** to attempt to persuade someone to copulate; to solicit someone to copulate. (See note 31.) □ *He tried to hustle her, but she ignored him.* □ *She was hustling him, which was exactly what he wanted.*

hustler ['həslɚ] a prostitute. (Other slang meanings having to do with cheaters and con artists.) □ *I was stopped by three hustlers between my car and my office door.* □ *She makes a pretty good living as a hustler.*

I

I don't give a flying-fuck AND **I don't give a French-fried-fuck** "I don't care at all." (See *flying-fuck.* Taboo. See note 4 for caution; see comment at note 32.) □ *I don't give a flying-fuck what you do.* □ *Walk out on me if you like. I don't give a flying-fuck.*

If that don't fuck all! an exclamation of surprise. (An elaboration of the colloquial "If that don't beat all!" See also *Fuck it all!* Taboo. See note 4 for caution; see comment at note 32.) □ *If that don't fuck all! You broke it, and it's my last one!* □ *My uncle left me $40,000! If that don't fuck all!*

If you can't use it, abuse it! "If you can't use your penis to copulate, then masturbate." (A phrase uttered frequently by both sexes on citizens band radio only a few years ago. See note 31.) □ *See you on the way back, Clyde. If you can't use it, abuse it!* □ *Getting any? If you can't use it, abuse it!*

im-fucking-possible [ɪm-fəkɪŋ-ˈpɑsəbl̩] totally impossible. (Typical of male-to-male talk and joking. Taboo. See comment at *abso-fucking-lutely.* See note 4 for caution; see comment at note 32.) □ *Who is that im-fucking-possible mungshit who just came in?* □ *I can't work this im-fucking-possible crossword puzzle!*

in deep shit in very serious trouble. (See *up shit creek (without a paddle).* See comment at note 32. Widely known.) □ *Man, you're in deep shit now.* □ *I broke the thing and really got myself in deep shit.*

inde-goddamn-pendent [ɪndi-gɑdæm-'pɛndənt] very indepen-
dent. (Typical of male-to-male talk and joking. See comment at
abso-fucking-lutely. See caution at note 11; see comment at note
32.) □ *She is so inde-goddamn-pendent that she can't even make
friends with anybody.* □ *Next time I'll take my goddamn car to
an inde-goddamn-pendent mechanic.*

in shit order in very bad order; messy; needing arranging or
cleaning. (Military. Typical of male-to-male talk. See comment at
note 32.) □ *This place is in shit order! Correct it immediately,
gentlemen!* □ *The papers were in shit order and it took hours to
get them straightened out.*

in the shit in a real mess; in severe trouble. (Pertains to a person.
See comment at note 32.) □ *Now I'm really in the shit! What'll I
do?* □ *By the time we got there, my foot was swollen, and my
whole life was in the shit.*

irre-fucking-sponsible [ɪri-fəkɪŋ-'spɑnsəbl̩] totally irresponsi-
ble. (Typical of male-to-male talk and joking. See comment at
abso-fucking-lutely. Taboo. See note 4 for caution; see comment
at note 32.) □ *Why are you so irre-fucking-sponsible?* □ *That
was a goddamn irre-fucking-sponsible thing to say.*

itie See *eytie*.

It's no skin off my ass. "It doesn't matter to me." (A version of
"It's no skin off my nose." Not widely known. See comment at
note 32.) □ *I don't care. It's no skin off my ass.* □ *Do whatever
you want. It's no skin off my ass.*

Ivan ['ɑɪvn̩] a [Russian] Soviet soldier; the average Russian. (A generic nickname. Not necessarily derogatory. See caution at note
1.) □ *See if Ivan wants some of this candy.* □ *Ivan isn't used to
having these kinds of choices to make.*

J

jack around to mess around; to waste time. (From *jack off.* Typical of teens and college student talk.) □ *Stop jacking around and get to work.* □ *You would finish on time if you didn't jack around so much.*

jack off See *beat off.*

jackoff See *jagoff.*

jack-shit **1.** a stupid and worthless person. (Usually refers to a male. Typical of male-to-male talk.) □ *Don't be such a stupid jack-shit!* □ *What a jack-shit! Not a brain in his head!* **2.** anything; anything at all. (Always in a negative expression. Typical of male-to-male talk. See comment at note 32.) □ *This whole thing isn't worth jack-shit!* □ *I wouldn't give you jack-shit for that!*

jag off See *beat off.*

jagoff AND **jackoff, jerkoff** [ˈdʒægɔf AND ˈdʒækɔf, dʒɚkɔf] **1.** a male who masturbates habitually. (See note 22 for examples.) **2.** a worthless jerk. (Usually refers to a male. From sense 1. Primarily male talk.) □ *I won't be bossed around by a jagoff like that.* □ *He's such a jackoff: a total jerk.*

jail-bait See *San Quentin jail-bait.*

jammy [ˈdʒæmi] the penis. (See note 8 for examples; see note 31.)

Jap [dʒæp] a person of Japanese nationality or descent. (War-time. Varying degrees of derogation. Often used as the obvious familiar abbreviation of "Japanese" with no ill intent. Potentially strongly derogatory. See also *nip*. See caution at note 1; see use as a slur at note 2.)

JAP [dʒæp] "Jewish American Princess"; "Jewish American Prince." (Refers to a young Jewish person who acts haughty and expects "royal" treatment. Intended and perceived as derogatory. Widely known and used by both sexes. See caution at note 1; see use as a slur at note 2.) □ *Oh, Sally, don't be such a JAP!* □ *He's a JAP and won't join in.*

Jeff [dʒɛf] a Caucasian. (Usually intended, but not always perceived, as derogatory. Also a term of address. Black. From "Jefferson Davis." See caution at note 1; see use as a slur at note 2.) □ *Who's that Jeff over there with the silky hair?* □ *Hey, Jeff, you got anything for sale?*

jerk off ['dʒɚk 'ɔf] to masturbate. (See *beat off*. The general slang term *jerk* meaning "a worthless person, usually male" is from this sense. See note 21 for examples; see note 31. See also *circle-jerk*.)

jerkoff See *jagoff*.

Jerry See *Gerry*.

Jesus (Christ)! a rude exclamation. (See note 11 for caution.) □ *Jesus Christ! I'm late! Oh, Jesus! What a mess!*

Jesus screamer ['dʒizəs 'skrimɚ] a Christian; an evangelical Christian. (See caution at note 1; see use as a slur at note 2.) □ *The Jesus screamers will be getting out of church soon. Let's eat before the rush.* □ *One of the Jesus screamers said something about my choice of words.*

Jew-boy [dʒu-bɔɪ] a Jewish male. (Intended and perceived as strongly derogatory and demeaning. Deeply resented. Also a term of address. May or may not be capitalized. See *boy*. User is considered to be bigoted and antisemitic. See caution at note 1; see note 3 for examples.)

jew(ish) flag   a dollar bill; any U.S. currency note. (Intended and perceived as derogatory. Refers to an allegedly unique devotion to earning money. Sometimes capitalized, although whether or not the phrase is capitalized is a matter of considerable dispute. For some people, it is more offensive if capitalized. User is considered to be bigoted and antisemitic. See caution at note 1; see use as a slur at note 2.)

jew someone down   to haggle down someone's price. (Not always of derogatory intent. Always perceived as derogatory by Jews. See note on capitalization in the previous entry. User is considered to be bigoted and antisemitic. See caution at note 1.) □ *Don't pay his price! Try to jew him down!* □ *Don't try to jew me down!*

jew someone out of something   to cheat someone out of something. (Derogatory. See note on capitalization in *jew(ish) flag*. User is considered to be bigoted and antisemitic. See caution at note 1.) □ *Don't try to jew me out of it. I saw it first.* □ *He was going to jew me out of more, but I held my own.*

jibagoo   See *jigaboo*.

jig   [dʒɪg] an American black. (Intended and perceived as derogatory. An old term that has become provocative and resented. Either a shortening or an elaboration of *jigaboo*. User is considered to be racially bigoted. See caution at note 1; see use as a slur at note 2.)

jigaboo AND **jibagoo**   ['dʒɪgəbu AND 'dʒɪbəgu] an American black. (Intended and perceived as derogatory, demeaning, and ridiculing. The main entry is the most common form; *jibagoo* is a parody of *jigaboo*. See also *jig*. Compare to *zigaboo*. User is considered to be racially bigoted. See caution at note 1; see use as a slur at note 2.)

Jim Crow ['dʒɪm 'kro] an American black; blacks in general. (Intended and perceived as derogatory. User is considered to be racially bigoted. See caution at note 1.) □ *Do you think that Jim Crow will patronize our store now?* □ *Jim Crow isn't going to put up with much more of that.*

jism AND **chism, gism, gizzum, jizz, jizzum** ['dʒɪzm̩ AND 'tʃɪzm̩, 'gɪzm̩ OR 'dʒɪzm̩, dʒɪz, 'dʒɪzm̩] semen. (Some spellings are widely known to both sexes. See note 31.) □ *Do you think jism is alive?* □ *This weird doctor took a sample of my gizzum and put it on a microscope slide.*

jive-ass ['dʒɑɪv-æs] lying; deceitful; boastful. (Originally black. Now widespread, especially among teens and college student users. See comment at note 32.) □ *I don't care about your stupid jive-ass story!* □ *I hate that jive-ass bastard!*

jizz See *jism.*

jizzum See *jism.*

jock [dʒɑk] the penis. (From *jockstrap.* Also a general slang term for an athlete as in *jockstrapper.* See note 8 for examples; see note 31.)

jock itch a stubborn and itchy fungal infection in the male genital area. (Universally known. Compare to *crotch rot.* See note 31.) □ *I got this case of jock itch that's driving me crazy.* □ *How can I get rid of this jock itch?*

jockstrap a male undergarment designed to support and protect the genitals. (See *jock.* Universally known and used. See note 31.) □ *They say he wears a pink jockstrap.* □ *He lost his jockstrap in the laundry.*

jockstrapper an athlete. (Usually, but not necessarily, refers to a male. See *jockstrap.*) □ *The jockstrappers eat at a special table where they can have all the food they want.* □ *The jockstrappers* *have to work extra hard in their classes when their sports are in season.*

john [dʒɑn] **1.** a toilet. (Usually with *the*. Sometimes capitalized. Universally known and used by both sexes of all ages.) □ *I gotta use your john.* □ *Where's the john around here?* **2.** a prostitute's customer. (Sometimes capitalized. See *trick*. Widely known.) □ *Tell me again what this john asked you to do!* □ *She can turn more johns in an hour than most hookers deal with in an evening.*

Johnson AND **Jones** [ˈdʒɑn(t)sn̩ AND dʒonz] the penis. (Originally black. Both terms are general terms for "thing." See note 8 for examples; see note 31.)

joint [dʒɔɪnt] the penis. (Also a drug slang term for a marijuana cigarette and an underworld term for a prison. See note 8 for examples; see note 31.)

Jones See *Johnson.*

joy stick the penis. (From the stick used to control small airplanes. See note 8 for examples; see note 31.)

Judas Priest! [ˈdʒudəs ˈprist] an exclamatory oath. □ *Did you see that plane! Judas Priest! It crashed into the cliff!* □ *Judas Priest! What a pair of knockers!*

jugs [dʒɝgz] a woman's breasts, especially if large. (Jocular and very popular, especially in male-to-male talk and joking. Usually plural. See notes 6 and 31; see note 7 for examples.)

jump **1.** to attack someone. (General slang.) □ *The gang jumped the old man and robbed him.* □ *The dope addicts will jump anybody for a few bucks to buy drugs.* **2.** to copulate [with] someone. (Transitive. See note 13 for examples; see note 31.)

jungle bunny an American black; an African. (Intended and perceived as derogatory. User is considered to be racially bigoted.

See caution at note 1; see examples at note 3; see use as a slur at note 2.)

junk [dʒəŋk] semen. (An avoidance. Not widely known. See note 31.) □ *Gee, that stuff looks like junk on your pants.* □ *They say that junk is alive with little wiggly things.*

K

kaka See *caca*.

kick-ass AND **bust-ass** ['kɪk-æs AND 'bəst-æs] powerful and vigorous. (Teens and college student users. See comment at note 32.) □ *The guy's a real kick-ass bastard!* □ *That was a real kick-ass party you had the other night!*

kick-ass on someone to give someone a hard time; to try to dominate or overwhelm someone. (Teens and college student users. See comment at note 32.) □ *Don't kick-ass on me! I'm not the one you're after.* □ *The cops were kick-assing on the guys and one of them got hurt.*

kick in the ass AND **kick in the butt, kick in the pants, kick in the rear** some kind of action that will motivate someone. (Rarely refers to an actual kick. See examples. Widely known and used by both sexes. See comment at note 32.) □ *What she needs is a kick in the ass!* □ *I thought that the failing grade would be the kind of kick in the butt you needed to get yourself going.* □ *A swift kick in the rear will show him who's boss.*

kick in the butt See the previous entry.

kick in the pants See *kick in the ass*.

kick in the rear See *kick in the ass*.

kick some ass (around) to raise hell with someone; to show someone who is boss. (Widely known and used by both sexes. See comment at note 32.) □ *If I have to come down there and kick some ass, there's going to be real trouble.* □ *I always have to kick some ass around to get anything done.*

kick the shit out of someone   See *beat the shit out of someone.*

kike [kɑɪk] a Jewish person. (Always with derogatory intent. Always perceived as strongly derogatory. Also a rude term of address. Sometimes capitalized. User is considered to be bigoted and antisemitic. See caution at note 1; see examples at note 3; see use as a slur at note 2.)

kikey ['kɑɪki] Jewish; of appeal to Jewish people. (Intended and perceived as strongly derogatory. See notes at the previous entry. User is considered to be bigoted and antisemitic. See caution at note 1.)

kink [kɪŋk] a person who is obsessed with adventuresome or perverse sexual acts. (Not widely known.) □ *They say that Wally is a real kink. Well, I can tell you that he's not.* □ *That's where the kinks hang out and play their little games.*

kinky AND **bent, twisted** ['kɪŋki AND bɛnt, 'twɪstəd] obsessed with adventuresome or perverse sexual acts; sexually deviant. (Widely known. See note 31.) □ *She's supposed to be sort of kinky and strange.* □ *He's bent and dangerous.*

kiss-ass ['kɪs-æs] **1.** someone who is servile and obsequious. (Typical of male-to-male talk. See comment at note 32.) □ *I'm fed up with that kiss-ass!* □ *Don't be such a sniveling kiss-ass!* **2.** servile and obsequious. (Typical of male-to-male talk. See comment at note 32.) □ *He can be so kiss-ass. It makes me sick.* □ *That's a silly kiss-ass way to go about something.*

Kiss my ass!   "Drop dead!"; "Go to hell!" (An angry retort. Widely known and used by both sexes.) □ *Kiss my ass, you creep!* □ *You can just kiss my ass!*

Kiss my tail! "Drop dead!" (Euphemistic for *Kiss my ass!* An angry retort. Widely known and used by both sexes.) ☐ *Kiss my tail, you insufferable jerk!* ☐ *If you want to talk like that, you can just kiss my tail!*

kiss someone's ass to kowtow to someone; to be servile and obsequious to someone. (Widely known and used by both sexes.) ☐ *I won't kiss her ass just to get a good grade.* ☐ *What do you want me to do, kiss your ass?*

klotz See *klutz.*

kluck See *dumb cluck.*

klutz AND **klotz** [klɔts AND klɑts] a stupid-acting person. (Also a term of address. Widely known and used by both sexes.) ☐ *You can be such a klutz without even trying.* ☐ *What klutz made this mess?*

knee deep in shit in very bad trouble. (Typical of male-to-male talk, but widely known. See comment at note 32. See also *in deep shit.*) ☐ *Man, I'm knee deep in shit! I gotta get a lawyer.* ☐ *What do you do when you're broke and knee deep in shit? Scream?*

knob-job ['nɑb-dʒɑb] an act of oral sex performed on the penis. (See also *get one's knob polished.* See note 31.) ☐ *She handed him a little list that had a bunch of prices and things like knob-job written on it.* ☐ *How much does the list say a knob-job is?*

knock a woman up to get a woman pregnant. (Widely known. See note 31.) ☐ *They say Sam knocked her up, but it could have been almost anybody.* ☐ *Don't knock anybody up, old buddy.*

knockers ['nɑkɚz] a woman's breasts. (Jocular and widely known. Usually plural. Typical of male-to-male talk and joking. See notes 6 and 31; see note 7 for examples.)

knock the shit out of someone See *beat the shit out of someone.*

know one's ass from a hole in the ground to be knowledgeable; to be alert and effective. (Usually negative. Widely known. Occurs in many similar forms.) □ *That stupid son of a bitch doesn't know his ass from a hole in the ground.* □ *She is so dumb, she doesn't know her ass from a hole in the ground.*

know shit about something to know anything about something. (Usually negative. Typical of male-to-male talk. See comment at note 32.) □ *He doesn't know shit about women.* □ *You've worked here for a month, and you don't know shit about this job.*

know shit from shinola [. . . ʃɑɪˈnolə] to know what's what; to be knowledgeable in the ways of the world. (Old and widely known. From the brand name of a shoe polish. See also *No shinola!*) □ *That jerk doesn't know shit from shinola! Don't even ask him about it!* □ *If you even knew shit from shinola, it would take all of your brain power.*

kraut [krɑʊt] **1.** a German. (Sometimes capitalized. Refers to sauerkraut, a popular German dish. Some jocular use. See caution at note 1; see use as a slur at note 2.) □ *Those krauts make some pretty good beer.* □ *A lot of krauts moved into the neighborhood and livened things up.* **2.** the German language. (See caution at note 1.) □ *I can say a few words in kraut, but not much.* □ *They say that kraut sounds guttural, but I don't know what that means.* **3.** pertaining to German things or the German language. (See caution at note 1.) □ *I really like that kraut beer.* □ *The best sauerkraut is kraut kraut.*

kweef [kwif] a vaginal fart. (Not widely known. See comments at *cunt fart.* See notes 6 and 31.) □ *I thought I heard a kweef, but no, she just cut one.* □ *Her little kweef startled him and he lost it.*

L

laid AND **layed** [led] copulated with. (The spelling *layed* is common but incorrect. Said of a male or a female. Widely known and used by both sexes. See notes 6 and 31.) □ *He's wanted to get laid since he was fourteen.* □ *She was laid first when she was sixteen.* □ *Man, I need to get laid!* □ *When was the last time you were layed?*

lard ass ['lɑrd æs] **1.** someone with very fat buttocks. (See also *booming*. Also a term of address. See note 31.) □ *Here comes that lard ass again.* □ *Get moving, lard ass! You've got to keep going!* **2.** very large buttocks. (See note 31.) □ *I'm gonna have to do something about this lard ass of mine.* □ *How'd you get that lard ass? Lots of potatoes, I'll bet.*

lay [le] **1.** to copulate [with] someone. (Transitive. See notes 6 and 31; see note 13 for examples.) **2.** to seduce or rape a woman. (Known and used by both sexes. See notes 6 and 31. More at *laid*.) □ *He set out to lay her, but they got to talking instead, and they became close friends.* □ *Each one in the gang laid her.* **3.** an act of copulation. (See notes 6 and 31; see note 16 for examples.) **4.** someone with whom to have copulation. (Known and used by both sexes. See notes 6 and 31.) □ *Tod's a good lay, but other than that, he's an asshole.* □ *She's okay as a lay, but that's about all.*

layed See *laid*.

leak **1.** to urinate. (See note 26 for additional examples.) □ *Your dog leaked all over my pants leg!* □ *He said somebody leaked in* *the hallway.* **2.** an act of urination. (Usually in *take a leak.*) □ *He stopped for a leak and a smoke.* □ *Time for a leak. Be right back.*

lech AND **letch** [lɛtʃ] **1.** a lecher. □ *Don't act like such a letch, Tod.* □ *I'm a lech and I know it.* **2.** to lust; to experience strong sexual desire. (See note 31.) □ *Don't come around here letching!* □ *Who's the jerk sitting in the corner leching at the girls?*

lech after someone AND **lech for someone** to lust for someone. (Sometimes also spelled "letch." See note 31.) □ *I think Bob has been leching after me for about a month.* □ *I'll lech for whomever I want, as long as I keep it a secret.*

leg a woman; a woman considered as a sexual object. (Typical of male-to-male talk and joking. See notes 6 and 31; see examples at note 23.)

leg-man a male who prefers females with good-looking legs; a male who is sexually aroused by well-shaped female legs. (Known and used by both sexes. See notes 6 and 31.) □ *Clyde is a leg-man, but almost everything will turn him on a little.* □ *I'm a leg-man myself. Knockers are okay, but legs drive me crazy!*

lemons [ˈlɛmənz] a woman's breasts, especially if small. (Usually plural. See notes 6 and 31; see note 7 for additional examples.) □ *I sure would like to squeeze those lemons.* □ *Alas, I found she had lemons where I wanted grapefruit.*

let a fart See *cut a fart.*

let one See *cut a fart.*

lez See the following entry.

lezbo AND **lez, lezzie** [ˈlɛzbo AND lɛz, ˈlɛzi] **1.** a lesbian. (Intended and perceived as derogatory. Also a term of address. Resented. Compare to *bulldiker.* See note 5 for examples and caution; see note 3 for examples.) **2.** having to do with lesbians or things lesbian. (Intended and perceived as derogatory.) □ *That's sort of a lezbo shirt she's got on.* □ *It was some sort of a lezzie place, but we left before we found out what kind.*

lezzie See *lezbo.*

lickety-split ['lɪkəti-'splɪt] an act of oral sex performed on the genitals of a female. (*Split* refers to the vulva. *Lickety* refers to licking. The entire phrase means "very fast" in colloquial English, as in "to run lickety-split." See note 31.) □ *Man, can he do lickety-split!* □ *Hey, baby, hows about a little lickety-split?*

lift his leg [for a male dog] to urinate. (Jocular when used for a human male. See note 31.) □ *Your damn mutt lifted his leg on my rose bushes!* □ *If that animal lifts his leg in this house, it's dead!*

lift up to get an erection of the penis. (See note 10 for examples; see note 31.)

like a bat out of hell very, very fast indeed. (Widely known and used by both sexes.) □ *She took off outa there like a bat outa hell!* □ *This car can go like a bat out of hell.*

Like fuck! an expression of total disbelief; *Like hell!* (Typical of male-to-male talk. Taboo. See note 4 for caution; see comment at note 32.) □ *Like fuck! You're full of shit!* □ *I'm the one who broke it? Like fuck, I did!*

Like fun! an exclamation of disbelief. (Euphemistic for *Like fuck!* Widely known.) □ *You expect me to do that? Like fun!* □ *Like fun, I will!*

like hell 1. an exclamation of disbelief. (Usually **Like hell!** See also *Like fuck!* Widely known and used by both sexes.) □ *Like hell, he did!* □ *Me? Go to the office? Like hell!* 2. very fast, very much, a general adverbial intensifier. (See examples. Widely known and used by both sexes.) □ *She can cook like hell, she can!* □ *You're gonna have to run like hell to get there on time.*

like pigs in shit a catchphrase describing a high degree of happiness and contentment. (Folksy. See examples.) □ *Just give them their beer and pretzels, and they're like pigs in shit.* □ *Look at them there, drinking and cutting the cheese! Just like pigs in shit.*

little shit a stupid and insignificant person. (Usually refers to a male. Typical of male-to-male talk. See comment at note 32.) □ *What's a little shit like him doing running a big company like this one?* □ *Tell the little shit to get his stuff together and get out.*

lock a Pole; a person of Polish nationality. (Intended as jocular and perceived as derogatory. Often plural. Based on *Polack*.) □ *We had some of that good lock grub, and she didn't even charge for it.* □ *A couple of locks walked into this bar and ordered a beer. Just one beer.*

love sausage ['lǝv sɔsɪdʒ] the penis. (Jocular and familiar. See note 8 for examples; see note 31.)

lunger ['lǝŋɚ] a gob of coughed-up mucus. (See note 31.) □ *That's not a fried egg. It's more like a lunger!* □ *He rumbled and coughed up another lunger. This one just dropped onto his shirt.*

M

macaroni [mækəˈroni] a person of Italian nationality or descent. (Intended as jocular and perceived as derogatory. See caution at note 1.) □ *Those macaronies can sure do wonderful things with noodles.* □ *If that fat macaroni thinks he can push me around like that, he's gonna get in trouble!*

mackerel-snapper See *fish-eater.*

make to urinate; to make water. (Mostly with children. See note 26 for examples; see note 31.)

make it with someone to copulate with someone; to succeed in copulating with someone. (Widely known and used by both sexes. One of the preferred expressions meaning "to copulate with someone." See note 31.) □ *He was hoping to make it with her, but she had other things on her mind.* □ *I really want to make it with you, baby.*

make out to pet; to pet and copulate. (Old. Used by both sexes.) □ *They were in the back seat making out.* □ *Okay, tell me. Did you make out or not?*

make-out artist AND **maker** someone who makes love well, frequently, or easily. (Old. See *make out.*) □ *Bob's a pretty feeble make-out artist. But he has beautiful eyelashes.* □ *What a make-out artist she is!*

maker See *make-out artist.*

mammy-jammer   See *mother(-fucker)*.

man-eater   ['mæn-itɚ] a female who performs oral sex on a male. (Mostly jocular. Not widely known. See also *cannibal*. See note 31.) □ *Sally is a man-eater and a damn good one, they say.* □ *I'd like to be stranded on a desert island filled with man-eaters.*

maracas   [məˈrɑkəz] a woman's breasts. (From the name of a Latin American gourd rattle. Based on the size and shape of the gourd and its shaking. Usually plural. See notes 6 and 31; see note 7 for examples.)

meat   [mit] **1.** the penis. (See note 8 for examples; see note 31.) **2.** the genitals of either sex; the sexual parts of either sex. (Partly jocular and partly euphemistic. The term serves well as a rude generic covering both sexes when no other term is known. See notes 12 and 8 for examples; see note 31.) **3.** a person of either sex considered sexually. (Also a slang term referring to a large and muscular male without any reference to genitals. See note 31.) □ *You could see that he was out looking for meat.* □ *If she didn't manage to wrap her legs around that big hunk of meat within the next twenty minutes, I'd lose my bet.*

melons   ['mɛlənz] a woman's breasts, especially if very large. (Jocular. Typical of male-to-male talk and joking. Usually plural. See note 7 for examples; see notes 6 and 31.)

mental   ['mɛntl̩] **1.** a person who is mentally deficient. (Perceived as cruel.) □ *Are you a mental or what?* □ *So Bob's a mental! So what? Help him rather than hurt him!* **2.** pertaining to a mentally deficient person; pertaining to mental deficiency. (Perceived as cruel.) □ *Are you mental or what?* □ *The guy's mental. He can't help it.*

Mex   [mɛks] a person of Mexican nationality or descent. (Nickname. Some derogatory intent. Perceived as derogatory. See caution at note 1; see use as a slur at note 2.)

m.f.   See *mother(-fucker)*.

Mick AND **Micky, Mike** [mɪk AND 'mɪki, maɪk] a male of Irish nationality or descent. (A generic nickname. Often intended and perceived as derogatory and provocative. Also a term of address. Potentially provocative. See caution at note 1; see examples at note 3; see use as a slur at note 2.)

Mike See the previous entry.

mind-fuck(er) a person, event, or a drug that disorients one's thinking or jars one severely. (Drug culture use. Compare to *headfucker.* Taboo. See note 4 for caution; see comment at note 32.) □ *Sam is a real mind-fucker. I hate his guts.* □ *This stuff is a mind-fucker!*

mind-fuck someone [for a person or a drug] to disorient someone's thinking or disturb someone in some way. (Originally drug culture use. Taboo. See note 4 for caution; see comment at note 32.) □ *Don't you try to mind-fuck me, you creep!* □ *They didn't educate us at that place, they mind-fucked us!*

mockie ['maki] a Jewish person. (Usually male. Not widely known. Intended and perceived as derogatory. User will be considered bigoted and antisemitic if the word is recognized. See caution at note 1; see use as a slur at note 2.)

monkey-fart AND **fiddle-fart** ['məŋki-fart AND 'fɪdl̩-fart] to waste time; to do something ineffectually or inefficiently. (A blend of "monkey around" and "fart around." Not widely known. See comment at note 32.) □ *Stop monkey-farting and get over here and get to work.* □ *He spent the day fiddle-farting with his motorcycle.*

moon [mun] to display the naked buttocks to someone, usually through the window of a moving car. (Transitive and intransitive.) □ *Two kids slowed down and mooned us, right on Main Street.* □ *Sally is probably the only girl I know who has ever mooned anybody.*

moose [mus] **1.** a prostitute. (Korean War. From Japanese *musume.*) □ *He went off somewhere with a moose.* □ *You just take ten steps from the ship, and you're surrounded by mooses.* **2.** a male's girlfriend. (Not widely known. Typical of male-to-male talk. See note 6.) □ *You stay away from my moose! You hear me?* □ *I'm taking out my moose tonight.*

mother(-fucker) AND **mammy-jammer, m.f., mother-grabber, mother-humper, mother-jumper, mother-lover, mother-rucker** a low and despised person, usually a male. (Widely known. Can be highly provocative. Also a provocative term of address. Taboo. See note 4 for caution; see note 3 for additional examples; see comment at note 32.) □ *You'd better watch out, mother-fucker!* □ *You stupid mother-jumpers are late!*

mother-fucking low; rotten; despised. (Widely known. Similar forms can probably be made on all the variations listed at *mother(-fucker).* Taboo. See note 4 for caution; see comment at note 32.) □ *Get your ugly mother-fucking face outa here!* □ *What a mother-fucking jerk.*

mother-grabber See *mother(-fucker).*

mother-humper See *mother(-fucker).*

mother-jumper See *mother(-fucker).*

mother-lover See *mother(-fucker).*

mother-rucker See *mother(-fucker).*

muff-diver AND **diver** one who performs oral sex on a woman. (See also *dive a muff.* Not widely known. See notes 6 and 31.) □ *John's a diver. That shocks some girls and intrigues others.* □ *He says he's a muff diver, and who can argue?*

muffins ['məfənz] a woman's breasts, especially small ones. (Usually plural. See notes 6 and 31; see note 7 for examples.)

muh-fuh ['mə-fə] a *mother-fucker.* (Black. See note 3 for examples.)

muncher-boy ['məntʃɚ bɔɪ] a male who performs oral sex on men. (See also *peter-eater.* See note 31.) □ *He made a living as a muncher-boy.* □ *Harvey is the original muncher-boy. He is obsessed with it.*

munch the bearded clam ['məntʃ ðə 'bɪrdəd 'klæm] to perform oral sex on a woman. (See explanation at *bearded clam.* See notes 6 and 31.) □ *He said his favorite pastime was munching the bearded clam.* □ *He asked her if he could munch the bearded clam, and she thought he was going to take her out for a seafood dinner.*

mungshit ['məŋʃɪt] a stupid and worthless person; an idiot. (Typical of low male-to-male talk. Also a term of address. See comment at note 32.) □ *God, what a stupid, slimy mungshit you are!* □ *I've never had to deal with such a mungshit before.*

murphies ['mɚfiz] a woman's breasts, especially if large. (Another word for *potatoes.* Usually plural. See notes 6 and 31; see note 7 for examples.)

My ass! an exclamation of surprise or disagreement. (See comment at note 32.) □ *You a cop! My ass!* □ *My ass! A whole dollar!*

My God! an exclamation of shock. (Very common. Universally known and used. See caution at note 11.) □ *My God! It's alive!* □ *Oh, my God! I'm late again.*

N

nads [nædz] the testicles. (From *gonads*. Partly jocular. See note 31.) □ *Man, whenever I see her my nads ache something awful!* □ *If you ever get close to her, they'll ache even more.*

N.D.B.F. [ˈɛn ˈdi ˈbi ˈɛf] a "needle-dicked bug-fucker," a worthless male. (Also a term of address. See also *bug-fucker*. See note 31.) □ *He's just an N.D.B.F. Forget him!* □ *Look, you N.D.B.F., just get your stuff together and get out of here, once and for all!*

needle dick AND **pencil dick** **1.** a male with a small penis. (Derogatory and demeaning. Also a term of address. See note 31.) □ *Hey, needle dick! Get a life!* □ *Tell pencil dick over there to ask for his money back. He really got gypped.* **2.** a small penis. (See note 8 for examples; see note 31.) **3.** a worthless male. (Also a term of address. See note 15 for examples; see note 31.)

negative [ˈnɛɡətɪv] an American black. (Intended as jocular and derogatory and perceived as derogatory. See caution at note 1.) □ *A carload of negatives drove by and nearly hit me.* □ *Get a load of that negative over there with the high platforms.*

nerd AND **nurd** [nɚd] a dull and witless person; an overly studious person. (Originally referred to a male. Also term of address. Universally known and used by both sexes.) □ *I am not a nerd. I am just a little eccentric.* □ *Who's the nurd in the plaid pants?*

nigger [ˈnɪɡɚ] a black American; an African. (Intended and perceived as extremely derogatory. Also a term of address. Provocative. User is considered to be racially bigoted. See caution at note

1; see note 3 for examples; see use as a slur at note 2. See the following entries and *buck nigger, house nigger, yellow nigger.*)

nigger-fishing fishing done standing on a riverbank. (See caution at note 1.) □ *He's down at the river, nigger-fishing.* □ *We used to go nigger-fishing on the weekends.*

nigger-lover someone, always a nonblack, who supports blacks and causes that favor blacks. (A strongly derogatory epithet in the South. Also a term of address. User is considered to be racially bigoted. See caution at note 1; see note 3 for examples.)

nigger toe the Brazil nut. (Now derogatory. See caution at note 1.) □ *I asked for two pounds of nigger toes at the store, and you'd have thought I farted in church.* □ *We used to call them nigger toes, just because that's what we called 'em. That's all.*

niggertown a section of town populated exclusively by blacks. (Extinct except in deliberate derogation. Perceived as derogatory. User is considered to be racially bigoted. See caution at note 1.) □ *He knows where you can get some real soul food over in niggertown.* □ *They still call this niggertown, except in the newspapers and in the city council.*

nigger-wool Negroid hair. (User is considered to be racially bigoted. See caution at note 1.) □ *I don't know what I'm gonna do with this nigger-wool. I guess I'll cut it.* □ *You're not supposed to do anything to that nigger-wool! That's you and it's beautiful.*

niggra ['nɪgrə] an American black. (An eye-dialect spelling of a Southern pronunciation. Not originally with derogatory intent. Now perceived as derogatory. User is considered to be racially bigoted. See caution at note 1; see note 3 for examples; see use as a slur at note 2.)

Nip [nɪp] **1.** a Japanese person. (From Nippon, the Japanese name for Japan. See also *Jap.* Usually derogatory or demeaning. Perceived as derogatory. See caution at note 1; see use as a slur at note 2. See also the following entry.) **2.** any East Asian [including

Japanese] person. (See caution at note 1.) □ *Let the Nips have the whole world! Hell, I don't care! At least they can cook.* □ *The island was full of Nips.*

nips [nɪps] nipples. (Not widely known. Used for male as well as female nipples. See note 31.) □ *And she had these neat little nips that always showed through her T-shirt.* □ *God, Tom, your nips are bigger than Sally's!*

nookie See the following entry.

nooky AND **nookie.** **1.** the female genitals; the vulva. (Typical of male-to-male talk and joking. Best known during wartime. No refined use. See notes 6 and 31; see note 12 for examples.) **2.** women considered as a receptacle for the penis. (Typical of low male-to-male talk. See notes 6 and 31; see examples at note 23.) **3.** male sexual release through copulation with a female. (Usually with *some*. See notes 6 and 31; see note 17 for examples.)

nose-lunger a glob of nasal mucus. (*Lunger* is an old slang term for a mass of coughed-up mucus. Low. Teens and college student use. See note 31.) □ *God, somebody blew a nose-lunger on my shoe!* □ *He sneezed, and this great nose-lunger flew across the room. Yechchch!*

noserag See *snotrag.*

No shinola! [...ʃaɪˈnolə] "No shit!" (From *know shit from shinola*. Cryptic and jocular.) □ *So you wanna be a radio announcer. No shinola!* □ *No shinola! I wouldn't lie to you!*

No shit! "You are kidding!" (Typical of male-to-male talk, especially with teens and college students. More female use recently.) □ *You're really gonna do it? No shit!* □ *No shit! She let you go all the way?*

notch [nɑtʃ] **1.** the female genitals; the vulva. (Primarily low male-to-male talk. See notes 6 and 31; see note 12 for examples.) **2.** women considered as a receptacle for the penis. (See notes 6 and 31; see examples at note 23.) **3.** male sexual release through copulation with a female. (Usually with *some*. See notes 6 and 31; see note 17 for examples.)

notch-house a brothel; a house of prostitution. □ *You can count on Clyde to find the closest notch-house whenever the ship docks.* □ *Where is the notch-house that has all those foreign girls?*

nuggets ['nəgəts] the testicles. (See note 31.) □ *Man, my nuggets are cold! Let's hurry up and get back in the car.* □ *I know this kid with three nuggets—a pair and a spare.*

number one urination; an act of urination. (Juvenile and euphemistic. Widely known and used by both sexes. See note 31.) □ *Jimmy made a mess in his pants. But don't worry. It's just number one.* □ *Mommy! I gotta go. Number one!*

number two defecation; an act of defecation. (Juvenile and euphemistic. Widely known and used by both sexes. See note 31.) □ *Mommy! I gotta do a number two.* □ *God, what's that smell? Number two?*

numb-nuts ['nəm-nəts] a stupid male. (Also a term of address.) □ *Come on, numb-nuts! We're late!* □ *What kind of a numb-nuts do you think I am?*

nurd See *nerd*.

nuts [nəts] the testicles. (Widely known. Typical of male-to-male talk. More female recently. See note 31.) □ *Unless you want me to kick you right in the nuts, you'd better keep moving.* □ *While he was running, his nuts slipped out of his jockstrap and caused him all kinds of grief.*

O

ofay AND **fay** ['ofe AND fe] a Caucasian. (Intended, but not always perceived, as derogatory. Black use only. *Fay* may or may not be derived from *ofay*, which is probably Pig Latin for *foe*. See caution at note 1.) □ *Who's the fay over there with Sarah?* □ *Some ofay came around asking about you. He was an insurance salesman.*

oiler ['oɪlɚ] a person of Mexican nationality or descent; a Hispanic person. (Intended and perceived as derogatory. Probably based on *greaser*. See caution at note 1.) □ *There was a bunch of oilers cutting the grass in the rain.* □ *I never would have guessed that Franco was an oiler.*

one-eyed pants mouse See *bald-headed hermit*.

one-night stand a sexual union that lasts only one night; a brief sexual affair. (Also the name of a musician's job that lasts for only one night. *Stand* may also refer to an erection of the penis. See note 31.) □ *She never knew affection. Just a series of one-night stands.* □ *I'm not the kind of girl who does one-night stands. Let's make it tomorrow night too.*

on one's ass See *flat on one's ass*.

on the make attempting to seduce [someone]. (Said of males or females. Widely known and used by both sexes. See note 31; see comment at note 32.) □ *She's on the make. Watch out!* □ *He's got a look in his eyes that tells you he's on the make.*

on the moon cycle [for a woman] to experience the monthly menstrual period. (See notes 6 and 31.) □ *My broad's on the moon cycle again. Happens every time I turn around.* □ *Isn't it better that she's on the moon cycle rather than off it?*

on the pill taking contraceptive pills or tablets. □ *Don't worry. I'm on the pill.* □ *She has been on the pill since she was twelve.*

on the rag AND **O.T.R.** [...'o 'ti 'ɑr] [for a woman] to experience the monthly menstrual period. (Widely known. Said typically to explain a woman's irritability. Typically in female use.) □ *She acts like she's on the rag all month long!* □ *Leave her alone! She's O.T.R.*

oreo ['orio] an American black who acts more like a white. (Intended and perceived as derogatory. Also a term of address. From the protected trade name of a chocolate cookie with a filling of white creme, i.e., black on the outside and white on the inside. See also *banana*. See caution at note 1; see use as a slur at note 2.)

O.T.R. See *on the rag.*

oyster ['ɔɪstɚ] a glob of mucus, either coughed up or blown from the nose. (Related to food-dirtying. See note 31.) □ *She hacked up a tremendous oyster, streaked with blood.* □ *What'll I do with this snotrag full of oysters?*

P

P. [pi] **1.** urine. (See note 25 for examples; see note 31. Both senses from *pee* or *piss*. Juvenile and euphemistic uses.) **2.** to urinate. (See note 26 for examples; see note 31.)

Packie ['pæki] a person of Pakistani nationality or descent. (Usually in derogatory contexts, but also a typical diminutive form. See caution at note 1; see use as a slur at note 2.)

Paddy ['pædi] a person of Irish nationality or descent. (From *Pat* or *Patrick*. Also a term of address. Potentially derogatory. See caution at note 1; see use as a slur at note 2.)

pain in the ass AND **pain in the butt, pain in the rear** a bother; a needless difficulty. (The phrase with "ass" is the strongest. "Rear" is euphemistic, and "butt" is heard more and more.) □ *She is such a pain in the ass!* □ *Don't be a pain in the butt, Chuck!*

pain in the butt See the previous entry.

pain in the rear See *pain in the ass.*

pair [per] a pair of breasts. (See notes 6 and 31; see note 7 for similar examples.) □ *Wow! What a pair!* □ *She's got a pair that would knock your socks off!*

pansy ['pænzi] a male homosexual, especially if effeminate. (Intended and perceived as derogatory. Also a term of address. See note 5 for examples and caution; see notes 3 and 31.)

pansy raid an attack against male homosexuals. (A play on "panty raid." Intended as jocular.) □ *The cops held a little pansy raid at the gay bar last night.* □ *The thugs staged a pansy raid in the dormitory.*

panther piss ['pænθɚ pɪs] strong liquor. (There are other names for strong liquor: **tiger piss, lion piss, cougar piss,** etc. See comment at note 32.) □ *Gimme another glass of that panther piss.* □ *That panther piss burned the skin off my throat.*

pants rabbit AND **seam squirrel** a louse. (Usually plural. Jocular.) □ *Are you scratching your pants rabbits?* □ *He's got seam squirrels, and that's why he's scratching.*

paps [pæps] the breasts, especially old and withered breasts. (Usually plural. An old, not very flattering word. See notes 6 and 31; see note 7 for examples.)

paste [pest] semen. (See note 31.) □ *Is that paste on your pants leg, or what?* □ *About how much paste does a dog make?*

patootie AND **patoot** [pə'tuti AND pə'tut] the buttocks; the anus. (Heard often on the television series *M*A*S*H*, especially as **horse's patoot.** Not to be confused with *sweet patootie,* "sweet potato," a term of endearment. See notes 29 and 30 for examples; see note 31.)

pecker ['pɛkɚ] the penis. (See note 8 for examples; see note 31.)

pecker-checker ['pɛkɚ-tʃɛkɚ] a doctor who examines men's genitals for signs of venereal disease. (Military. Contrived and jocular. See note 31.) □ *Around here I'm just a pecker-checker. I never get any interesting diseases to deal with.* □ *See if you can get the pecker-checker to give you some aspirin for your headache.*

peckerhead **1.** the head or end of the penis. (See note 31.) □ *He said he had a little red sore on his peckerhead.* □ *It was so cold* *that all I had left was a little peckerhead playing peekaboo.* **2.** a stupid and ignorant male. (See note 15 for examples.)

peckerwood AND **wood**   a Caucasian; an American white, especially in the South. (*Wood* is newer than *peckerwood*. Old Southern. Usually considered derogatory. From the common name for the red-headed woodpecker which has a red neck.) □ *Hey, peckerwood! Come over here and say that!* □ *Go over and ask wood there if he knows where he is.*

peddle ass AND **peddle one's ass**   to sell one's body as a prostitute. (Low. Not widely known.) □ *I don't want to have to peddle ass the rest of my life.* □ *She's spent three years of her life peddling ass so she could retire and live off her investments.*

pee [pi] **1.** urine. (Both are euphemistic and primarily juvenile. A spelling-out of *P.* From *piss.* See note 25 for examples; see note 31.) **2.** to urinate. (See note 26 for examples; see note 31.)

peed off [pid 'ɔf] a euphemism for *pissed-off.* (A jocular euphemism. People who would avoid *pissed-off* might also avoid this and similar expressions.) □ *Man, is she peed off!* □ *You'd be peed off too, if that had happened to you.*

pee hole **1.** the vagina. (A misunderstanding. Primarily low or juvenile male-to-male talk or joking. See notes 6 and 31; see note 12 for examples.) **2.** the urinary *meatus*; the point at which urine emerges from the body. (May be used when the speaker does not know the proper name. See note 31.) □ *I got some sort of a sore on my pee hole.* □ *If you don't give me a straight answer, I'll stick something up your pee hole.*

peenie ['pini] the penis; a child's penis. (Juvenile. See note 8 for examples; see note 31.)

peep [pip] to urinate. (From *pee-pee.* See note 26 for examples; see note 31.)

pee-pee ['pi-pi] **1.** to urinate. (Juvenile. See note 26 for examples; see note 31.) **2.** urine. (Juvenile. See note 25 for examples; see note 31.) **3.** the penis, especially that of a child. (Juvenile. See note 8 for examples; see note 31.)

peer-queer ['pir-kwir] a homosexual male who likes to watch sexual activity. (See note 5 for additional examples and caution.) □ *He says he's a peer-queer. He likes to peep and watch.* □ *There was a peer-queer next to me in the john.*

pencil dick See *needle dick.*

penis breath a negative term of address or an epithet. (Occurred in the most popular children's movie of all times, *E.T.* See comment at note 32.) □ *Mommy, Jimmy called me a penis breath!* □ *Shut up, penis breath!*

pepper-belly ['pɛpɚ-bɛli] a Mexican. (Intended and perceived as derogatory. Also a term of address. Because of the spicy food eaten. See also *beaner, rice-belly.* See caution at note 1; see use as a slur at note 2.)

peter ['pitɚ] the penis. (See note 8 for examples; see note 31.)

peter-cheater a sanitary napkin for use during a woman's monthly menstrual cycle. (The napkin prevents the *peter* from entering the vagina. See note 31.) □ *When are you going to get rid of those peter-cheaters? You had them on for days.* □ *I gotta go change my peter-cheater.*

peter-eater someone who performs oral sex on the penis. (See *peter.* See note 31.) □ *He's a peter-eater. You know, a professional muncher-boy.* □ *The girls all said that Freddy is a peter-eater. But how would they know?*

piccolo-player See *flute(r).*

piece of ass AND **hunk of ass, hunk of tail, piece of snatch, piece of tail** **1.** someone considered as a partner in copulation.

(Low. Usually male talk. See notes 6 and 31.) □ *Man, isn't she a fine looking piece of ass?* □ *Man, isn't he a fine looking piece of snatch?* **2.** an act of copulation; copulation with someone. (Both senses originated with females as the target, but use is also recorded in a homosexual context. See notes 6 and 31.) □ *God, if I don't get a piece of tail pretty soon, I'm gonna come to no good.* □ *If Tod doesn't get a hunk of tail once a day, he's real grouchy.*

piece of snatch See the previous entry.

piece of tail See *piece of ass.*

pile of shit **1.** a mass of lies. (Low. Typical of male-to-male talk. Refers to *bullshit.*) □ *He came in and told me this great pile of shit about how his alarm clock was in the shop.* □ *Don't give me that pile of shit! I know the truth!* **2.** any worthless structure or device. (Low. Typical of male-to-male talk.) □ *Take this pile of shit back where you bought it and get your money back.* □ *The car is nothing but a pile of shit.* **3.** a totally worthless person. (Low and provocative. Typical of male-to-male talk.) □ *Tod, you are the biggest pile of shit I've ever seen.* □ *Don't be such a pile of shit!*

pill a contraceptive pill or tablet. (Universally known.) □ *The pill made her really sick, so she stopped taking it.* □ *Her doctor prescribed the pill, but it didn't work.*

pimp [pimp] **1.** a male procurer for the prostitutes he manages. □ *He's a pimp, a drug addict, a drug pusher, a murderer, and he thinks he can get elected alderman? Lordy!* □ *Her pimp always beat her up.* **2.** to procure customers for a prostitute. □ *He spends a lot of time pimping for his girls.* □ *I don't do much. I pimp. I sell drugs. Nothing exciting.*

pimpish ['pimpɪʃ] flamboyant; flashy; in the manner or style of a pimp. □ *That's a pimpish way to walk, don't you think?* □ *That is the most pimpish hat I've ever seen!*

pimpmobile **1.** a very large and showy car with lots of chrome and decorative elements as might be driven by a wealthy pimp. (Usually an exaggerated derogation for a big fancy car. Jocular.) □ *Did you see that pimpmobile that just passed us?* □ *I'm gonna buy me the biggest pimpmobile and drive around the old neighborhood.* **2.** AND **cunt-wagon** a pimp's car, which carries prostitutes to customers. (Compare to *cock-wagon.* Low.) □ *One of those cunt-wagons stopped at the corner and two real hookers got out.* □ *The pimpmobile drew up and discharged its whoresome load.*

pimp someone over to cheat and deceive someone. (Typical of low male talk. See comment at note 32.) □ *God, that jerk really pimped me over. He'll never do it again!* □ *They were pimping over some poor drunk who wandered by.*

pimpstick ['pɪmpstɪk] a machine-made cigarette. (Named at a time when machine-made cigarettes were considered flashy and unmasculine.) □ *You won't catch me smoking any of them pimp-sticks!* □ *Lemme try one of those pimpsticks, huh?*

pimp up to dress up in very fancy clothing. (Typical of male-to-male talk. See comment at note 32.) □ *It'll take a little while for me to pimp up, but I'll be right with you.* □ *Let's get pimped up and take the girls out tonight.*

pimp walk a kind of a strut thought to be typical of flamboyant, wealthy pimps. (Low. See comment at note 32.) □ *Look at the pimp walk that guy's doing! What a clown!* □ *He came in the door with sort of an exaggerated pimp walk.*

piss [pɪs] **1.** to urinate. (One of the English "four-letter words." See note 26 for examples; see note 31. See also the following entries and *half-pissed, panther piss, take a piss, take the piss out of someone.*) **2.** urine. (See note 25 for examples; see note 31.) **3.** bad beer; bad liquor; any bad-tasting or poor quality liquid. (Typical of low male talk. See comment at note 32.) □ *How about another can of that piss you serve here?* □ *I've had enough of this damn piss!*

piss and vinegar **1.** arrogance. (See comment at note 32.) □ *He still has a lot of piss and vinegar left in him. This ought to fix him.* □ *Of all the piss and vinegar! You are rude, crude, and ugly!* **2.** vigor. (See comment at note 32.) □ *Here I am with lots of piss and vinegar.* □ *Come on! Put some piss and vinegar into it.*

pissant [pɪs-ænt] **1.** a wretched and worthless person. (Not originally taboo. Now avoided. See comment at note 32.) □ *Look, you silly pissant, beat it!* □ *Wally is such a little pissant!* **2.** worthless. (See comment at note 32.) □ *I don't want this little pissant piece of pie. Give me a real piece.* □ *Who is this pissant shithead who thinks he can tell me what to do?*

pissant around to waste one's time; to spend time doing something worthless. (An elaboration of *piss around*. See comment at note 32.) □ *Don't pissant around asking a lot of silly questions. Get right to the point.* □ *Stop pissanting around and get to work.*

piss around to waste time; to be inefficient at something. (Typical of male-to-male talk. See comment at note 32.) □ *She's just pissing around. She'll never finish.* □ *I can't piss around here all day! Let's get going!*

piss-ass **1.** a wretched and disliked person. (Low and provocative. Typical of male-to-male talk. See comment at note 32.) □ *You are the biggest and stupidest piss-ass I know!* □ *Get some piss-ass over here to clean up this mess!* **3.** wretched; worthless. (Low. Typical of male-to-male talk. See comment at note 32.) □ *Who left this piss-ass piece of stale pizza on that table?* □ *What a stupid, piss-ass thing to say!*

piss blood AND **sweat blood** **1.** to experience great anxiety. (Typical of male-to-male talk.) □ *He made me piss blood before he agreed.* □ *I really had to sweat blood in order to land that contract.* **2.** to expend an enormous amount of energy. (Typical of male-to-male talk.) □ *I pissed blood to come in first in the race.* □ *All the crew sweat blood and got it done on time.*

piss call the bugle call that indicates it's time to get up; time to get up. (Military.) □ *He's been in a bad mood since piss call.* □ *What time is piss call in the morning?*

piss-cutter AND **piss-whiz** an extraordinary person; someone who can do the impossible. (Low. Typical of teens and college student talk. See comment at note 32.) □ *Sam is a real piss-cutter when it comes to running.* □ *Tod's no piss-whiz as a batter, but he can really pitch!*

pissed [pɪst] drunk. (Widespread. See also the following entry.) □ *She was too pissed to stand up.* □ *He's totally pissed every night at this time.*

pissed (off) (at someone or something) AND **pissed off about someone or something** very angry with or about someone or something. (Originally far more rude than at present. Still frowned on by many people as rude, this expression can be heard in public almost anywhere. It is also sometimes heard in informal conversation on the radio. See comment at note 32.) □ *She's always pissed off about something.* □ *Man, is that guy pissed off!*

piss elegant [ˈpɪs ˈɛləgənt] very pretentious; overly elegant. (Not widely known. Primarily male talk. See comment at note 32.) □ *Man, this place is piss elegant. Look at them lamp shades!* □ *I ain't never seen such a piss-elegant bathroom!*

pisser [ˈpɪsɚ] **1.** a urinal; a place [room, restroom] to urinate. (See note 31.) **2.** a remarkable thing or person. (Compare to *piss-cutter.* See comment at note 32.) □ *Man, isn't he a real pisser! Have you ever seen anybody bat like that?* □ *She's no pisser, but she can get the job done.* **3.** the penis; the female genitals. (Low and rude. See notes 8 and 12 for examples; see note 31.) **4.** a terribly funny joke. (You laugh so hard you wet your pants. Jocular.) □ *He told a real pisser and broke up the entire class.* □ *Hey, you wanna hear a real pisser?*

piss factory a bar, tavern, or saloon. (Because it makes the drinker urinate. Low. Typical of male-to-male talk.) □ *I stopped* *in at the piss factory for a round or two.* □ *Fred spends far too much time at the piss factory.*

piss freak someone who derives special sexual pleasure from urine. (Usually in a homosexual context. See also *golden shower.* See note 31.) □ *Wally, it turns out, is a total piss freak, and suggested something unbelievable to Ernie.* □ *He said he was a piss freak and wanted me to urinate where I most likely had never urinated before.*

piss hard-on an early morning erection of the penis; a urinary erection. (Caused by the need to urinate rather than sexual arousal. See note 9 for examples; see note 31.)

pisshead **1.** a wretched and disgusting person. (Low and provocative. Typical of male-to-male talk. See comment at note 32.) □ *Hey, pisshead! Clean up that mess!* □ *How can you even think of going out with a pisshead like Sam?* **2.** a drunkard; a drunken person. (Low. See *pissed.*) □ *Some old pisshead in the gutter must have given you that hat.* □ *The cops hauled in a couple of pissheads and locked them up.*

pisshouse **1.** a privy; a toilet room. (Low. Not widespread.) □ *He's out in the pisshouse. Be back in a minute.* □ *I gotta stop at the pisshouse for a minute.* **2.** a police station. (Low. Typical of male-to-male use, especially underworld talk. See comment at note 32.) □ *I spent four hours in the pisshouse waiting for my lawyer.* □ *Can you believe it? They locked me up in the pisshouse for two days!*

pissing ['pɪsɪŋ] worthless; minimal. (Low. Typical of male-to-male talk. Refers to the short duration of an act of urination.) □ *I'll be there in one pissing minute. Be quiet.* □ *I got a pissing amount of coffee for a buck and a quarter.*

pissing-match an argument; a pointless competition. (Typical of male-to-male talk. See comment at note 32.) □ *Let's call a halt to this pissing-match and get to work.* □ *That was no meeting. It was a silly pissing-match.*

pissing-spell AND **farting-spell**   a short period of time, just long enough to urinate or break wind. (Typical of low male-to-male talk. See comment at note 32.) □ *I'll be there in a pissing-spell.* □ *He said he'd be through in a farting-spell, but that was an hour ago.*

Piss in it!   "To hell with it!" (An exclamation of exasperation. Not literal. Compare to *Shit on it!*") □ *Oh, piss on it! I've had enough!* □ *The damn car will never start! Piss on it!*

piss in the wind   to do something that is futile and counter-productive; to waste one's time doing something. (Typical of male-to-male talk.) □ *Shut up! You're just pissing in the wind!* □ *I'm tired of pissing in the wind. I'm gonna look for a new job.*

piss-mean   very mean; cruel. (Typical of male-to-male talk. See comment at note 32.) □ *Her pimp is piss-mean and looking for blood.* □ *He's a piss-mean son of a bitch.*

piss off AND **P.O.**   to depart; to go away. (Usually a command. See also *piss someone off.* Typical of male-to-male talk. See comment at note 32.) □ *Piss off, you jerk! Get out!* □ *P.O.! Get out!*

piss on someone or something   **1.** to urinate on someone or something. (Typical of male-to-male talk. See note 31.) □ *That dog pissed on my shoe!* □ *Hey, watch out! Don't piss on me!* **2.** to degrade or denigrate someone or something. (Compare to *do a number on someone.* See comment at note 32.) □ *He spent three paragraphs pissing on the play, then he said to go see it.* □ *He pissed on me, and then said I tried my best. What does that mean?*

pisspiration [pɪspɚˈeʃn̩] sweat. (From *perspiration.* Intended as jocular. Typical of male-to-male talk. See comment at note 32.) □ *Man, look at the pisspiration bespangling his brow!* □ *I'm soaked with pisspiration! I gotta have a shower.*

piss-poor   **1.** of very poor quality. (Typical of male-to-male talk. See comment at note 32.) □ *This is piss-poor coffee. Pay the bill* *and let's go.* □ *That's one piss-poor car you got there.* **2.** without any money; broke. (Emphatic. Typical of male-to-male talk. See comment at note 32.) □ *I'm so piss-poor, I can't afford a newspaper.* □ *Tell those piss-poor jerks to go beg somewhere else.*

piss someone off to make someone angry. (Originally far more rude than at present. Still frowned on by many people as rude, this expression can be heard in public almost anywhere used by both sexes. It is also sometimes heard in informal conversation on the radio. See also *pissed (off) (at someone or something).* See comment at note 32. More at *pissed off.*) □ *Whatever you do, don't piss him off.* □ *That really pisses me off!*

piss something away to waste all of something, such as time or money. (Typical of male-to-male talk. To let something flow or rush away as easily as releasing urine.) □ *He pissed away the best possible chances.* □ *Don't piss the day away sleeping! Get up and get to work!*

piss-ugly ['pɪs 'əgli] very ugly. (See also *fugly.* Typical of low male talk. See comment at note 32.) □ *Your baby is the most piss-ugly thing I ever saw—or is that a monkey?* □ *Man, isn't she piss-ugly?*

piss-warm warm; lukewarm; the temperature of new urine. (Typical of male-to-male talk.) □ *This coffee is just piss-warm. Heat it up.* □ *I can't stand piss-warm milk.*

piss-whiz See *piss-cutter.*

piss(y)-faced ['pɪs(i)-fest] drunk. (Widespread. See comment at note 32.) □ *He was so piss-faced he could hardly stand up.* □ *How many beers does it take to get you pissy-faced, anyway?*

pity fuck an act of copulation permitted by a woman who feels sorry for the man. (Jocular. Taboo. See note 4 for caution; see note 16 for related examples; see note 31.) □ *You don't love me. This is just a pity fuck.* □ *You slime. All I could ever give you is a pity fuck!*

pizza face See *crater-face.*

play doctor to examine and fondle someone's genitals, assuming the privileges of a physician. (Based on an activity normally practiced by small children. Also used for adult sexual play. See note 31.) □ *When he said he wanted to play doctor, I thought he was going to take my pulse!* □ *They were in the back seat playing doctor when somebody knocked on the car window.*

play grab-ass **1.** to attempt to touch or feel someone's buttocks. (Used by both sexes. See note 31.) □ *He walked right through the main lobby playing grab ass with all the clerks.* □ *That new guy is always trying to play grab ass!* **2.** to participate in sexual play. (See note 31.) □ *You can't stand here playing grab-ass all day.* □ *How about we go upstairs and play a little grab-ass?*

play hide the salami AND **play hide the sausage, play hide the weenie** to copulate. (See note 13 for related examples; see note 31.)

play house [for a man and woman] to live together and copulate, unmarried. (Mostly euphemistic.) □ *They're just playing house. They even have their own apartments elsewhere.* □ *I don't want to spend the rest of my life playing house with you!*

play with oneself to play with one's own genitals; to masturbate. (See note 19 for examples; see note 31.)

P.O. See *piss off.*

pocket pool the act of a male playing with his genitals with his hand in his pants pocket. (Mostly jocular. Used by both sexes, especially in teasing. See note 31.) □ *The stupid jerk stands on the street corner playing pocket pool all day.* □ *Stop playing pocket pool and get to work.*

P.O.d ['pi 'od] the same as *pissed-off.* (See comments at *piss someone off*) □ *I get so P.O.d at you!* □ *The teacher was P.O.d at the whole class.*

pogie ['pogi] the vagina. (More joking than rude. Male-to-male talk and use among teens and college students. See notes 6 and 31; see note 12 for examples.)

pogostick swirl ['pogostɪk 'swɚl] a prostitute's service performed on the penis. (Not widespread. See note 31.) □ *She told about something called pogostick swirl which she reckoned she would do for thirty-five dollars.* □ *The john wanted to know if the hooker had a patent on her pogostick swirl.*

poke [pok] to copulate [with] a woman. (Transitive. See notes 6 and 31; see note 13 for examples.)

poker the penis; the erect penis. (Sometimes with "hot," referring to the heat of passion. From the name for the iron rod used to stir fires. See notes 8 and 9 for examples; see note 31.)

poke through the whiskers to copulate [with] a woman. (The whiskers are the pubic hair. See note 13 for related examples; see note 31.)

Polack ['polɑk] a Pole; a person of Polish descent. (This is the Polish word for a male Pole. Often intended and perceived as derogatory. Potentially provocative. See caution at note 1; see note 3 for examples; see use as a slur at note 2.) □ *Well, that's the way we Polacks are.* □ *I'm proud to be a Polack, and you'd better remember it!*

poo [pu] **1.** dung; feces. (Euphemistic or juvenile. See note 27 for examples; see note 31.) **2.** to defecate. (See note 28 for examples; see note 31.)

poon tang AND **poontang** ['pun 'tæŋ] **1.** the female genitals; the vulva. (Originally military or Southern. Probably from a foreign word, such as French *putain*. Now used in low male-to-male talk and joking. This sense is less common than those that follow. See notes 6 and 31; see note 12 for examples.) **2.** women considered as a receptacle for the penis. (See notes 6 and 31; see examples at note 23.) **3.** male sexual release through copulation with a female. (Usually with *some*. See notes 6 and 31; see note 17 for examples.)

poop [pup] **1.** dung; feces. (Euphemistic or juvenile. See note 27 for examples; see note 31.) **2.** to defecate. (Usually juvenile. See note 28 for examples; see note 31.) **3.** information; explanation. (General slang. No reference to dung in this sense. Old and widespread.) □ *What's the poop on the new building they're putting up on Main Street?* □ *Have you heard the poop on the mayor's cousin's wedding?*

poophead a stupid-acting person. (Heard in the children's movie *Mary Poppins*. Also a term of address.) □ *Don't vote for Franco. He's a silly poophead.* □ *All right, poophead! That's enough!*

poopied ['pupid] drunk. (See *shit-faced*. Mostly jocular.) □ *Only four beers and she was totally poopied!* □ *God, I'm poopied! Which way is up?*

poo-poo ['pu-pu] (All senses are juvenile or jocular.) **1.** feces; dung. (See note 27 for examples; see note 31.) **2.** to defecate. (See note 28 for examples; see note 31.) **3.** an act of defecation. □ *Billy has to do a poo-poo.* □ *Who made the poo-poo in the garage?*

(poor) white trash financially and culturally impoverished Caucasians in the South; a derogatory name for any Caucasian in the South or elsewhere. (Potentially provocative. See caution at note 1.) □ *Back in them hills you find poor white trash and a few wild pigs. Can't always tell which is which.* □ *Don't call me white trash!*

pork [pork] to copulate [with] a woman. (Widespread. In the movie *European Vacation*. Transitive. See note 13 for examples; see note 31.)

porked [porkt] copulated [with]; [of a female] deflowered. (Widespread. In the children's movie *Monster Squad*. See note

31.) □ *Well, have you been porked?* □ *I don't think I'd like to get porked by you, thank you.*

porker ['porkɚ] **1.** one who copulates. (Usually refers to a male. Mostly jocular. See note 31.) □ *Old Max is a real porker. He's always going at it.* □ *Sally is a porker and will make it with anyone.* **2.** AND **porky** ['porki] a Jewish person. (Intended as jocular and derogatory; perceived as derogatory. From the Biblical injunction against eating pork. User is considered to be bigoted and antisemitic. See caution at note 1; see use as a slur at note 2.)

porky See under *porker.*

Portugoose ['portʃugus] a person of Portuguese nationality or descent. (Jocular wartime. An imaginary singular form of the word "Portuguese," playing on "goose/geese." See caution at note 1.)

potatoes [pə'tedoz] a woman's breasts. (See also *murphies.* Usually plural. See notes 6 and 31; see note 7 for examples.)

potty mouth See *toilet mouth.*

pound off See *beat off.*

pound one's meat See *beat the dummy.*

powder burn ['paudɚ bɚn] an American black. (Intended and perceived as derogatory. Not widely known. See caution at note 1; see use as a slur at note 2.)

prick [prɪk] **1.** the penis. (See note 8 for examples; see note 31. See the following entries and *spare prick.*) **2.** a stupid or obnoxious male. (See note 15 for examples; see note 31.)

prick-teaser AND **cock-tease(r)** **1.** a female who leads a male on sexually, but refuses to copulate. (See notes 6 and 31.) □ *She is such a prick-teaser. Don't get your hopes up.* □ *You are such a cock-tease. I'm surprised he will still go out with you!* **2.** an overly flirtatious woman. (See note 6.) □ *What a prick-teaser! Look at her flutter those eyelashes.* □ *Look at that cock-tease swing her ass!*

primed [prɑɪmd] pertaining to a female who is ready for copulation. (See also *pump*. See note 31.) □ *She was all primed when the phone rang.* □ *It took three hours to get her primed, but it was worth it.*

pud [pəd] the penis. (Possibly from *pudendum.* See *pull one's pud.* See note 8 for examples; see note 31.)

puke [pjuk] **1.** to vomit. (See note 31.) □ *I thought I would puke when I smelled it.* □ *Who puked in the john?* **2.** vomit. (See note 31.) □ *There's puke on the bathroom wall.* □ *Tod put a big hunk of fake plastic puke on the teacher's desk.* **3.** a totally disgusting and obnoxious person. (Provocative.) □ *God, I hate you, you puke!* □ *What an ugly puke. Make him leave! Make him handsome!*

puke hole **1.** someone's mouth. (Rude. Typical of male-to-male talk. One vomits through the mouth.) □ *Put some of that in your puke hole and see how you like it!* □ *Shut up, or I'll bash you one right in the puke hole!* **2.** a toilet. (Typical of male-to-male talk and joking.) □ *How many times have I told you? Leave the lid up on the puke hole!* □ *Go flush this down the puke hole. It's not fit to eat.*

pull a train [for a female] to copulate with a sequence of males, voluntarily. (See note 31.) □ *She's never happier than when she's pulling a train.* □ *Pulling a train doesn't sound like fun. It sounds disgusting and messy.*

pull oneself off See *beat off.*

pull one's pud See *beat the dummy.*

pull one's wire See *beat the dummy.*

Pull your finger out! "Wake up!"; "Get moving!"; "Become alert!" (Probably means to pull one's finger out of one's rectum. In widespread use, typically in athletics.) □ *Move it, you toads! Pull your finger out!* □ *Pull your finger out! Show some speed!*

pump [pəmp] to copulate [with] a woman. (Said of the male. Transitive. See note 13 for examples; see note 31.)

pump ship **1.** to vomit. (See note 31.) □ *God, I think I gotta pump ship.* □ *She crept over to the bushes and pumped ship for a while.* **2.** to urinate. (See note 26 for examples; see note 31.) **3.** to masturbate. (See note 19 for examples; see note 31.)

pussy ['pʊsi] **1.** the female genitals; the vulva. (Very widespread and well known. For some people, a reasonable, familiar diminutive. For others, it is rude. Primarily, but not exclusively, male talk. See notes 6 and 31; see note 12 for examples.) **2.** women considered as a receptacle for the penis. (See notes 6 and 31; see examples at note 23.) **3.** male sexual release through copulation with a female. (Usually with *some*. See notes 6 and 31; see note 17 for examples.)

pussy-bumping ['pʊsi-bəmpɪŋ] a type of lesbian sexual activity. (See *flat-fuck, tummy-fuck*. See note 31.) □ *Pussy-bumping doesn't sound like it's a lot of fun, but what the hell.* □ *There was a couple in the corner pussy-bumping or something like that.*

pussy fart See *cunt fart*.

pussy-posse ['pʊsi-pɑsi] a vice squad; the police unit in charge of suppressing prostitution. (See also *cathouse detail*. Jocular and contrived.) □ *The pussy-posse broke up a little household on Monday night.* □ *One of the neighbors called the pussy-posse to investigate all of Sally's visitors.*

pussy-simple AND **pussy-struck** obsessed with copulation. (Said of a male. See note 31.) □ *The dumb clod is pussy-simple. No brains at all.* □ *He's pussy-struck now, but he'll probably outgrow it.*

pussy-struck   See the previous entry.

pussy-whipped   ['pʊsi-ʍɪpt] totally dominated by a female; ruled by a woman; henpecked. (Refers to a male. See comment at note 32; see note 6.) □ *The guy is so pussy-whipped, he's afraid of his own shadow.* □ *He was pussy-whipped before he was married a month.*

put it in   to place the penis into the vagina. (Colloquial. See note 31.) □ *He tried to put it in, but he was too clumsy.* □ *All his life Wallace J. Ott had been waiting for the chance to put it in, but he would have to wait a while longer.*

put it to someone   **1.** to proposition someone for sexual activity. □ *She put it to him, and he fled the room blushing.* □ *He put it to her, and she slapped him.* **2.** [for a male] to copulate [with] a woman. (See note 13 for related examples; see note 31.)

put lipstick on his dipstick   [... 'lɪpstɪk ... 'dɪpstɪk] [for a woman] to perform oral sex on a man's penis. (Jocular and contrived. See note 31.) □ *She's the kind of dame who'd rather put lipstick on your dipstick than kiss.* □ *What do you want me to do? Put lipstick on your dipstick? What turns you on, anyway?*

put one's ass on the line   See the following entry.

put one's balls on the line AND **put one's ass on the line**   to risk something important in some endeavor; to put an important part of oneself into jeopardy for something important. (Typical of male-to-male talk and joking. See comment at note 32.) □ *I really put my balls on the line for this project, and I don't intend to see you fuck it up.* □ *I'll never put my ass on the line again if you won't back me up.*

put (some) balls on something   to make something stronger and more powerful. (This could be done to music, a speech, a declaration, etc. Typical of male-to-male talk. See note 31; see comment at note 32.) □ *It's too wimpy. It sounds feeble. Put* *some balls on it.* □ *Your lines need power and drive. Put some balls on it and try it again.*

put the blocks to someone to put pressure on someone, usually a female, to copulate. (See note 31.) □ *He put the blocks to her and she broke up with him.* □ *Bob put the block to her, and she turned out to be a real bed-bunny.*

put the hard word on her to attempt to seduce a woman; to proposition a female. (See note 31.) □ *He waited three weeks before he put the hard word on her, but she was already screwing everybody in town by then.* □ *He wanted to put the hard word on her, but didn't have the courage.*

put the make on someone to attempt to seduce someone. (See note 31.) □ *She tried to put the make on him, but he wouldn't have any of it.* □ *You can always tell when they're getting ready to put the make on you. Their eyes get all squinty.*

putz [pəts] **1.** the penis. (From Yiddish. See note 8 for examples; see note 31.) **2.** a stupid or obnoxious male; a stupid person. (Typically a male. Compare to *prick*.) □ *What a stupid putz!* □ *Don't be a putz. Come on over here!*

putz around to waste time; to do something ineffectually. (Widespread. Used by both sexes. Some users do not connect this sense with *putz*, above.) □ *Get busy and stop putzing around.* □ *I spent the whole day just putzing around.*

Q

queer [kwir] **1.** a homosexual person. (Originally and typically refers to a male. Intended and perceived as strongly derogatory. Also a term of address. Always deeply resented. See note 5 for examples and caution; see note 3 for examples.) □ *Stop acting like a queer, even if you are one.* □ *The bar was full of queers rubbing up against one another.* **2.** homosexual; pertaining to homosexual people or things. (Usually male, but also for females.) □ *Have you ever been to a queer bar?* □ *What sort of queer things do they do?*

queer as a three-dollar bill obviously homosexual. (See *queer*.) □ *The guy's as queer as a three-dollar bill! He couldn't have raped her.* □ *Somebody said that Tod is as queer as a three-dollar bill.*

queer-beer ['kwir-bir] **1.** a homosexual male. (An elaboration of *queer*. Also a term of address. See note 5 for examples and caution.) **2.** strange; undesirable. (No homosexual connotations. Standard English.) □ *What a queer-beer thing to do!* □ *That's a queer-beer idea.*

queervert ['kwirvɚt] a homosexual person, especially a male. (A combination of *queer* and *pervert*. See note 5 for examples and caution.)

quickie See the following entry.

quick one AND **quickie** **1.** a quickly drunk drink, especially a beer. (Universally known and used.) □ *Hey, how about a quickie?* □ *We had a couple of quick ones while we were waiting.* **2.** a hasty act of copulation. (See note 16 for examples; see note 31.)

R

Rachel [ˈretʃl] a Jewish female. (Derogatory when used generically. User is considered to be bigoted and antisemitic when used generically. See caution at note 1; see use as a slur at note 2.)

racked [rækt] struck in the testicles. (Used by both sexes. See note 31.) □ *The quarterback got racked and didn't play the rest of the quarter.* □ *I got racked once. It's not fun.*

rag a sanitary napkin; a perineal pad. (See notes 6 and 31. Typical of low male talk.) □ *She had to go to the lady's can to change a rag, I guess.* □ *Don't flush rags down the john.*

rag-head See *towel-head.*

rag time a woman's menstrual period. (A reinterpretation of the term for an early type of syncopated jazz. See notes 6 and 31.) □ *Well, it's rag time again at my house.* □ *Rag time has its drawbacks, but I'd hate to have it stop suddenly.*

ram-job the customary act of copulation involving male thrusting. (Typical of male-to-male talk. See note 31.) □ *She likes the regular old ram-job the best of all.* □ *The hustler charged a little less for a quick ram-job.*

ramrod [ˈræm-rɑd] the penis, especially when erect. (See notes 8 and 9 for examples; see note 31.)

rat-bastard ['ræt-bæstɚd] a really wretched or despised person. □ *You dirty rat-bastard! I could kill you!* □ *Stay away from Max, he's a real rat-bastard when he's drunk.*

Rat fuck! a curse expressing anger or exasperation. (Taboo. See note 4 for caution.) □ *Oh, rat fuck! I broke a nail!* □ *Rat fuck! I'm outa gas!*

ream [rim] **1.** a poke or *goose* in the anus. (See note 31.) □ *Sam gave Tom a ream, and Tom nearly killed him.* □ *Why would anyone want to give somebody a ream?* **2.** to poke or *goose* someone in the anus. (See note 31.) □ *He reamed him but good.* □ *Don't you ever ream me again—if you know what's good for you!*

ream-job See *rim-job.*

rear end the buttocks; the *bottom.* (Euphemistic. See note 29 for examples; see note 31.)

red-assed ['rɛd-æst] very angry; red with anger. □ *Man, she was so red-assed, I thought she'd explode.* □ *The cop was boiling mad at us, and we were red-assed, too.*

redeye ['rɛdaɪ] the anus. (See note 30 for examples; see note 31.)

red-light district [... 'dɪstrɪkt] a district of prostitution in a town. (A widely known euphemism.) □ *There were many hustlers down in the red-light district.* □ *The cops raid the red-light district periodically.*

red-light sister a prostitute. □ *A couple of red-light sisters wearing leather everything walked by, swinging their butts all over the place.* □ *He drove by and signaled to a red-light sister.*

red sails in the sunset a catchphrase referring to a woman's menstrual period. (The "red" refers to the blood of the menses. See notes 6 and 31.) □ *Well, it's red sails in the sunset again. No* *joy for old Tom tonight.* □ *Every time I turn around, it's red sails in the sunset!*

redskin ['rɛdskɪn] an American Indian. (Known mostly through Western movies. Not necessarily derogatory in its original context. Now resented. See caution at note 1; see use as a slur at note 2.)

rice-belly ['raɪs-bɛli] an East Asian or Southeast Asian person. (Intended and perceived as derogatory. Because of the amount of rice eaten. See also *beaner, pepper-belly.* User is considered to be racially bigoted. See caution at note 1; see use as a slur at note 2.)

rich-bitch ['rɪtʃ-bɪtʃ] a rich person, male or female. (For the sake of the rhyme. See comment at note 32.) □ *Here comes that rich-bitch in his big car.* □ *Call me a rich-bitch if you want. I earned it all by the sweat of my back.*

ride the cotton bicycle AND **ride the rag, ride the white horse** [... 'katn̩...] [for a woman] to have her period; to experience the monthly menstrual period. (The cotton refers to the sanitary napkin. Jocular euphemism. See notes 6 and 31.) □ *Well, it's time to ride the rag again.* □ *I wish you could ride the cotton bicycle for a while, Chuck.* □ *She's riding the white horse. That's why she's a little cranky.*

ride the porcelain train [... 'pɔrsələn...] to sit on the toilet. (Typical of teens and college student talk. Compare to *drive the porcelain bus.* See note 31.) □ *Man, I gotta go ride the porcelain train for a while.* □ *If I don't ride the porcelain train pretty soon, I'm gonna bust wide open.*

ride the rag See *ride the cotton bicycle.*

ride the white horse See *ride the cotton bicycle.*

rim-job AND **ream-job** ['rɪm-dʒab AND 'rim-dʒab] an oral sex act involving licking the anus. (See note 31.) □ *They talked about* *something called a rim-job. Sounds vile to me.* □ *This hustler claimed she could do the best ream-job in town.*

rocks the testicles. (See *stones*. See also *hot-rocks*. See note 31.) □ *I was afraid I'd get kicked in the rocks, so I stayed back.* □ *Careful of the rocks, doc! I got plans for them.*

roll in the hay See *toss in the hay.*

Roosian ['ruʃn̩] a Russian. (Primarily an older folksy pronunciation of "Russian." Some derogatory use. See caution at note 1.) □ *The Roosians can have the whole damn country for all I care.* □ *We're going to Moscow to visit the Roosians.*

royal fucking See the following entry.

royal screwing AND **royal fucking** a total defeat or other bad treatment at the hands of someone. (Used by both sexes. Taboo. See note 4 for caution; see comment at note 32.) □ *We gave their team a royal screwing.* □ *The gang gave the mugger a royal fucking he'll never forget.*

rubber a condom. (See *fucking-rubber*. Widely known and used by both sexes. Care should be taken to avoid confusing British English *a rubber*, meaning an eraser, with this sense. *A rubber* used by itself in American English is assumed to mean condom.) □ *He showed up with a gross of rubbers.* □ *She found a rubber in her birthday card.*

rug [rəg] the female pubic hair. (The standard word for a carpet, large or small. See also *wool*. See notes 6 and 31; see note 24 for examples.)

rug muncher ['rəg məntʃɚ] a lesbian. (See *rug*. See note 5 for examples and caution; see note 31.)

rump [rəmp] the buttocks. (Mild and euphemistic. The same term is used for the muscular rear of large four-legged animals. See note 29 for examples; see note 31.)

runs [rənz] diarrhea. (Always with *the*. Compare to *trots*. Because one has to run to the toilet frequently or because the feces are runny. See note 31.) □ *Man, I got the runs! See you!* □ *I can't eat that stuff. It give me the runs.*

Russki ['rəski OR 'ruski] a Russian. (Originally military. Potentially derogatory. See also *Ivan*. See caution at note 1; see use as a slur at note 2.)

S

safety ['sɛfti] a rubber condom. (See note 31.) □ *You better stop at a drugstore and get a safety.* □ *I got a safety in my wallet. It's an antique, in fact.*

San Quentin jail-bait See the following entry.

San Quentin quail AND **jail-bait, San Quentin jail-bait** ['sæn 'kwɛntn̩ 'kwel AND 'dʒel-bet . . .] a female below the legal age to consent to copulation. (San Quentin is a prison. *Quail* is one of a series of "bird" nicknames for a woman. See note 31.)

save someone's ass to save someone's life, neck, reputation, or sense of well-being. (Typical of male-to-male talk, but used by both sexes. See comment at note 32.) □ *My only thought was to save my ass. Nobody else was going to.* □ *You better figure out some other way to save your ass.*

S.B.D. ['ɛs 'bi 'di] "silent but deadly," referring to a soundless but horrendous smelling release of intestinal gas. (Old. Typical of male-to-male talk, especially with teens and college students. See note 31.) □ *Somebody just did an S.B.D.!* □ *Who let the S.B.D.?*

scared fartless See the following entry.

scared shitless AND **scared fartless** very frightened. (See comments at *scare the shit out of someone.* So frightened as to contain no more feces or intestinal gas. Typical of male-to-male talk. See comment at note 32.) □ *He was scared shitless because of the exam.* □ *The whole business had him scared fartless.*

scare the hell out of someone to frighten someone badly. (Universally known and used.) □ *Oh, you scared the hell out of me!* □ *Let's jump out and scare the hell out of Martha.*

scare the shit out of someone to frighten someone very badly. (As if one were frightened enough to defecate in one's clothing. Widely used. See comment at note 32.) □ *Wow! You really scared the shit out of me with that gorilla mask!* □ *Let's jump out and scare the shit out of her.*

schmuck See *shmuck.*

score [skor] **1.** to achieve sexual intercourse. (Usually said of a male achieving copulation with a female. Typical of teens and college student talk. See note 31.) □ *He's been trying to score since he was 14 years old.* □ *He finally scored. At least he said he did.* **2.** an act of copulation. (See note 16 for examples; see note 31.)

screaming queen ['skrimɪŋ 'kwin] a very obvious or blatant male homosexual. (See note 5 for examples and caution.)

screw [skru] **1.** to copulate [with] someone. (Transitive and intransitive. See notes 6 and 31; see notes 13 and 14 for examples. More at *screwed.*) **2.** to cheat or deceive someone. □ *The sales clerk screwed me on this watch.* □ *You can count on somebody screwing you at a traveling carnival.* **3.** an act of copulation. (See notes 6 and 31; see note 16 for examples.) **4.** a person with whom one can copulate. (Typical of low male talk. See notes 6 and 31.) □ *They say she's a good screw.* □ *His teeth are crooked and his hands are calloused, but he's a good screw.*

screw around **1.** to mess around; to waste time. □ *Stop screwing around and get to work!* □ *Are you going to screw around all day?* **2.** to copulate with someone. (See note 13 for related examples; see note 31.) **3.** to copulate casually with anyone. (Widely known. Compare to *sleep around.* See note 31.) □ *She screws around with everybody.* □ *He screws around almost every night.*

screwed [skrud] **1.** copulated with. (See notes 6 and 31.) □ *Oh, Bill, I really feel screwed.* □ *I got myself good and screwed, and I haven't felt better in months.* **2.** cheated. □ *Wow, you got screwed on that watch.* □ *I was screwed something awful on my vacation.*

screwed, blued, and tattooed ['skrud 'blud n̩ 'tæ'tud] cheated severely. (See *screw.*) □ *I came away from that deal screwed, blued, and tatooed.* □ *Tod got screwed, blued, and tatooed when he bought that car.*

screw off to waste time; to do something inefficiently. □ *He's always screwing off when he should be working.* □ *Stop screwing off and get busy!*

screw someone or something up to mess someone or something up. (Euphemistic for *fuck someone or something up.*) □ *Who screwed up my stereo?* □ *He got screwed up in college.*

screw up to mess up; to do something badly. (From *screw.*) □ *I hope I don't screw up.* □ *The Army screwed up, and I got sent home for good.*

Screw you! "To hell with you!" (Euphemistic for *Fuck you!* Provocative. See comment at note 32.) □ *Screw you! I won't do it!* □ *Oh, screw you! I'm outa here!*

scrog [skrɔg] **1.** to copulate [with] someone. (Transitive and intransitive. See notes 13 and 14 for examples; see note 31.) **2.** to cheat or deceive someone. □ *The stereo dealer scrogged everybody who bought stuff from him.* □ *Are you trying to scrog me?*

scrump [skrəmp] to copulate [with] someone. (Transitive and intransitive. See notes 13 and 14 for examples; see note 31.)

scum [skəm] **1.** a totally worthless and disgusting person. (Also a rude and provocative term of address.) □ *You scum! Get out of here!* □ *Freddy has become such a scum, I can't stand him.* **2.** low-life in general; disgusting and worthless people. □ *Fourth*

Street is where all the scum in town hangs out. □ *I can't stand this scum! I'm getting out.* **3.** semen; seminal fluid. (See note 31.) □ *God, I don't want your old scum in me, you bastard! Go find a whore!* □ *You'd better clean up the scum from the back seat before you take the car home.*

scumbag ['skəmbæg] **1.** a condom; a used condom. (See note 31.) □ *I saw a used scumbag in the school parking lot.* □ *Well, what the hell do you do with a scumbag, after?* **2.** a totally disgusting person. (Used by both sexes, especially teens and college students. Also a term of address.) □ *Oh, he's a scumbag. I wouldn't be seen dead with him!* □ *She's not such a scumbag. She got great tits.*

scum-sucking ['skəm-səkɪŋ] "semen-sucking," totally disgusting; pertaining to a disgusting person. (See *scum*. Provocative. See note 31.) □ *You rotten, scum-sucking mother-fucker! Get out!* □ *I can't deal with a scum-sucking idiot like you.*

seam squirrel See *pants rabbit.*

septic stick ['septɪk 'stɪk] a formed fecal rod. (Used for writing nasty words. See note 31.) □ *Somebody wrote something on the wall with a septic stick.* □ *Is that a septic stick over there by the rose bush?*

serve head to perform oral sex on the penis. (Homo- and heterosexual. Compare to *give head.* See note 31.) □ *She sure can serve head.* □ *You just keep me around because I answer the phone nice and serve great head.*

shack up with someone to live with and copulate with someone. (Widely known euphemism.) □ *She shacked up with him for a month or two.* □ *He only wanted to shack up with me. What a jerk!*

shade [ʃed] an American black. (Intended and perceived as derogatory. User is considered to be racially bigoted. See examples at note 2; see caution at note 1.)

shag ass (out of some place)   See *bag ass (out of some place)*.

shanty Irish   ['ʃænti 'aɪrɪʃ] impoverished Irish families or a group of Irish people. (See caution at note 1; see use as a slur at note 2.)

shat   [ʃæt] an imaginary past tense of *shit*. (See note 31.) □ *I shat and shat. I've never been so full of stuff in my life.* □ *The cat shat on the back stairs.*

Shee-it!   ['ʃi-'ɪt] the exclamation **Shit!**, prolonged and emphasized. (Typical of male-to-male talk. See comment at note 32.) □ *Shee-it! What a mess!* □ *You here again? Shee-it!*

Sheeny   ['ʃini] a Jewish person. (Intended and perceived as strongly derogatory. User is considered to be bigoted and antisemitic. See caution at note 1; see note 3 for examples.)

shine   [ʃaɪn] an American black. (Intended and perceived as derogatory. No longer common. User is considered to be racially bigoted. See caution at note 1; see use as a slur at note 2.)

shit   [ʃɪt] (See also the following entries and the list at the end of this entry.) **1.** dung. (See note 27 for examples; see note 31.) **2.** to defecate. (See note 28 for examples; see note 31.) **3.** any trash or unwanted material. □ *Get this shit out of here!* □ *Clean up this shit and don't let this place get so messy.* **4.** a wretched person; a despised person. (Also a term of address. See comment at note 32.) □ *You stupid shit! Look what you did!* □ *Come here and say that again, you little shit!* **5.** one's personal belongings. (See also *get one's shit together*. See comment at note 32.) □ *I gotta get my shit from the kitchen and get outa here.* □ *Is this your shit? Move it!* **6.** lies; nonsense. (See comment at note 32.) □ *I'm tired of your shit!* □ *All I ever hear out of you is shit.* **7.** drugs, especially heroin or marijuana. □ *This is pretty good shit.* □ *You are going to have to get off this shit or you're gonna die.* (See also *apeshit, bad shit, bat-shit, beat the shit out of someone, big shit, birdshit, built like a brick shithouse, bullshit, bullshit artist, bullshitter, chicken shit, chick(en) shit habit, cling like shit to a shovel, cowshit, crock (of shit), day the eagle shits, diddly-shit,* *dipshit, doodly-shit, dumbshit, Eat shit!, fuck-shit, full of shit, get one's shit together, G.I. shits, give a shit (about someone or something), go apeshit over someone or something, good shit, have a shit-fit, have shit for brains, Holy dog shit!, Holy shit!, horseshit, hot shit, in deep shit, in shit order, in the shit, jack-shit, kick the shit out of someone, knee deep in shit, knock the shit out of someone, know shit about something, know shit from shinola, like pigs in shit, little shit, mungshit, No shit!, pile of shit, scared shitless, scare the shit out of someone, shoot the shit, sticks like shit to a shovel, take a shit, tough shit, up shit creek (without a paddle), when (the) shit hit the fan.)*

shit a brick to be very upset; to be extremely angry. (Not literal, obviously.) □ *I was so mad, I almost shit a brick!* □ *Don't shit a brick. Just calm down.*

shit-ass **1.** a disgusting and wretched person. (See comment at note 32.) □ *Max is the world's worst shit-ass.* □ *The guy's a shit-ass. What're you gonna do?* **2.** pertaining to someone or something disgusting and wretched. (See comment at note 32.) □ *He's nothing but a shit-ass bastard!* □ *Help me move this shit-ass box of junk.*

shit-ass luck very bad luck. (See comment at note 32.) □ *Of all the shit-ass luck!* □ *I've had nothing but shit-ass luck all my life.*

shit-bag **1.** an unpleasant or inept person. (Typical of male-to-male talk. See comment at note 32.) □ *I don't want that shit-bag working for me anymore!* □ *Who is that shit-bag who just fell off the barstool?* **2.** a collection of unpleasant problems or annoyances. (Especially with "whole." See comment at note 32.) □ *You can just take your whole shit-bag and bother somebody else with it.* □ *This place has been a regular shit-bag of grief this morning.*

shitcan ['ʃɪtkæn] **1.** a toilet; an outhouse. (Typical of low male talk.) □ *I gotta spend some time on the shitcan.* □ *Where's the shitcan around here?* **2.** a trash can. (Military. See comment at note 32.) □ *Just throw all this stuff in the shitcan.* □ *Somebody'd better dump the shitcan. It's full.*

shit-eating pertaining to a really wretched or disgusting person. (Low. See comment at note 32.) □ *Tell the shit-eating jerk to collect his pay and clean out his locker.* □ *You're just a shit-eating cop, and I know my rights!*

shit-face a despised person. (Typical of male-to-male talk. See comment at note 32.) □ *What a shit-face you have grown to be!* □ *I can't deal with a shit-face like you. Outa my way!*

shit-faced ['ʃɪt-fest] drunk. (See also *poopied*. Widespread. See comment at note 32.) □ *He was so shit-faced, he couldn't walk.* □ *She got shit-faced on only four beers.*

Shit-fire and damnation! See *Hell-fire and damnation!*

shit-fit ['ʃɪt-fɪt] a temper tantrum; a display of anger. (Contrived. Exists for shock and the sake of the rhyme. See *throw a shit-fit*. See comment at note 32.) □ *What a shit-fit she had. You'd think the roof had caved in on her.* □ *Don't throw a shit-fit at me! I didn't do it!*

shit for the birds **1.** someone or something totally worthless. (See comment at note 32.) □ *He's just shit for the birds. Forget him!* □ *This idea is shit for the birds. Try another.* **2.** nonsense. (See comment at note 32.) □ *Don't give me that shit for the birds! You're a liar!* □ *I'm tired of listening to your shit for the birds. Beat it!*

shit-fuck (Taboo in both senses.) **1.** to copulate anally. (See note 4 for caution; see note 31.) □ *Those guys shit-fuck one another all the time.* □ *The principal caught them shit-fucking in the john.* **2.** an act of anal copulation. (See note 31.) □ *He said he preferred a shit-fuck, but I think he was obsessed with it.* □ *The prisoner had at least one shit-fuck a day.*

shit green to defecate green dung in fear or surprise. (Imaginary. See *shit in one's pants.* See examples for contexts. See note 31.) □ *When we went around that last curve, I nearly shit green.* □ *I shit green just thinking about what might have happened.*

shithead ['ʃıthɛd] a stupid and obnoxious person, usually a male. (Also a term of address. Provocative. Typical of low male talk. See comment at note 32.) □ *You stupid shithead! Get out of my life!* □ *Who needs a shithead like him around?*

shitheaded ['ʃıthɛdəd] stupid and obnoxious. (Typical of low male talk. See comment at note 32.) □ *Of all the stupid, shitheaded things to do!* □ *The shitheaded fool just walked away from a million bucks.*

shit-hole 1. the anus. (See note 30 for examples; see note 31.) 2. a hole in which to defecate; an outdoor toilet. (Typical of low male talk. See note 31.) □ *I gotta go out and spend some time at the old shit-hole.* □ *The shit-hole's out in back if you need it.*

shit-hooks See *cunt-hooks.*

shit-hot 1. very exciting or excited; powerful and effective. (Typical of male talk and joking. See comment at note 32.) □ *That's a fine, shit-hot idea! Let's talk it over.* □ *The new play is really shit-hot! Go see it!* 2. very hot. (See comment at note 32.) □ *That soup is too shit-hot to eat.* □ *It's shit-hot in here. Open the window!*

shit-house AND **crap-house** an outdoor toilet; an outhouse. (Typical of male-to-male talk.) □ *There is a hornet's nest in the crap-house.* □ *Some boys tipped over the shit-house, and I've got no place to go.*

shit-house poet ['ʃıt-haʊs 'poət] someone who writes dirty graffiti on bathroom walls. (Widely known. See comment at note 32.) □ *Some shit-house poet has messed up the wall of the john.* □ *Them shit-house poets think some real deep thoughts, you know.*

shit in one's pants to defecate in one's pants out of fear or surprise. (A catchphrase indicating the degree of fright or surprise one has experienced. See the examples below, and see note 31.) □ *I nearly shit in my pants when I heard that.* □ *Tod was so frightened that he almost shit in his pants.*

shit-kicker a backwards, rural person; a farmer. (Also a term of address. Typical of male-to-male talk. See comment at note 32.) □ *Some old shit-kicker spit his tobacco juice on my shoe.* □ *The shit-kickers are the ones with the rifles in the back windows of their pick-up trucks.*

shit-kicking having to do with rural things or people; having to do with farmers. (Low. See comment at note 32.) □ *What a rotten, shit-kicking pigsty you live in. Move to the city, why don't ya?* □ *There are too many shit-kicking jerks in the legislature.*

shit-list AND **crap-list** a list of people who are as worthless as dung; a list of problem people. (The phrase with "crap" is milder. See also *shit parade.* See comment at note 32.) □ *From now on you are on my shit-list!* □ *Trouble with Tom is that everybody he knows is on his crap-list.*

shitload of something a whole lot of something. (Typical of low male talk. See comment at note 32.) □ *I ended up with a whole shitload of bills and no job.* □ *That woman is a whole shitload of trouble.*

shit locker ['ʃɪt lɑkɚ] the bowels; the stomach. (Originally naval. At sea, every storage unit is called a "locker." See comment at note 32.) □ *Doc, I got some sort of problem in the old shit locker.* □ *The sailor punched the cop right in the shit locker.*

shit on a shingle [... 'ʃɪŋgḷ] creamed chipped beef on toast; *S.O.S.* (See also *creamed foreskins.* Military. See comment at note 32.) □ *Oh, no, it's shit on a shingle again tonight.* □ *This shit on a shingle tastes like what it is.*

Shit on it!   "Forget it!"; "Take it away!" (Usually said in anger or disgust. Compare to *Piss on it!*) □ *I don't want it! Shit on it!* □ *What a rotten day! Shit on it!*

shit on someone   **1.** to defecate on someone. (See note 31.) □ *That damn cat shit on me!* □ *Watch out! That cow almost shit on you!* **2.** to treat someone very badly. (Widespread. Used by both sexes, especially teens and college students.) □ *The prof shit on the whole class by assigning a paper due Monday morning.* □ *The Internal Revenue Service really shit on me this year.*

shit on wheels   someone who does something very skillfully. (See comment at note 32.) □ *Look at him go! He really thinks he's shit on wheels, doesn't he?* □ *She's shit on wheels when it comes to tennis.*

Shit or get off the pot!   "Do something or go away!"; "Do something or give someone else a chance!"; "Hurry up!" (Based on an encouragement to either defecate or leave the bathroom. Low catchphrase.) □ *Hurry up with it, Fred! Shit or get off the pot!* □ *Shit or get off the pot! Make up your mind.*

shit out of luck   completely out of luck; unfortunately out of luck. (Originally military. See comment at note 32.) □ *I was shit out of luck and ended up on this lousy island.* □ *You're shit out of luck, chum. All the good ones are gone.*

shit parade   ['ʃɪt pə'red] a list or collection of unpleasant people or things. (Jocular and contrived. Based on "hit parade," a list of hit songs and the name of a radio and, later, a television program. See comment at note 32.) □ *You are right at the top of my shit parade.* □ *That town is on my shit parade, for sure.*

shits   diarrhea. (Always with *the.* Typical of low male talk. See comment at note 32; see note 31.) □ *Man, I got a case of the shits!* □ *I can't eat that stuff. It always gives me the shits.*

shit-scared   very frightened; frightened enough to defecate in one's pants. (Typical of low male talk. See comment at note 32;

see note 31.) □ *God, I was shit-scared when the car turned over.* □ *Don't be so shit-scared. Dogs can smell fear.*

shitsky [ˈʃɪtski] a really stupid and obnoxious person. (Usually refers to a male. Also a term of address. From *shit*. See comment at note 32.) □ *He's a rotten shitsky, and I can't stand him!* □ *Who is that shitsky in the plaid pants?*

shitstick [ˈʃɪtstɪk] **1.** a wretched and undesirable person. (Usually refers to a male. Also a provocative term of address. See comment at note 32.) □ *Why are you such a shitstick all the time?* □ *Is that little shitstick giving you trouble, Doreen?* **2.** a rod of dung. (Typical of low male talk. See comment at note 32; see note 31.) □ *How would you like a shitstick in your lap?* □ *Who left the shitsticks floating in the john?*

shit-stomper [ˈʃɪt-stɑmpɚ] a farmer who must walk on much dung in the farmyard. (Also a term of address. Intended as jocular. See comment at note 32.) □ *Some old shit-stomper fell off his tractor and got everybody all upset.* □ *I can't work from dawn to dusk like a shit-stomper.*

shit-stompers [ˈʃɪt-stɑmpɚz] large and heavy shoes or boots of the type worn by farmers. (See *shit-stomper*. See comment at note 32.) □ *I got me a new pair a shit-stompers to go hiking in.* □ *Whose crappy shit-stompers are those in the hallway?*

Shitsure! [ˈʃɪtʃɚ] very, very sure. (Typical of male-to-male talk. See comment at note 32.) □ *Shitsure you can! Just help yourself!* □ *Don't be so shitsure about it!*

shitter [ˈʃɪtɚ] **1.** a toilet; an outdoor toilet. (Low male talk.) □ *Mind if I use the shitter for a minute?* □ *Somebody really made a mess of that shitter.* **2.** a person who tells lies, boasts, or deceives people; a *bullshitter*. (Typical of low male talk.) □ *Don't pay any attention to her. She's just a shitter. Lies, lies, lies.* □ *All those television news guys are shitters.*

shitty [ˈʃɪti] **1.** covered or soiled with dung. (See note 31.) □ *I got my shoes all shitty.* □ *Get that shitty shovel out of the garage and clean it.* **2.** lousy; rotten. (See comment at note 32.) □ *This has been a real shitty trip for me.* □ *I'm tired of being treated like I'm some sort of shitty bum.*

shitty end of the stick the bad side of a bargain; the troublesome part of a transaction. (Typical of male-to-male talk. See comment at note 32.) □ *If you don't want to get stuck with the shitty end of the stick, you'd better make your plans carefully.* □ *Well, it looks like I got stuck with the shitty end of the stick again.*

shit-work menial work; work that no one else wants to do. (Does not usually have anything to do with dung. Much recent female use in reference to menial work. See comment at note 32.) □ *I always get stuck with the shit-work!* □ *As far as I'm concerned, all work is shit-work.*

shmuck AND **schmuck** [ʃmək] **1.** the penis. (Yiddish. See note 8 for examples; see note 31.) **2.** a stupid or inept male. (Yiddish. Also a term of address. See note 15 for examples; see note 3 for examples.)

shoofly [ˈʃuflaɪ] an American black. (Intended and perceived as derogatory. User is considered to be racially bigoted. See caution at note 1; see examples at note 2.)

shoot one's wad [ˈʃut ˈwənz ˈwɑd] to ejaculate a mass of semen. (See *wad*. Also general slang meaning to spend all of one's money or use up everything, the latter being more widely known. See note 31.) □ *He shot his wad right in mid-air.* □ *Some kid must have shot his wad in the movie. You could sort of tell.*

shoot the bull See *shoot the shit.*

shoot the crap See the following entry.

shoot the shit AND **shoot the crap, shoot the bull**   to engage in small talk; to gossip and brag. (Widely known and used.) □ *Well, dude, let's sit down and shoot the shit.* □ *We were just shooting the bull.*

short-arm   the penis. (Military. Refers to the penis as a short gun compared to a rifle. See note 8 for examples; see note 31.) □ *Man, my short-arm is lonely.* □ *I got my short-arm all ready for a little target practice.*

short-arm inspection AND **small-arm inspection**   an examination of the male genitals for signs of venereal disease. (Military. The penis is referred to as a small gun. See also *tool-check, pecker-checker.* See note 31.) □ *All right, you guys! Line up for short-arm inspection!* □ *I bet that doc likes to give short-arm inspections. She doesn't seem at all shy.*

Shove it (up your ass)!   a rude invitation intended as an insult. (Provocative. Usually said in anger.) □ *You can just shove it up your ass!* □ *If you think I'll do that, you can shove it up your ass!*

siff   See *syff.*

silk   [sɪlk] an American Caucasian. (Black. Intended as derogatory, but not always perceived as derogatory. See use as a slur at note 2; see caution at note 1.)

sin-bin   See *cock-wagon.*

sixty-nine   an act of mutual oral sex. (Based on the interlocking numerals in "69." See note 31.) □ *The old lady caught them in the bushes doing a sixty-nine.* □ *He prefers sixty-nine. She prefers booze.*

skeet   [skit] a glob of nasal mucus. (Teens and college student use. See note 31.) □ *There's a big skeet about to drop on your shirt.* □ *Don't blow that skeet out around here.*

skeet-shooting [ˈskit-ʃutɪŋ] blowing the nose with the thumb. (See *skeet*. Teens and college student use. See note 31.) □ *Who's been skeet-shooting around here?* □ *Stop skeet-shooting and use a snotrag.*

skid mark [ˈskɪd mɑrk] an American black. (Intended and perceived as derogatory. Refers to the black marks left by skidding tires. User is considered to be racially bigoted. See caution at note 1; see use as a slur at note 2.)

skin flick [ˈskɪn flɪk] a film featuring naked people. (Usually women. See note 31.) □ *Did you see that skin flick down at the Roxy?* □ *I'm sick of watching skin flicks. I'm looking for something live.*

skin flute the penis as used in oral sex. (Not widely known. See *flute(r), piccolo-player.* See note 8 for examples; see note 31.)

skin-mag a magazine showing pictures of naked people. (Usually pictures of women. Widely known and used. See note 6.) □ *That shop keeps a huge selection of skin-mags under the counter.* □ *Those skin-mags are expensive.*

skirt **1.** a woman; a woman considered as a sexual object. (See notes 6 and 31; see examples at note 23.) **2.** an act of copulation with a woman; male sexual release through copulation with a woman. (Usually with *some*. See notes 6 and 31; see note 17 for examples.)

slant See *slope.*

slanteye(s) See *slope.*

slash [slæʃ] **1.** the female genitals; the vulva. (Compare to *gash*. Primarily low male-to-male talk and joking. See notes 6 and 31; see note 12 for examples.) **2.** to urinate. (See note 26 for examples; see note 31.) **3.** an act of urination. (See note 31.)

sleep with someone to copulate with someone. (Compare to *go to bed with someone.* No sleep is involved. See note 13 for related examples; see note 31.)

slime [slaɪm] **1.** semen. (See note 31.) □ *Keep your old slime to yourself.* □ *God, Sam, is that slime on your trousers, or what?* **2.** a truly disgusting person; a *slime bucket.* (Widely known, especially among teens and college students.) □ *You damn slime! Get out!* □ *Somebody get that slime outa here before I kick the shit out of him.*

slime bucket ['slaɪm bəkɪt] a truly disgusting person. (Typically a male.) □ *What a slime bucket he is!* □ *I have never met such a low slime bucket in all my life!*

slit [slɪt] the female genitals; the vulva. (Primarily low male-to-male talk. See notes 6 and 31; see note 12 for examples.)

slop-chute See *dirt-chute.*

slope AND **slant, slanteye(s)** [slop AND slænt, 'slæntaɪz] an East Asian [including Japanese] or Southeast Asian person having the "oriental" epicanthic folds. (Intended and perceived as derogatory. User is considered to be racially bigoted. See caution at note 1; see use as a slur at note 2.)

sloppy seconds an act of male-to-female copulation that immediately follows a previous act of copulation on the part of the woman. (Refers to the remains of the products of the first act of copulation. See also *sloppy sex.* See note 31.) □ *Man, sloppy seconds is not my cup of tea.* □ *That lousy hustler wanted to charge me for sloppy seconds.*

sloppy sex sexual activity that involves some sort of a wet mess. (A variety of *sloppy seconds.* See note 31.) □ *Why do you have to have sloppy sex all the time?* □ *Why don't you ever want to have sloppy sex?*

slot the female genitals; the vulva. (Primarily male-to-male talk. See notes 6 and 31; see note 12 for examples.)

slut [slət] a sexually free woman who will copulate with anyone. (Provocative. Also a term of address. Standard English. See note 6.) □ *She is the most notorious slut in town.* □ *You slut! Get out!*

small-arm inspection See *short-arm inspection.*

smart-ass AND **wise-ass** 1. a smart aleck; an arrogant person. (See *wise-ass(ed).* Widely known and used by both sexes. See comment at note 32.) □ *Look, wise-ass, I've had about enough outa you!* □ *This smart-ass thinks he can push people around!* **2.** arrogant; smart alecky. (See comment at note 32.) □ *No more of your smart-ass answers, you hear?* □ *Get your wise-ass face outa my way, or I cut it, see?*

smear [smir] an American black. (Intended and perceived as derogatory. User is considered to be racially bigoted. See examples at note 2; see caution at note 1.)

Smell me! AND **Well, smell me!** "Well, la-di-dah!"; "So, you think you are special!"; "Drop dead!"; "So, what!" (Both *smell* and *me* are drawn out for a long time. A vague negative comment.) □ *Thinks he's a big guy, huh? Well, smell me!* □ *Smell me, if you think I give a damn what you do!*

smell the place up to have a bowel movement, creating a bad odor in the bathroom. (A rudely jocular expression. Typical of male-to-male joking. See note 31.) □ *I gotta smell the place up. Back in a minute.* □ *Hey, who smelled the place up?*

SNAFU ['snæ'fu] "situation normal, all fucked up." (Originally military. A euphemistic version uses *fouled* rather than *fucked*.) □ *That was one hell of a SNAFU yesterday.* □ *This place is just one SNAFU after another.*

snatch [snætʃ] **1.** the female genitals; the vulva. (Primarily low male-to-male talk or joking. Widely known. See notes 6 and 31; see note 12 for examples.) **2.** women considered as a receptacle for the penis. (See notes 6 and 31; see examples at note 23.) **3.** male sexual release through copulation with a female. (Usually with *some.* See notes 6 and 31; see note 17 for examples.)

snot [snɑt] **1.** nasal mucus, wet or dry. (Universally known. See note 31.) □ *Don't blow your snot all over the place.* □ *There's snot on my mirror. Somebody clean it up!* **2.** a vile-acting person; an impudent person. (There are no polite synonyms for this sense. Also a term of address. Universally known. Provocative.) □ *Don't be such a snot—if you can help it.* □ *Sally has been such a snot to me lately. What did I do to that bitch?*

snotnose(d) (kid) **1.** a child whose nose is dripping nasal mucus. □ *Three little snotnosed kids were hanging around the door when we went in.* □ *I ain't felt so bad since I was a snotnosed kid.* **2.** a young and inexperienced person; one so ineffective that one can't even wipe one's nose. □ *He's just a snotnosed kid. He can't handle this contract!* □ *My boss is a snotnose kid. I don't think she's even had her first period yet.*

snotrag AND **noserag** ['snɑtræg AND 'nozræg] **1.** a handkerchief. (Widely known and considered impolite.) □ *Where's my snotrag.* □ *Old Chuck never uses a noserag.* **2.** a despicable and contemptible person. (Also a term of address.) □ *You crummy snotrag! Get out!* □ *You have to be the world's greatest noserag!*

snotted ['snɑtəd] very drunk. □ *She gets totally snotted almost every night.* □ *That guy was really snotted!*

snotty ['snɑti] **1.** impudent; rude. □ *That clerk was really snotty to me.* □ *I didn't mean to sound so snotty.* **2.** covered with snot. (See note 31.) □ *Your handkerchief is all snotty.* □ *The little kid has a snotty upper lip.*

S.O.B. [ˈɛs ˈo ˈbi] a *son of a bitch.* (Also a provocative term of address.) □ *You silly S.O.B.!* □ *Don't be such an S.O.B.! Give me a break!*

soft-ass(ed) [ˈsɔft-æs(t)] weak and docile; pliant. (Used by both sexes.) □ *She is such a soft-ass wimp!* □ *He's really soft-assed when it comes to talking back to a woman.*

someone's ass is grass "someone has had it"; "It is the end for someone." (Catchphrase. Used by both sexes. For the sake of the rhyme. See comment at note 32.) □ *You do that again, and your ass is grass!* □ *If I don't get there on time, my ass is grass.*

son of a bitch AND **sonovabitch** **1.** a wretched and disgusting person. (Usually refers to a male. Also a term of address. See note 3 for examples.) **2.** an exclamation of anger or surprise. (Usually **Son of a bitch!, Sonovabitch!**) □ *Son of a bitch! He did it again!* □ *I got it right! Son of a bitch!*

sonovabitch See the previous entry.

sorry-ass(ed) [ˈsɑri æs(t)] **1.** sad and depressed. (See comment at note 32.) □ *Why do you look so sorry-assed?* □ *Man, old Charlie was about the most sorry-ass dude you ever saw.* **2.** worthless; poor quality. (See comment at note 32.) □ *This is really a sorry-ass movie. I want my money back.* □ *How much longer do I have to drive this sorry-ass excuse for an automobile?*

S.O.S. [ˈɛs ˈo ˈɛs] **1.** "Shit on a shingle," creamed chipped beef on toast. (Military. The same as *creamed foreskins, shit on a shingle.* See comment at note 32.) □ *This S.O.S. stuff isn't all that bad!* □ *Put a little pepper sauce on that S.O.S., and pretend it's something edible.* **2.** "Same old shit," another round of the same thing (as before). (See comment at note 32.) □ *Well it's the S.O.S. again. It's really getting boring.* □ *She started in on my bad breath again. S.O.S. all over again.*

spade [sped] an American black. (Intended and perceived as derogatory and provocative. Also a term of address. From the blackness of the ace of spades in a deck of cards. See also *ace of spades*. User is considered to be racially bigoted. See caution at note 1; see note 3 for examples; see use as a slur at note 2.)

spare prick someone who is totally useless. (From the phrase "as useful as a spare prick." See *prick*.) □ *Who's that standing around like a spare prick?* □ *Tom, you're a real spare prick. Come on and give us a hand so we can get this done.*

spear-chucker ['spir-tʃəkɚ] an American black. (With reference to the Africans' use of spears as a weapon. Partly jocular, but derogatory and provocative nonetheless. Also a term of address. See caution at note 1; see use as a slur at note 2.)

spic [spɪk] a person of Mexican nationality or descent; a Hispanic person. (Supposedly from the word "speak" as pronounced with a Spanish accent. Intended and perceived as derogatory and provocative. Also a term of address. User is considered to be bigoted. See caution at note 1; see note 3 for examples; see use as a slur at note 2.)

splib [splɪb] an American black. (Intended and perceived as derogatory. Not widely known. See caution at note 1; see use as a slur at note 2.)

split-tail ['splɪt-tel] a woman considered sexually. (Intended as jocular. See notes 6 and 31; see examples at note 23.)

spook [spuk] an American black. (Intended and perceived as strongly derogatory. Also a term of address. User is considered to be racially bigoted. See caution at note 1; see note 3 for examples; see use as a slur at note 2.)

spread beaver a view of the female genitals. (See *beaver*. See notes 6 and 31.) □ *That movie was just one spread beaver after another.* □ *You wouldn't think that a star like that would pose for a spread beaver, would you?*

spud [spəd] **1.** a person of Irish nationality or decent. (Refers to the heavy use of potatoes in the Irish diet.) □ *Of course, the cop's a spud!* □ *I love to listen to those spuds talk. It's real music.* **2.** a woman's breast. (Usually plural, **spuds.** See *murphies,* another nickname for the potato. See notes 6 and 31; see note 7 for examples.)

squeeze the lemon ['skwiz ðə 'lɛmən] to urinate; to empty the bladder thoroughly. (See note 26 for additional examples; see note 31.) □ *Come on, Billy. Squeeze the lemon so we can leave now.* □ *You'd better squeeze the lemon good. It's two hours till the next rest stop.*

star-fucker ['stɑr-fəkɚ] someone, usually a teenage female, who follows performers, especially rock performers, from town to town offering herself sexually. (Taboo. See note 4 for caution; see note 31.) □ *She's the type who will be a star-fucker for a year or two and then go to graduate school.* □ *The guy is surrounded by star-fuckers everywhere he goes.*

Stick it! a rude exclamation, inviting one to stick something up one's ass. (Low. Typical of male-to-male talk.) □ *Don't do that again! Stick it!* □ *If you think I care, you can just stick it!*

stick like shit to a shovel See *cling like shit to a shovel.*

stiffy ['stɪfi] an erection of the penis; an erect penis. (See note 9 for examples; see note 31.)

stones **1.** the testicles. (Also a standard English euphemism. See also *rocks.* Other terms for testicles are: *alls-bay, balls, chones, cojones, crystals, dodads, dohickies, family jewels, nads, nuggets, nuts, rocks.* See note 31.) □ *He got hit in the stones.* □ *You scared me so much, I almost lost my stones.* **2.** courage; bravado. □ *Hey, man, you got no stones!* □ *Come on, Wally, show some stones!*

street-meat ['strit-mit] a street-walking prostitute; a *street-walker.* (A jocular avoidance.) □ *If you want street-meat, you'll* *find it on Fourth Street.* □ *When I finish with you, you'll have no home; you'll have no job; you'll be nothing but street-meat!*

street pimp a male who procures business—on the streets of a town or city—for the prostitutes that he manages. (Viewed as a low type of *pimp*.) □ *Freddy is a no-good street pimp. He'll do anything for a buck, no matter who he hurts.* □ *The town is overrun with street pimps and their hustlers.*

street sister a prostitute; a *streetwalker.* □ *Fourth Street is just a long parade of street sisters.* □ *Some of those street sisters have very serious diseases.*

streetwalker ['stritwɔkɚ] a prostitute; a prostitute who solicits business on the streets of a city or town. (A standard English euphemism.) □ *The town was asleep by midnight, save for a few streetwalkers in tall boots and short skirts.* □ *The life of a streetwalker is not a happy one.*

stroke [strok] to masturbate a male; to stimulate a male by stroking his penis. (Transitive. See note 20 for examples; see note 31.) □ *We could see her through the blinds, stroking away on Tod.* □ *If you want to turn him on, stroke him a little.*

stud [stəd] **1.** a sexually attractive young male. (Now replaced by *hunk*. Also a term of address. Widely known and used by both sexes.) □ *Look at the muscles on him! What a stud!* □ *See if you can catch the eye of that stud over there.* **2.** a sexually active young male. (Also a term of address. Widely known and used by both sexes.) □ *That guy's a real stud. He's always running around with some dame.* □ *Hey, stud! Getting any?*

stupid-ass See *dumb-ass.*

suck [sək] to be annoying, disgusting, or worthless. (Always in a sentence, such as **It sucks!** Widespread use among all ages and both sexes. Originally teens. See also *bite the big one*.) □ *This is lousy. It sucks!* □ *Take away this crappy food. It sucks!* □ *This stupid test sucks!*

suck-ass ['sək-æs] **1.** a hopeless flatterer; a sycophant. (Typical of male-to-male talk. See comment at note 32.) □ *Stop being such a suck-ass, Wally! Earn your grades!* □ *Bob's a suck-ass. He can't help buttering up people.* **2.** in the manner of a flatterer. (Typical of male-to-male talk. See comment at note 32.) □ *Stop your lousy suck-ass flattery!* □ *Tell the suck-ass jerk to get to work and earn his promotion.* **3.** totally rotten; lousy. (Typical of male-to-male talk. See comment at note 32.) □ *Get your suck-ass car out of my parking space, or I'll bash in the headlights.* □ *What a suck-ass day!*

suck queen ['sək kwin] a male homosexual who prefers oral sex involving sucking. (See note 5 for examples and caution; see note 31.)

suck someone off to perform oral sex on someone and cause an orgasm. (See note 31.) □ *She wanted to suck him off, but he went to sleep.* □ *Come on, don't suck me off! I wanna work for it!*

suck someone's hind tit [. . . 'haɪnd 'tɪt] to kowtow or toady to someone; to be obsequious to someone. (Meaning to go to enormous pains to please someone. Refers to either sex. Never literal. See comment at note 32.) □ *What does he want me to do, suck his hind tit or something?* □ *Yeah, I got it signed, but I had to suck the old bag's hind tit to get her to agree to it.*

sucky-fucky ['səki-fəki] an act of sex involving both oral and genital sex. (An act that can be requested by name of a prostitute. Taboo. See note 4 for caution; see note 31.) □ *The john wanted some sucky-fucky, but couldn't come up with the scratch.* □ *What's the standard sucky-fucky going for now?*

sugar pimp a sweet-talking pimp. (Low. Prostitute's jargon.) □ *He's just a sugar pimp, and he's no damn good.* □ *Watch out for those sugar pimps, they'll beat you up after they've got you on the job.*

sunshine [ˈsənʃɑɪn] an American black. (Potentially derogatory. Mostly forgotten. Also a term of address. See caution at note 1.)

sweat blood See *piss blood.*

swing to perform adventuresome sexual acts, usually with strangers with similar interests. (Widely known. See note 31.) □ *Do you swing?* □ *We met this couple who said they would like to swing, and we thought they meant to dance or something.*

swing both ways to be bisexual; to desire sexual intercourse with persons of either sex. (See *swing.* Widely known and used as a euphemism by both sexes. See note 31.) □ *They say Tod swings both ways. What d'you think about that?* □ *Some people swing both ways. They say it's less dull that way.*

swinger a person who performs adventuresome sexual acts, usually with strangers with similar interests. (See also *twister.* See note 31.) □ *These two swingers asked me if I wanted to come up and see their etchings.* □ *What's a swinger like you doing at a church retreat like this?*

S-word [ˈɛs-wɚd] the word "shit." (A euphemism or avoidance. Widely known and used by both sexes.) □ *The movie is okay, except that it's full of the S-word.* □ *When one of the actors said the S-word, a middle-aged lady got up and walked out.*

syff AND **siff** [sɪf] the venereal disease syphilis. (See note 31.) □ *God, I don't wanna catch syff.* □ *Don't worry about siff, they can cure that. It's AIDS that's going to kill you.*

T

taco [ˈtɑko] an attractive Mexican female. (A jocular, but derogatory, nickname. See similar food terms at *beaner, bean-eater.* See note 6; see caution at note 1; see use as a slur at note 2.)

tail [tel] **1.** the female genitals; the vulva. (Primarily male talk. Not as well known as the following senses. See notes 6 and 31; see note 12 for examples.) **2.** women considered as a receptacle for the penis. (See notes 6 and 31; see examples at note 23.) **3.** male sexual release through copulation with a female. (Usually with *some.* See also *piece of tail.* See notes 6 and 31; see note 17 for examples.)

take a crap See *take a shit.*

take a dump See *take a shit.*

take a leak See the following entry.

take a piss AND **take a leak** to urinate. (Low. See note 26 for examples; see note 31.)

take a shit AND **take a crap, take a dump, take a squat** to defecate. (It is always "taken," not "given," "done," or "put." *Shit* is the most offensive with *crap, dump,* and *squat* following in descending order of offense. See note 28 for examples; see note 31.)

take a squat See the previous entry.

take it out in trade   to repay someone with sexual favors. (From a colloquial expression referring to repaying someone by working off the debt or by offering a favorable price on goods that the debtor sells.) □ *This woman then suggested that I take it out in trade, but hell, I needed the money instead.* □ *Well, I'll take it out in trade, if you've got the time.*

take oneself in hand   to masturbate. (Said of a male, about himself. Jocular. See examples at note 19.)

take the piss out of someone   to humble someone; to make someone—usually a male—less cocky, perhaps by violence. (Typical of male-to-male talk.) □ *You need somebody to take the piss outa you!* □ *He failed his test again. That'll take the piss outa him.*

T. and A.   See *tits and ass.*

target practice   copulation; sexual intercourse. (See note 17 for examples; see note 31.)

tea   urine. (Homosexual contexts. See note 25 for examples; see note 31.)

tee-tee   ['ti-ti] (Both senses juvenile and euphemistic.) **1.** urine. (See note 25 for examples; see note 31.) **2.** an act of urination. (Juvenile. See note 31.) □ *Billy has to stop now for a tee-tee.* □ *Time to go do a tee-tee.*

The hell you say!   "I don't believe you!" (An exclamation of surprise.) □ *No! The hell you say! I don't believe it!* □ *The garage fell over! The hell you say!*

There will be hell to pay.   there will be real problems to be solved and that will cause you a lot of trouble. □ *If you keep doing that kind of thing, there will be hell to pay.* □ *There will be hell to pay because you are late again.*

thicklips ['θɪklɪps] an American black; an African. (Intended and perceived as derogatory and demeaning. Also a term of address. User is considered to be racially bigoted. See caution at note 1; see note 3 for examples; see use as a slur at note 2.)

thing 1. the penis. (See note 8 for examples; see note 31.) 2. the female genitals. (A reasonably polite and vague euphemism. See notes 6 and 31; see note 12 for examples.)

third leg the penis. (See note 8 for examples; see note 31.)

third sex homosexuality. (Usually with *the*.) □ *He's playing around with the third sex right now.* □ *The third sex has gotten very political in the last few years.*

throne [θron] a toilet; a toilet seat. (Usually with *the*. Widely known and used by both sexes.) □ *There I was, sitting on the throne, when some part of a plane fell right through the ceiling and crashed into the bathtub!* □ *Man, I gotta sit on the throne for a while!*

throw the bull AND **throw the crap** to gossip, brag, and trade stories. (The *bull* is *bullshit*. Widely known and used by both sexes.) □ *We spent a few hours throwing the bull.* □ *We were just throwing the crap. We meant no harm.*

throw the crap See the previous entry.

tight-ass a person who is uptight about moral matters; an overly rigid person. (More at *tight-ass(ed)*. See comment at note 32.) □ *Don't be such a tight-ass, Mervin! Loosen up!* □ *Here comes old Bill, the world's tightest tight-ass.*

tight-ass(ed) having to do with an overly rigid person who is uptight about moral matters. (See comment at note 32.) □ *I'm tired of your old tight-assed attitude about life.* □ *We live in a very tight-ass society.*

tinkle [ˈtɪŋkl̩] **1.** to urinate. (Usually juvenile. Jocular when used by adults. See note 26 for examples; see note 31.) **2.** urine. (Usually juvenile. Jocular when used by adults. See note 25 for examples; see note 31.)

tip the penis; the head of the penis. (See note 8 for examples; see note 31.)

tired-ass(ed) tired and depressed; weary and droopy. □ *Why do you look so tired-assed all the time?* □ *He's the little tired-ass guy standing by the door.*

tit hammock [ˈtɪt hæmək] a brassiere. (Typical of male-to-male talk and joking. See notes 6 and 31.) □ *I don't think she's wearing a tit hammock, but I can't tell.* □ *Look at the size of that tit hammock hanging on the line.*

tit job [ˈtɪt dʒɑb] a surgical operation to alter the size and shape of a woman's breasts. (See notes 6 and 31.) □ *They say she had a tit job, but she looks the same to me as she always did.* □ *When I can save up enough money, I wanna get a tit job.*

titless wonder **1.** an oafish or awkward person. (Can refer to male or female. See note 6.) □ *That stupid jerk is the classic titless wonder. What a twit!* □ *What can you expect from a titless wonder like that?* **2.** an unsatisfactory thing or situation. (See note 6.) □ *This day has been a perfect titless wonder. I'll be thrilled to death when it's over.* □ *I've got to take this titless wonder into the shop for an oil change.*

tits a woman's breasts. (Often used disparagingly, especially by women, with reference to the power breasts seem to have over men. Singular or plural. See notes 6 and 31; see note 7 for additional examples. See the following entries and *go tits up, suck someone's hind tit, Tough titties!*) □ *She's nothing but tits and teeth! Not a brain in her head!* □ *All she needs to do is make her tits quake a bit, and she's got the job.*

tits and ass AND **T. and A.** ['tɪts n̩ 'æs AND 'ti n̩ 'e] the phenomenon of bare breasts and buttocks as displayed in magazines, movies, and stage shows. (Occurs in the Broadway show *Chorus Line*. Widely known and used by both sexes. See notes 6 and 31.) □ *All you see in the movies these days is tits and ass.* □ *It's one of your typical Broadway shows, lots of T. and A.*

titty ['tɪti] A woman's breast. (Plural: **titties**. Not too far from standard English. See notes 6 and 31; see note 7 for examples.)

tochis AND **tokkis, tokus, tuchis** ['tokəs AND 'tokɪs, 'tokəs, 'təkəs] the buttocks. (Yiddish. There are many spellings. See note 29 for examples; see note 31.)

toe jam ['to dʒæm] a nasty, smelly substance that collects between the toes of unwashed feet. (Compare to *crotch-cheese*. Intended as jocular and disgusting. See note 31.) □ *These socks are heavy with toe jam.* □ *Wash your feet, you turkey! I don't want you tracking all your toe jam all over the room!*

To hell with that! **1.** "That is not true!" □ *You say he's coming here? To hell with that!* □ *To hell with that! You are dead wrong!* **2.** "I'm finished with that!"; "No more of that!" □ *To hell with that! Never again!* □ *To hell with that! No more! I'm through!* **3.** "I refuse!" □ *You want me to go over there for you? To hell with that!* □ *To hell with that! It's a rotten idea! I won't do it!*

toilet mouth AND **potty mouth** ['tɔɪlət mɑʊθ AND 'pɑti mɑʊθ] **1.** someone who uses foul words constantly. (Also a term of address. Used by both sexes.) □ *Hey, toilet mouth! Watch your language!* □ *What a potty mouth you've turned out to be!* **2.** the mouth of someone who uses foul words constantly. (Used by both sexes.) □ *He's got a real toilet mouth on him.* □ *She's developed quite a potty mouth since she went away to school.*

tokkis See *tochis.*

tokus See *tochis.*

Tom   See *Uncle Tom.*

tongue-fuck   ['təŋ fək] (Taboo in both senses.) **1.** an act of oral sex involving the use of the tongue on the genitals. (See note 4 for caution; see note 31.) □ *Can't you catch something from a tongue-fuck?* □ *One more tongue-fuck, and we'll call it quits.* **2.** to perform an act of oral sex involving the tongue on someone. (See note 31.) □ *She wanted me to tongue-fuck her, but I begged off.* □ *We caught these two dames tongue-fucking, and they didn't stop till they were through.*

tonsil hockey   ['ton(t)sl̩ hɑki] **1.** an act of oral sex performed on the penis; fellatio. (Refers to the tonsils at the back of the throat being struck with the penis or with semen. Mostly jocular. See note 31.) □ *How about a little tonsil hockey, babe?* □ *Give him a good round of tonsil hockey, and you've got a customer for life.* **2.** an act of French kissing. □ *The two kids spent the rest of the evening playing tonsil hockey.* □ *No tonsil hockey for me. I don't want to catch something.*

Tonto   ['tɑnto] an Amerindian who betrays his race to Caucasian Americans. (Patterned on *Uncle Tom.* Refers to the Amerindian character who played a supporting and perhaps subservient role to the Lone Ranger in the radio and television series *The Lone Ranger.* Also a term of address. See caution at note 1; see use as a slur at note 2.)

tool   [tul] **1.** the penis. (See note 8 for examples; see note 31.) **2.** a stupid or obnoxious male. (Compare to *prick.*) □ *You stupid tool! You really got cheated!* □ *Don't be such a tool! Fight for your rights.*

tool bag   the scrotum. (See *tool.* See note 31.) □ *He's got a little itch on his tool bag, I guess. That's why he's scratching.* □ *Are you fiddling with your tool bag, or what?*

tool-check   a check of the male genitals for venereal disease. (Military. See also *pecker-checker.* Intended as jocular. See note 31.)

□ *All right, you guys, line up for tool-check!* □ *Time for a tool-check. Everybody up on deck!*

toolshed the vagina. (A jocular match for the *tool*. Not widely known, but easily understood. See notes 6 and 31; see note 12 for examples.)

toot [tut] **1.** to break wind anally. (A euphemism for *fart*. See note 31.) □ *Who tooted?* □ *Man, I gotta get outa here and toot.* **2.** a noisy release of intestinal gas through the anus. (See note 31.) □ *Who made that rotten-smelling toot?* □ *That wasn't a toot, that was a thunderstorm.*

toss in the hay AND **roll in the hay** an act of sex, especially if spontaneous or hasty. (As if the act were performed hidden in a stack of hay. See note 31.) □ *She's good for a toss in the hay anytime.* □ *I need more outa life than just a roll in the hay every now and then.*

toss off See *beat off.*

tough shit AND **T.S.** ['təf 'ʃit AND 'ti 'ɛs] tough luck; too bad. (Often an exclamation: **Tough shit!** Low. Used by both sexes.) □ *If you really think I did wrong, then tough shit! I don't care.* □ *T.S., Fred. That's really too bad.*

Tough titties! ['təf 'titiz] "Too bad!"; "Tough luck!" (See note 6.) □ *Well, tough titties! Nobody has it easy all the time.* □ *So you don't like it. Tough titties!*

towel-head AND **handkerchief-head, rag-head** someone who wears a turban as part of a national costume. (With or without the rest of the costume. Often an East Indian. See caution at note 1; see use as a slur at note 2.)

town pump a woman who is readily available for copulation with any of the men in town; a *tramp* or harlot. □ *She's nothing more than the town pump.* □ *After a few years as the town pump, she* *started charging. In three years she made enough to endow the town's library.*

tramp [træmp] a sexually free woman; a sexually promiscuous woman. (Widely known and used by both sexes.) □ *They say she's a tramp. But how would anyone really know?* □ *You're nothing but a cheap tramp! You bitch!*

transy ['træn(t)si] a transvestite. (Usually a male who dresses as a woman in public and derives great pleasure from doing so. See note 31.) □ *A couple of transies wandered by and gave us the eye.* □ *She wears so much makeup, she looks like a transy or a cheap hustler.*

trick   **1.** a sex act of any type as performed by a prostitute. (Widely known.) □ *Okay, chum, do you want a trick or don't you? I don't have time to sit here and talk.* □ *I sell it trick at a time. No package deals. None of this all-you-can-get-in-an-hour stuff.* **2.** a prostitute's customer. (See *john.* Also a general slang term referring to a woman. Widely known.) □ *Barbara's with a trick now. Will Sally do?* □ *Tell the trick I'll be right there, and not to start without me.*

troller ['trolɚ] a male exhibitionist; a *flasher.* (Jocular. See note 31.) □ *The cops hauled in a couple of trollers and two drunks. Not much for a warm Saturday night.* □ *Why is it trollers seem to favor public libraries for their little shows?*

trots [trɑts] a case of diarrhea. (Usually **the trots.** Compare to *runs.* Because one has to trot to the toilet in a hurry. See note 31.) □ *God, I've got the trots! Outa my way!* □ *I had the trots for two days running last week.*

T.S.   See *tough shit.*

tuchis   See *tochis.*

tummy-fuck AND **flat-fuck**   simulated copulation between two people, usually of the same sex, who rub their genitals together.

(Taboo. See note 4 for caution; see note 31.) □ *She said they were doing a tummy-fuck.* □ *They just did a flat-fuck, nothing really happened.*

turd [tɚd] **1.** a formed mass of fecal material; a fecal bolus. (One of the English "four-letter words." See note 31. See also *turd face, bird-turd, ghost turd.*) □ *Don't step on that dog turd.* □ *There's a turd floating in the swimming pool!* **2.** a wretched or worthless person. (Usually a male. Also a rude term of address. See note 3 for examples; see comment at note 32.) □ *You stupid turd!* □ *Don't be such a goddamn turd!*

turd face a wretched and obnoxious person. (Provocative. Also a term of address. See comment at note 32; see note 3 for examples.)

turk [tɚk] a sadistic male homosexual. (Compare to *butch*. See note 5 for examples and caution; see note 31.)

turn a trick to perform a sex act for pay as a prostitute. (Widely known. See note 31.) □ *Wanda said she turned four tricks before midnight.* □ *If I don't turn a trick soon, I'm gonna be in trouble with Freddy.*

tush AND **tushy** [tuʃ AND 'tuʃi] the buttocks. (From the Yiddish *tochis*. See note 29 for examples; see note 31.)

tushy See the previous entry.

twanger ['twæŋɚ] the penis; the erect penis. (See notes 8 and 9 for examples; see note 31.)

twat [twɑt] **1.** the female genitals; the vulva. (One of the English "four-letter words." Used in male-to-male talk and joking. Not widely known. See notes 6 and 31; see note 12 for examples.) **2.** women considered as a receptacle for the penis. (See notes 6 and 31; see examples at note 23.) **3.** male sexual release through copulation with a female. (Usually with *some*. See notes 6 and 31; see note 17 for examples.)

twisted   See *kinky.*

twister   a person obsessed with adventuresome or perverse sexual acts. (See also *swinger.* See note 31.) ☐ *Wally is a real twister. In fact, he's weird. In fact, he's sick.* ☐ *A bunch of twisters hung out in the apartment upstairs and made a lot of noise around the clock.*

U

Uncle Tom AND **Tom**   an American black [male] who betrays his race in the manner of the character Uncle Tom in *Uncle Tom's Cabin*. (Also a term of address. Considerable black-to-black derogatory use. See caution at note 1; see use as a slur at note 2.)

undy-grundy   ['əndi-grəndi]   a poke or *goose* in the anus that soils the victim's underwear. (Typical of teens and college student talk. See note 31.) □ *Sam gave Tom an undy-grundy and started a serious fight.* □ *Let's sneak up on Sam and show him what an undy-grundy is like.*

un-fucking-conscious   [ən-fəkɪŋ-'kɑntʃəs]   completely unconscious. (Taboo. See note 4 for caution; see comment at note 32.) □ *Man, did I sleep last night. I was un-fucking-conscious!* □ *Tom knocked Max un-fucking-conscious.*

un-fucking-sociable   [ən-fəkɪŋ-'soʃəbl̩]   very unsociable. (Typical of male-to-male talk. Taboo. See note 4 for caution; see comment at note 32.) □ *Why are you so un-fucking-sociable? You didn't even say hello.* □ *That was a real un-fucking-sociable thing to do!*

unt-cay   ['ənt-ke]   "cunt." (Pig Latin for all senses of *cunt*. See the entry *cunt* for meanings and examples. See notes 6 and 31.)

upchuck   See *chuck up.*

Up it!   See *Up your ass!*

up shit creek (without a paddle) AND **up the creek (without a paddle)** in very great difficulty. (The difficulty is that one has to wade or swim. The second version with *the* instead of *shit* is acceptable informal English, because many users do not recognize it as euphemistic for the version with *shit*. See comment at note 32.) □ *I'm really up the creek. Could I borrow $50?* □ *You're gonna be up shit creek without a paddle if you don't watch your step.*

Up your ass! AND **Up it!, Up yours!, Up your brown!** "Whatever the problem is, stick it up your rectum!" (A rude response to someone. Provocative. Typical of male-to-male talk.) □ *Up your ass, you stupid jerk!* □ *Up yours, you faggot!*

Up your brown! See *Up your ass!*

Up yours! See *Up your ass!*

urp See *earp.*

V

vagina juice See *cunt juice.*

V.D. ['vi 'di] "venereal disease." (A standard English euphemism. See note 31.) □ *I don't wanna catch V.D. or anything like that.* □ *Sally got V.D. from just playing around.*

velcro head ['vɛlkro hɛd] a black American. (Intended as jocular and perceived as derogatory. Not common. Refers to Negroid hair. See caution at note 1; see use as a slur at note 2.)

vige [vɑɪdʒ] the vagina. (Collegiate. Not limited to male talk and not necessarily vulgar. See notes 6 and 31; see note 12 for examples.)

W

waccoon [wæˈkun] a black WAC; a black woman who is in the WACs, the Women's Air Corps. (Military, World War II. See *coon.* Intended as jocular and perceived as derogatory. See note 6; see caution at note 1; see use as a slur at note 2.)

wack off to masturbate. (The same as *whack off.* See *beat off.* See note 21 for examples; see note 31.)

wad [wɑd] a glob of semen. (Also general slang for a stack or roll of currency or a large amount of money. See also *shoot one's wad.* Typical of male-to-male talk. See note 31.) □ *Why is there a wad floating in the john, Sam? You been pulling your pud?* □ *That's no wad. It's a nose-lunger.*

walk-up fuck a woman who permits copulation without much fuss. ("Just walk up and ask." Taboo. See note 4 for caution; and see note 31.) □ *Hell, she's just a walk-up fuck. She never said no to anybody.* □ *Why don't you comb your hair? You look like some walk-up fuck. We are high-priced professionals.*

wand-waver an exhibitionist; a *flasher.* (Jocular. See note 31.) □ *The cops hauled in the usual Saturday-night collection. Three dozen drunks and a wand-waver or two.* □ *I saw one of those wand-wavers once, right on Michigan Avenue.*

wang See *whang.*

wank off to masturbate. (The same as *whank off.* See *beat off.* See note 21 for examples; see note 31.)

WASP [wɑsp] **1.** a "white Anglo-Saxon Protestant," the stereotypical generic Caucasian American. (Originally derogatory. See caution at note 1; see use as a slur at note 2.) **2.** AND **WASPY** pertaining to a "white Anglo-Saxon Protestant," the stereotypical generic Caucasian American. □ *We live in that WASP house on the corner.* □ *I don't like your WASPY attitude.*

wazoo **1.** the penis. (See note 8 for examples; see note 31.) **2.** See *bazoo.*

weenie AND **wienie** ['wini] **1.** a stupid and inept male. (Could also be a female. Also a term of address. See note 15 for examples.) **2.** the penis. (See *wiener.* See note 8 for examples; see note 31.)

wee-wee ['wi-wi] (All senses juvenile.) **1.** urine. (See note 25 for examples; see note 31.) **2.** to urinate. (See note 26 for examples; see note 31.) **3.** the penis. (See note 8 for examples; see note 31.)

well-hung AND **hung** **1.** having large [male] genitals. (Widely known and very old. See note 31.) □ *God, that guy is well-hung.* □ *If Tom was as hung as he thinks he is, he wouldn't even say anything at all.* **2.** having large breasts. (Derived from the first sense. Not as widely known as sense 1. See note 31.) □ *God, is she well-hung!* □ *She is so hung, she's top-heavy.*

Well, smell me! See *Smell me!*

wetback ['wɛtbæk] a person of Mexican nationality or descent. (Intended and perceived as derogatory when used generically. Also a term of address. Implies that Mexicans have wet backs from swimming the Rio Grande river to sneak into the U.S. User is considered to be bigoted. See caution at note 1; see note 3 for examples; see use as a slur at note 2.)

whacker ['ʍækɚ] a male masturbator. (See note 22 for examples; see note 31.)

whacking material See *whanking material.*

whack off   See *beat off.*

wham-bam-thank-you-ma'am   a catchphrase referring to a quick act of copulation with a few words of gratitude to the female. (See notes 6 and 31.) □ *He smiled impishly at her, there were zipping sounds, then "wham-bam-thank-you-ma'am." He called it love.* □ *They ran into the spare room, and in no time— wham-bam-thank-you-ma'am—there had been a honeymoon.*

whang AND **wang**   [ʍæŋ AND wæŋ] the penis. (See note 8 for examples; see note 31.)

whanger   ['ʍæŋɚ] the penis; an erect penis. (Compare to *twanger.* See notes 8 and 9 for examples; see note 31.)

whanker   ['ʍæŋkɚ] a male masturbator. (See *whank (off).* See note 22 for examples; see note 31.)

whanking material AND **whacking material**   magazines with pictures of naked women used by males to stimulate fantasies to accompany or enable masturbation. (Seen in the movie *Airplane.* See note 31.) □ *He was very blunt about calling girlie magazines "whanking material."* □ *Sam said he had to stop off at the newsstand and pick up some whacking material.*

whank (off)   to masturbate. (The same as *wank off.* See *beat off.* See note 21 for examples; see note 31.)

whank-pit   a place where a young male masturbates. (Usually refers to a bed. See *whank off.* See note 31.) □ *Man, I'm tired. I gotta go home and get into the whank-pit.* □ *I haven't changed the sheets in my whank-pit for about a month. Or is it two?*

What (in) the fucking hell!   an angry and surprised elaboration of "What?" (Typical of male-to-male talk. Taboo. See note 4 for caution; see comment at note 32.) □ *What the fucking hell! Who are you and how'd you get in here?* □ *What in the fucking hell! The light's burned out!* □ *What the fucking hell do you think you are doing?*

What (in) the hell! an exclamation of surprise; an exclamation uttered when one is surprised or confused. (Widely known and used by both sexes.) □ *What in the hell! My wallet's gone!* □ *What the hell do you mean by that?*

What the fuck! a surprised elaboration of the exclamation "What?" (Typical of male-to-male talk. Taboo. See note 4 for caution; see comment at note 32.) □ *What the fuck! Who are you?* □ *What the fuck! My wallet's gone!*

when (the) shit hit the fan when the trouble broke out; when things became difficult. (A catchphrase usually appearing as "Where were you when the shit hit the fan?" See examples.) □ *We had one hell of an afternoon around here. Where were you when the shit hit the fan?* □ *When the shit hit the fan, we were in Argentina, thank heavens.*

whip off See *beat off.*

whip one's wire See *beat the dummy.*

whip the dummy See *beat the dummy.*

whiskey dick ['ʍɪski 'dɪk] **1.** an impotent penis due to too much alcohol. (Typical of teens and college student talk. See note 31.) □ *What's wrong with you is a case of whiskey dick.* □ *He drinks to get a whiskey dick. Some sort of strange birth control.* **2.** a male too drunk to get an erection of the penis. (Also a term of address. Typical of teens and college student talk. See note 31.) □ *Hey, whiskey dick! Getting any?* □ *The guy's a chronic whiskey dick. Why doesn't he give up the booze?*

white face a Caucasian. (Also a term of address. See caution at note 1.)

white meat a Caucasian woman considered sexually. (See also *dark meat.* Based on the white and dark meat of the chicken. Also a term of address. See notes 6 and 31; see examples at note 23; see caution at note 1.) □ *She's not bad-looking for white* *meat.* □ *I've never been around so much white meat in my life. Not sure's I like it.*

white trash   See *(poor) white trash.*

whitey   ['ʍɑɪti] **1.** a Caucasian. Sometimes intended, but not always perceived, as derogatory. Used by blacks for whites. Also a term of address.) □ *What's that whitey think she's doing down here in this neighborhood?* □ *Hey, whitey. Go back where you belong!* **2.** Caucasians in general. (Derogatory. Used by blacks for whites. Also a term of address. See caution at note 1.) □ *How does whitey expect us to find a job when he moves all the factories outa the city?* □ *I hear whitey passed some more laws and made some more programs to ease his conscience.*

whiz   [ʍɪz] **1.** to urinate. (See note 26 for examples; see note 31.) **2.** an act of urination. (See note 31.) □ *He stopped back there for a whiz.* □ *It's time for a whiz. Be with you in a minute.* **3.** urine. (See note 25 for examples; see note 31.)

Who (in) the hell!   a surprised or shocked exclamation elaborating "Who?" (Widely known and used by both sexes.) □ *Who in the hell do you think you are?* □ *Who in the hell! I thought you were dead!*

whore   [hor] **1.** a prostitute. (Usually, but not necessarily, a female. Standard English, but subject to the same restrictions as taboo language. See note 31.) □ *The entire city was overrun by whores during the convention.* □ *Some whore stopped me on the street and asked for a match.* **2.** to rent out one's body for sexual purposes. □ *She whores to make enough money to feed her kids.* □ *Stop whoring and get a job.* **3.** to patronize prostitutes. □ *His hobby is whoring and drinking.* □ *He stopped whoring when he got a disease.*

whorehouse   ['horhɑʊs] a brothel; a house of prostitution. (Standard English. Has acquired a taboo status in polite company because of its subject matter. See note 31.) □ *That's not a hotel, it's* *a whorehouse!* □ *The cops closed down a whorehouse on Fourth Street.*

Who the fuck! an angry and surprised exclamation elaborating "Who?" (Taboo. See note 4 for caution; see comment at note 32.) □ *Who the fuck! How'd you get in here?* □ *Who the fuck are you, and what do you think you're doing here?*

Why (in) the fuck! an angry and surprised exclamation elaborating "Why?" (Taboo. See note 4 for caution; see comment at note 32.) □ *Why the fuck do you think I put the lock on the door?* □ *Why in the fuck! What's the matter with you? Why'd you do that?*

Why (in) the hell! an angry and surprised exclamation elaborating "Why?" (Universally known and used by both sexes.) □ *Why in the hell are you so mad?* □ *Why the hell didn't you say so?*

wiener ['winɚ] the penis. (Compare to *weenie*. See note 8 for examples; see note 31.)

wienie See *weenie.*

wild-ass(ed) wild; unruly. (Applies to persons or things. Typical of male-to-male talk. See comment at note 32.) □ *We had a real wild-ass time at John's party.* □ *Who's that wild-assed dude I saw you with at the races?*

winkie ['wɪŋki] the penis. (Juvenile. See note 8 for examples; see note 31.)

winkle ['wɪŋkl̩] the penis. (Juvenile or jocular. See note 8 for examples; see note 31.)

wise-ass See *smart-ass.*

wise-ass(ed) smart-alecky; arrogant; cocky. (See comment at note 32.) □ *Don't be such a wise-ass jerk!* □ *What a smart-ass thing to do!*

wog AND **WOG** [wɑg] someone from an Eastern or Middle Eastern country. (A generalized racial and ethnic nickname. Originally British. Probably from "golliwog." See also *gook*. User is considered to be racially bigoted. See caution at note 1; see note 3 for examples; see use as a slur at note 2.)

woman-flesh a woman; a woman considered sexually. (See notes 6 and 31; see examples at note 23.)

wood See *peckerwood*.

woody ['wʊdi] an erection of the penis. (See note 9 for examples; see note 31.)

wool [wʊl] **1.** the female pubic hair. (See notes 6 and 31; see note 24 for examples.) **2.** women considered as objects for copulation. (See notes 6 and 31; see examples at note 23.)

wop [wɑp] an Italian; a person of Italian descent. (Usually and perceived as derogatory. Possibly from Italian dialect *guappo*. Sometimes capitalized. User is considered to be bigoted. See caution at note 1; see note 3 for examples; see use as a slur at note 2.)

wop special any sort of "special" Italian food, such as a salad or pasta dish. (Considered derogatory. This has appeared on restaurant menus.) □ *The man came into the restaurant and ordered the wop special.* □ *Look at this menu! It lists a salad called a wop special! Imagine!*

working girl a prostitute. (Euphemism.) □ *How many tricks does a working girl have to turn a week to make ends meet?* □ *Fourth Street has become a meeting place for working girls and the like.*

work one's ass off AND **work one's butt off**   to work very hard. (Widespread. See comment at note 32.)   □ *It was really busy at the shop. I worked my ass off all day.*   □ *I'm tired of working my butt off for low pay.*

work one's butt off   See the previous entry.

worms   [wɚmz] noodles; spaghetti noodles. (A food-dirtying term.)   □ *Oh, it's worms again tonight!*   □ *Wouldn't you like another helping of worms?*

worms in blood   ['wɚmz ɪn 'bləd] Spaghetti noodles in tomato sauce. (A food-dirtying term.)   □ *There's nothing I like better than worms in blood for dinner.*   □ *Are we having worms in blood again tonight?*

Y

yank one's strap See *beat the dummy.*

yank someone's crank [ˈjæŋk...ˈkræŋk] to tease a male sexually. (Literally, to tug at his penis. Also in general slang use with no sexual reference or restriction. See note 31.) □ *Don't pay any attention to her. She's just yanking your crank.* □ *Come on, stop yanking my crank and let's get it on!*

yellow-black an American black whose skin is a yellowish color. (Compare to *high-yellow.* Intended and perceived as derogatory. User is considered to be racially bigoted. See caution at note 1; see note 3 for examples.)

yellow nigger an East Asian [including Japanese] or Southeast Asian; a person of the Mongoloid race. (Intended and perceived as derogatory and demeaning. User is considered to be racially bigoted. See caution at note 1; see note 3 for examples; see use as a slur at note 2.)

yid [jɪd] a Jewish person. (Intended and perceived as derogatory. From *Yiddish.* User is considered to be bigoted and antisemitic. See caution at note 1; see note 3 for examples; see use as a slur at note 2.)

ying-yang [ˈjɪŋ-jæŋ] the penis. (Jocular and juvenile. See note 8 for examples; see note 31.)

You bet your (sweet) ass!   "You can be quite certain about that!"; "You are absolutely correct!"   □ *I'll be there all right. You bet your sweet ass!* □ *You bet your ass I'll be on time! Don't worry about it!*

Z

zigaboo [ˈzɪgəbu] an American black. (Intended and perceived as derogatory. Not common. Compare to *jigaboo,* on which this word may be patterned. User is considered to be racially bigoted. See caution at note 1; see note 3 for examples; see use as a slur at note 2.)

zig-zig [ˈzɪg-zɪg] copulation. (Based on a French expression. Originally military. See note 17 for examples.)

zip [zɪp] a stupid person, especially the enemy during wartime. (Usually applied to a foreigner. From "zero intelligence potential." Also a term of address. User is considered to be racially bigoted. See caution at note 1.) □ *If these zips don't get into the cave where it's safe, there's gonna be a lot less of 'em.* □ *Where is that zip with my coffee? What do I pay him for, anyway?*

NOTES

Many of the notes are followed by lists of words to which the notes apply. Sometimes the user is advised to consult the individual entries for each expression in the list for further information. Many of the notes have examples that show how the words in the lists are actually used. Each example begins with the □ symbol. In some instances, each of the words in the list can be inserted into each example. The swung dash symbol "~" shows where the expressions in the lists fit in each example. In some of the notes there are suggested alternate terms that are not usually forbidden in American English. For many of the categories of terms, there are no polite substitutions, however.

Note 1.

Use caution with nicknames and epithets for personal or national types. Use of these expressions may cause trouble for the person who uses them. If used in the presence of a person described by the term, the person may be insulted, angered, or provoked to violence. Even when a person described by one of these terms is not present, the very use of one of these terms may suggest to other people that the user is irrationally hostile to members of the group being described. Persons in whose presence these terms are used can be offended, believing that the users of such terms assume that their audience agrees with the insults. Virtually none of these terms would *ever* be used by a polite, educated person, and only less refined and poorly educated persons use them on an exclusive basis.

Note 2.

LIST A contains terms that have been used as verbal weapons for national, ethnic, and personal types. The caution at note 1 applies to all of these terms. Although these terms are usually recognized as racial, national, ethnic, or religious slurs, some of them are used as intimate epithets between members of the group described or under other special conditions.

LIST A. *ace boon coon, ace of spades, alligator bait, banana, bean-eater, beaner, boogie, brown, buck nigger, Buddha head, burrhead, Canuck, chili-eater, chink, chocolate, chocolate drop, Christ-killer, clipped-dick, coals, coon, cut-cock, Dago, darky, dinge, dink, dothead, eggplant, gink, gook, goulash, goy, gray, greaser, gringo, ground ape, Guinea, halfbreed, handkerchief-head, Hebe, Heeb, Heebie, high-yellow, hooknose, house nigger, Hun, hunkie, hunky, JAP, Jap, Jeff, Jesus screamer, jew(ish) flag, jibagoo, jig, jigaboo, jungle bunny, kike, kraut, Mex, Mick, mockie, nigger, niggra, Nip, oreo, Packie, Paddy, pepper-belly, Polack, porker, porky, powder burn, Rachel, raghead, redskin, rice-belly, Russki, shade, shanty Irish, shine, shoofly, silk, skid mark, slant, slanteye(s), slope, smear, spade, spear-chucker, spic, splib, spook, taco, thicklips, Tom, Tonto, towel-head, Uncle Tom, velcro head, waccoon, WASP, wetback, wog, wop, yellow nigger, yid, zigaboo.*

Examples of slurs: □ *You stupid ~! Go back where you came from!* □ *I'd always heard you ~s were dumb, but I didn't know how dumb till now!* □ *Wouldn't you know that a ~ would do something like this?* □ *I didn't know they let ~s in here.* □ *You Goddamn stupid ~! Go back to your ~ friends!* □ *There's a million or two too many ~s on this planet.*

Specific examples of intimate epithets: □ *Come over here, you silly old coon, and give me a kiss.* □ *You may be a wop, but you're my wop and I love you.* □ *Come on! We slants*

gotta stick together. □ *Speaking as one spade to another,
there's gotta be some changes made around here.*

Note 3.

LIST B contains terms that have been used as strong verbal
weapons. See caution at note 1. The terms in LIST B are
usually uttered with the intention of punishing or hurting.
All of them are provocative to some extent and all are used
as a substitute for physical violence or to accompany physical violence. See also the comments at notes 1 and 2.

LIST B. *A.H., A-hole, asshole, ass-wipe, bastard, boy,
buck nigger, bug-fucker, bulldiker, bull-dagger, bulldyker,
Christ-killer, clipped-dick, cocksucker, coon, cut-cock,
Dago, dick-sucker, dike, dyke, fag, faggot, fairy, fruit, fruitcake, fruiter, fuckhead, fuck-shit, fuck-up, ground ape,
homo, Jew-boy, jungle bunny, kike, lez, lezbo, lezzie, Mick,
Micky, Mike, mother(-fucker), muh-fuh, nigger, nigger-
lover, niggra, pansy, Polack, queer, Sheeny, shmuck, son
of a bitch, spade, spic, spook, thicklips, turd, turd face,
wetback, wog, wop, yellow-black, yellow nigger, yid, zigaboo.*

□ *You listen to me, you stupid ~. Shut up and get out!* □
You Goddamn ~! I hate your guts! □ *What can you expect
from a ~ like that?* □ *Hey, ~! What're you doing here?* □
I won't even talk to a ~ like him.

Note 4.

LIST C contains the words and expressions containing the
taboo word *fuck*. The taboo is in effect primarily when the
intended audience MAY contain women, children, and/or
genteel males. Otherwise these expressions are in wide, but
not universal, use. Genteel persons of either sex would
never use any of the following expressions. Such persons
might not even know what the following expressions mean
and might not know anyone who does know or use them.
The use of this type of expression is frequent in all-male

groups, especially in the military services. There is ample reason to believe that there is more female use of the word in the last two decades, but the basic prohibition against their free use in public persists. Examples of use are found at the individual entries.

LIST C. *abso-fucking-lutely, ass-fuck, bug-fucker, bullfuck, bunny fuck, butt-fuck, cluster fuck, dry fuck, fast-fuck, father-fucker, F-ing around, finger-fuck, fist-fuck, flat-fuck, flying-fuck, free-fucking, French-fried-fuck, fuck, fuckable, Fuck a dog!, Fuck a duck!, fuck around, fuck around with someone, fuck around with something, fuck-athon, fuck-brained, fuck bunny, fucked out, fucked up, fucker, fuckery, fuck-film, fuck-freak, fuckhead, fuck-headed, fuck-hole, fuck-house, fucking, fucking machine, fucking-rubber, Fuck it!, Fuck it (all)!, fuck like a bunny, fuck off, fuck one's fist, fuck-shit, fuck someone around, fuck someone or something up, fuck someone over, fuck someone's mind (up), fuck up, fuck-up, Fuck you!, fuck with someone or something, give a fuck about someone or something, Go fuck a duck!, Go fuck yourself!, head-fucker, Holy fuck!, honey fuck, I don't give a flying-fuck, I don't give a French-fried-fuck, If that don't fuck all!, im-fucking-possible, irre-fucking-sponsible, Like fuck!, m.f., mind-fuck(er), mind-fuck someone, mother(-fucker), mother-fucking, pity fuck, Rat fuck!, shit-fuck, star-fucker, sucky-fucky, tongue-fuck, tummy-fuck, un-fucking-conscious, un-fucking-sociable, walk-up fuck, What (in) the fucking hell!, What the fuck!, Who the fuck!, Why (in) the fuck!*

Note 5.

LIST D contains rude names for homosexual men and women. The caution in note 1 applies to all these terms. All the following terms are usually used as verbal weapons. Some of them can be used as intimate or jocular nicknames as with LIST A in note 2. Polite terms include *gay [person], homosexual [man], male homosexual, lesbian, homosexual woman,* and *female homosexual.*

LIST D. *ag-fay, aunt, aunteater, auntie, bufu, bulldiker, bull-dagger, bull-dyker, butterfly queen, chicken queen, closet queen, closet queer, dike, dinge queen, drag queen, dyke, fag, faggot, fairy, father-fucker, flamer, flaming queen, foot queen, fruit, fruitcake, fruiter, gay, homo, lez, lezbo, lezzie, pansy, peer-queer, queer, queer-beer, queervert, rug muncher, screaming queen, suck queen, turk.*

☐ *I won't sit next to no ~!* ☐ *The whole bar was full of ~!* ☐ *I heard that Bill has declared himself a ~.* ☐ *There's too many damn ~s around here!* ☐ *Let's go out and bash a ~ or two tonight.*

Note 6.

Women may take exception to the terms in LIST E. That does not mean they would not use them, but that they are potentially "offensive," often because of the topic, but also because of the "slant" or "profane intent" of the expression. To treat the subject of women or women's bodies in a trivial or mocking fashion is regarded as highly offensive by some women. LIST E contains the terms to which could offend. These terms are also forbidden on other grounds also.

LIST E. *ass, ass-man, ball-breaker, ball-busting, balloons, ballsy, bazoom(s), bazoongies, bearded clam, beaver, beaver-flick, beaver-retriever, beaver shot, begonias, bezongas, big brown eyes, bitch, bitchy, boody, boosiasms, bottom, box, bra-buster, broad, bumps, bunch-punch, bush, can, cans, chichis, clit, clitty, cock-teaser, cooch, coozey, coozie, crack, crawl, cream, cunt, cunt cap, cunt fart, cunt hair, cunt-hooks, cunt hound, cunt juice, cuntrag, cunt-sucker, cunt-teaser, curse, dark meat, decunt, dicked, diver, dogess, douche-bag, dugs, feel someone up, finger-fuck, flat-chested, flopper-stopper, friend, fuck, fuckable, fuckathon, fuck bunny, fucker, fuck-hole, fur-pie, gang-bang, gang-shag, garbanzos, gash, geechie, george, Get any?, get a piece of ass, get some ass, get some cunt, Getting any?, hair-pie, headlights, ho, hole, honkers, hooters, hose, hunk of ass, hunk of tail, jugs, knockers, kweef, laid, lay, leg, leg-man, lemons, maracas, melons, moose, muff-diver, muffins, munch the bearded clam, murphies, nookie, nooky, notch, on the moon cycle, on the rag, O.T.R., pair, paps, pee hole, piece of ass, piece of snatch, piece of tail, pogie, poke, poon tang, potatoes, prick-teaser, pussy, pussy-fart, pussy-whipped, rag, rag time, red sails in the sunset, ride the cotton bicycle, ride the rag, ride the white horse, rug, screw, screwed, skin-mag, skirt, slash, slit, slot, slut, snatch, split-tail, spread beaver, spud, taco, tail, T. and A., thing, tit hammock, tit job, titless wonder, tits, tits and ass, titty, toolshed, Tough titties!, twat, unt-cay, vagina juice, vige, waccoon, wham-bam-thank-you-ma'am, white meat, woman-flesh, wool.*

Note 7.

LIST F contains terms for the human [female] breasts. With the exception of *boob(s)* and *tits*, these terms are mostly used by males, usually in appreciation. *Paps* and *dugs* are disparaging. A woman discussing her own breasts with another woman is likely to use the term breasts or perhaps *boobs* if less formal language is used. Polite terms include *breasts* and *bosom*. (The examples are all plural even when the entry forms in LIST F are singular. See the individual entries for comments on singular and plural.)

LIST F. *balloons, bazoom(s), bazoongies, begonias, bezongas, big brown eyes, boobs, booby, boosiasms, bra-buster, bumps, cans, chichis, dugs, garbanzos, headlights, honkers, hooters, jugs, knockers, lemons, maracas, melons, muffins, murphies, paps, potatoes, spuds, tits, titties.*

□ *Wow, look at the ~ on that dame!* □ *What a pair of ~!*
□ *How would you like to have a date with a chick with ~ like that?* □ *If I had ~ like that, I'd be in the movies, or something that would take me out of this rat hole.* □ *One*

look at her ~ and Wally knew he was going to have a fine evening.

Note 8.

LIST G contains terms for the penis. Most of these terms are jocular, and many refer to shape or sexual function. Some terms on this list have special meanings, and each entry should be consulted for special comments. See also note 15. Polite terms include *penis* and *phallus.* Euphemisms include: *[male] member* and *[male] organ.* The terms *privates* and *private parts* refers to both the penis and testicles, and these terms are also used for the female genitalia. See *stones* for a list of terms for the testicles.

LIST G. *bald-headed hermit, bug-fucker, cock, crank, crotch-cobra, dick, ding-dong, dingle, dingle-dangle, dingus, dingy, dink, dipstick, dong, doodle, dork, dummy, fucker, hammer, hose, jammy, jock, Johnson, joint, Jones, joy stick, love sausage, meat, needle dick, one-eyed pants mouse, pecker, peenie, pee-pee, pencil dick, peter, pisser, poker, prick, pud, putz, ramrod, shmuck, short-arm, skin flute, thing, third leg, tip, tool, twanger, wang, wazoo, weenie, wee-wee, whang, whanger, wiener, winkie, winkle, ying-yang.*

☐ *Hey, cover your ~ before you come running down the hall!* ☐ *As his towel dropped, one hand darted down to conceal his ~.* ☐ *God, Tom, is that ~ all you got when they were passing them out?* ☐ *With a ~ like that, you ought to be in movies—or something.* ☐ *He was in love with his ~ from the day he was born!* ☐ *When he thought of her, his ~ began to come alive.*

Note 9.

LIST H contains terms for an erection of the penis. The subject is usually forbidden. The only candidate for a polite term is *erection.* Anatomical expressions include: *erection [of the penis]* and *[penile] erection.* An evasive adjectival expression is *aroused.*

LIST H. *bone, boner, fucker, hammer, hard-on, piss hard-on, poker, ramrod, stiffy, twanger, wang, whanger, woody.*

□ *He got a ~ during the movie.* □ *I never wanted to dance with a girl, because I was always afraid of getting a ~.* □ *He rocked and rocked, trying to remember what it was like to have a steel-hard ~.* □ *A man's ~ is just another piece of mechanical equipment that he must keep finely tuned and ready to function.* □ *The more he tried to suppress his ~, the harder it got.*

Note 10.

LIST I contains terms meaning to have or get an erection. Consult the individual entry for specific information. The examples below are for the specific entries.

LIST I. *get it on, get it up, have a bone on, have a hard-on, have lead in one's pencil, lift up.*

Specific examples: □ *Tod couldn't remember when he last had a bone on.* □ *He hasn't had lead in his pencil for years.* □ *Excuse me, I have a hard-on.* □ *Come on, get it up, you wimp!* □ *I'm too drunk to get it on.* □ *The sea air made him lift up.*

Note 11.

Use caution with the use of the name of God and related expressions. It is regarded as offensive by many people of various religions to make reference to the deity in a profane or blasphemous manner. Nonetheless, such expressions now dominate everyday conversation, and they are often heard on radio and television. This does not mean that such expressions are acceptable to everyone. Examples are given at each entry. There is a vast number of additional terms in this category.

LIST J. *Godamighty!*, *God-awful*, *Goddamn (it)!*, *Holy Christ*, *Holy God!*, *Holy Kerist!*, *inde-goddamn-pendent*, *Jesus (Christ)!*, *My God!*

Note 12.

LIST K contains terms for the female genitals. Most such expressions are considered rude and are typically heard in male-to-male talk and very low female talk. These terms would not be used in polite or genteel company under any circumstances. Some expressions are meant to be jocular. Many are very well-known and approach being vulgar—but standard—English. See the individual entries for further information. The most typical, polite term is *vagina,* even when not referring solely to the vaginal canal. Otherwise, *female genitals* and *female genitalia,* usually expressed as "her genitals," is used. Anatomical terms tend to be specific Latin terms for the individual structures that make up the female urinary and reproductive organs: *vulva, labia majora, labia minora, clitoris, urethra, vagina, cervix,* and *uterus.* Some of the terms in LIST K actually make reference to the individual structures. The terms *privates* and *private parts* can be used, but these terms are also used for the male genitalia.

LIST K. *ass, bearded clam, beaver, boody, bottom, box, can, cock, cooch, coozey, coozie, cunt, fuck-hole, gash, hole, meat, nookie, nooky, notch, pee hole, pisser, pogie, poon tang, pussy, slash, slit, slot, snatch, tail, thing, tool-shed, twat, vige.*

☐ *Man, I'd really like to get into her* ~. ☐ *I bet she has a fine* ~. ☐ *Damn! You can see her* ~ *through her bikini!* ☐ *I've got something special for her* ~. ☐ *I've got a little friend who's longing for all the comforts of her* ~. ☐ *I'd go exploring in her* ~ *any day.*

Note 13.

LIST L contains transitive verbs meaning to copulate with someone. These expressions mean for someone, usually a male, to perform the sexual act upon someone else, usually a female. Since there is no unambiguous, standard, transitive verb in English that bears this meaning, the meaning is expressed in the definitions with the phrase "copulate [with] someone." All these terms, in addition to being too rude for genteel people, are euphemistic to some degree. Some terms on the list have special meanings. Consult the individual entries for details. See also note 14. Polite terms are euphemistic or evasive: *make love to someone, have sex with someone, have intercourse with someone.*

LIST L. *ball, bang, bob, boff, boink, bonk, bop, crawl, dick, do, fork, frig, fuck, gang-bang, george, hose, hump, jump, lay, poke, pork, pump, screw, scrog, scrump.*

□ *I really would like to ~ her!* □ *How can I possibly have a good time when all you can talk about is how much you want to ~ me?* □ *I wouldn't let that guy ~ me if he offered me the moon!* □ *He drank so much that by the time he got around to ~ing her, his stamina left him.* □ *Her pimp said she could let him ~ her or she could die. It was her choice.*

Note 14.

LIST M contains intransitive or reflexive verbs meaning to copulate. This is almost the same set of verbs as in note 13, but these are used intransitively or reflexively. Polite terms are euphemistic or evasive: *make love, have sex, have intercourse.*

LIST M. *ball, bang, bob, boff, boink, bonk, boogie, bop, dick, fork, frig, fuck, gang-bang, george, get down, grind, hose, hump, screw, scrog, scrump.*

□ *They both wanted to ~ so bad, they could taste it.* □ *The headmaster caught them ~ing in the closet.* □ *Did you two sneak off somewhere to ~?* □ *Hey, babe, let's go ~!* □

They set out to ~ each other four times, and they almost made it.

Note 15.

LIST N contains expressions referring to the penis used as epithets for despised males. These phallic terms are used as derogatory terms for males of any age. The most common is *prick*, followed closely by *shmuck* and *dork*. The latter two have been in use for a despised male for so long that they are more widely known in this sense than for penis. *Dork,* in particular, is even applied to females, especially by young people. Most of the terms can be used as verbal weapons in the appropriate context. See the individual entry for specific details.

LIST N. *dickhead, dildo, dipstick, dork, needle dick, peckerhead, prick, shmuck, tool, weenie.*

□ *What a stupid ~!* □ *Look here, you ~, watch where you are going!* □ *What a ~! They don't make 'em any dumber.* □ *God, what a ~!* □ *I shouldn't expect any better from a ~ like you.*

Note 16.

LIST O contains terms for a specific single act of copulation. A polite expression is "an act of [sexual] intercourse." Most of the expressions in LIST O are specialized.

LIST O. *bang, bunny fuck, fast-fuck, flying-fuck, fuck, hump, lay, pity fuck, quick one, quickie, score, screw.*

Specific examples: □ *He's good for a lay.* □ *I need a good screw. How about it?* □ *All you ever want from me is a hump! I can cook too, you know!* □ *He stopped off at his girlfriend's house for a lay.* □ *They like to start off the day with a bang.* □ *Don't you ever want any more than a fast-fuck?* □ *He's good for a bunny-fuck, but that's all.* □ *You don't really love me. That was just a pity fuck!* □ *I thought only cartoon characters did flying-fucks.*

Note 17.

LIST P contains general terms for an act or period of copulation; i.e., some copulation. Compare to the terms listed at note 23 which focus on the bodies of women. The meaning can be expressed politely and evasively as *sexual release*.

LIST P. *ass, boody, boom-boom, bush, cooch, coozey, coozie, crack, cunt, nookie, nooky, notch, poon tang, pussy, skirt, snatch, tail, target practice, twat, zig-zig.*

Specific examples: □ *God, I need some pussy!* □ *I gotta get off this boat and get some cooch!* □ *Let's go out and get some snatch!* □ *It's skirt that you need, old boy, some of that good old skirt.* □ *Where can a gentleman get some target practice in this hellhole of a town?* □ *If I don't get some ass pretty soon, I'll die.* □ *Some tail would cure me. No question about it.* □ *I need some shore time for zig-zig and stuff like that.*

Note 18.

LIST Q contains expressions for an act of masturbation, usually for a female. See the individual entries for specifics.

LIST Q. *finger-fuck, finger-job, hand job.*

□ *I think she'd rather have a ~ than the real thing.* □ *She snuck off during the picnic for a solitary ~.* □ *Who would think a prim old girl like Gert would go for a ~?* □ *This weird movie was just one shot after another of the same dame doing a ~.*

Note 19.

LIST R contains phrases meaning to masturbate. Most of the phrases meaning to masturbate refer to male masturbation, and most of them are clever, colorful disguises. The technical term is *masturbate*. An evasive euphemism is *abuse oneself*.

LIST R. *beat the dummy, beat the meat, beat one's meat, beat the pup, choke the chicken, frig oneself, fuck one's fist, get a hold of oneself, play with oneself, pound one's meat, pull one's pud, pull one's wire, pump ship, take oneself in hand, whip one's wire, whip the dummy, yank one's strap.*

□ *He left the room in a hurry. Probably went out to ~.* □ *I guess he can ~. He can't seem to do anything else right.* □ *He was so tired, he couldn't even ~.* □ *The old man suggested that the recruit ought to ~ rather than risk disease.* □ *Oh, go ~, you horny bastard!*

Note 20.

LIST S contains transitive verb expressions meaning to masturbate someone, usually a male. *Finger-fuck* is for females only, as in □ *She finger-fucked her friend who had come for the weekend.*

LIST S. *diddle, finger-fuck, fist-fuck, stroke.*

Examples (excluding *finger-fuck*): □ *She ~ed him for a while, then he did it again.* □ *He wanted to take his friend somewhere and ~ him.* □ *Do you want me just to ~ you, or did you have something else in mind?*

Note 21.

LIST T contains expressions meaning [for a male] to masturbate himself. Most of them could also be used transitively.

LIST T. *ball off, beat off, diddle, fist-fuck, fuck off, jag off, jack off, jerk off, pull oneself off, toss off, wack off, wank off, whack off, whank off, whip off.*

Specific examples: □ *I don't ball off anymore because it gives me pimples.* □ *So they all got in a circle to jack off together.* □ *Don't pull yourself off so much! It'll stunt your growth.* □ *Fred learned to whank off quickly and quietly while everyone else was asleep.* □ *He preferred to diddle himself rather than have to negotiate with the haughty women of the streets. □ He stood in the corner, whipping off. □ He ran to the john to toss off, and then he came back all red in the face.*

Note 22.

LIST U contains derogatory expressions for a male who masturbates, usually habitually.

LIST U. *chicken-choker, jackoff, jagoff, jerkoff, whacker, whanker.*

□ He doesn't care for women. He's a confirmed ~. □ I can't spend the rest of my life as a ~! □ Every kid goes through a stage when he's a hopeless ~. □ At least you ~s will not catch anything from your hands.

Note 23.

LIST V contains names for women or women's bodies considered as objects of sexual interest. Compare to the terms at note 17 that focus on the sexual act itself. The terms are frequently used with *piece of.* Some of these terms are specialized. See the appropriate entry.

LIST V. *ass, beaver, boody, bush, cooch, coozey, coozie, cunt, dark meat, leg, nookie, nooky, notch, poon tang, pussy, skirt, snatch, split-tail, tail, twat, white meat, woman-flesh, wool.*

Specific examples: *□ The beach was wall-to-wall twat! □ What the place needed was a little poon tang for decoration. □ Sharon is one fine little split-tail, don't you think? □ That campus is just overrun with hot snatch. □ Have you ever seen so much gorgeous woman-flesh? □ There's some good boody in L.A., for sure!*

Note 24.

LIST W contains terms for the pubic hair, usually female pubic hair.

LIST W. *bush, cunt hair, rug, wool.*

□ *She had (a) lush ~ that hid almost everything.* □ *He wanted her to shave her ~, but she said no.* □ *Your ~ is coming out the side of your bathing suit, sweetie.* □ *Wally wanted a woman with no ~.*

Note 25.

LIST X contains terms for urine. It is the juvenile terms for bodily wastes that dominate. See also notes 26 through 28.

LIST X. *P., pee, pee-pee, piss, tea, tee-tee, tinkle, wee-wee, whiz.*

□ *Is this ~ or cider?* □ *Why is ~ yellow?* □ *There's ~ all over the floor!* □ *The doctor wanted me to put my ~ in a bottle.*

Note 26.

LIST Y contains terms meaning to urinate.

LIST Y. *go, leak, make, P., pee, peep, pee-pee, piss, pump ship, slash, squeeze the lemon, take a leak, take a piss, tinkle, wee-wee, whiz.*

□ *I gotta ~.* □ *He would never ~ in public.* □ *She left the room to ~.* □ *Let's go ~ and have a smoke.*

Note 27.

LIST Z contains terms meaning dung. Many of them refer to specific kinds of dung. Consult the individual entries for specifics.

LIST Z. *bat-shit, birdshit, bird-turd, caca, cack, crap, crapola, doo-doo, grunt, horseshit, kaka, poo, poop, poo-poo, shit.*

□ *You got some ~ on your shoe.* □ *That stuff smells like ~ or something similar.* □ *Is that ~, or what?* □ *His coat was about the color of fresh ~.*

Note 28.

LIST AA contains terms meaning to defecate.

LIST AA. *cack, doodle, doo-doo, drop one's load, dump, dump one's load, george, go, grunt, poo, poop, poo-poo, shit, take a crap, take a dump, take a shit, take a squat.*

□ *He said he had to ~.* □ *I gotta go ~.* □ *It's better if you ~ in the morning.* □ *He ducked off into the woods to ~.*

Note 29.

The expressions in LIST BB below all refer to the human buttocks. See also note 30 for terms used specifically for the anus.

LIST BB. *ass, boody, bottom, buns, butt, can, patoot, patootie, rear end, rump, tochis, tokkis, tokus, tuchis, tush, tushy.*

□ *Man, look at the ~ on that guy!* □ *When they were passing out ~, you got more than your share.* □ *A lot of broads don't care about what you got in front as long as you got (a) good ~.* □ *When he turned his back, she kicked him square in the ~.* □ *I like a man with a nice tight and tiny ~.*

Note 30.

The expressions in LIST CC below refer to the anus, usually of humans. See also note 29 for terms used specifically for the buttocks.

LIST CC. *asshole, bazoo, brown, brown hole, bunghole, butthole, cornhole, dirt-chute, patoot, patootie, redeye, shit-hole, slop-chute, wazoo.*

☐ *Well, doc, you see, I got this pain in my* ~. ☐ *Looks like this stuff came outa somebody's* ~. ☐ *If you don't like it, you can stick it up your* ~. ☐ *There's this little fish that swims right up your* ~ *if you don't watch out.* ☐ *If the universe has a(n)* ~, *it's somewhere in this city.*

Note 31.

The very large collection of expressions found in LIST DD below represents all the expressions in this dictionary that are forbidden because of *what they refer to,* not necessarily because the particular words used in the expression are taboo. That is, all the expressions in LIST DD refer to forbidden *topics* or *subjects.* Any additional words for the same subjects would also be forbidden. Compare with LIST EE at note 32.

LIST DD. *ass-fuck, asshole, ass-wipe, bald-headed hermit, ball, ball off, balls, B. and D., bang, barf, bat-shit, bazoo, bearded clam, beat off, beat the dummy, beat the meat, beat one's meat, beat the pup, beaver, beaver shot, beef, beef-hearts, bend down for someone, bent, bi, bigass, birdshit, bite the big one, bi-trade, blow, blow a fart, blow job, blue balls, B.M., bob, boff, boink, bone, bone addict, boner, bonk, boob, booby, boody, booger, boom-boom, boosiasms, bop, bottom, box, box lunch, boy, bra-buster, break someone's balls, bring someone off, bring someone on, brown, brown hole, bufu, bug-fucker, bullfuck, bumps, bunch-punch, bunghole, bunny fuck, bush, butt, butter, butt-fuck, butthole, butt-wipe, caca, cack, can, cannibal, cans, cheezer, cherry, chichis, chicken-choker, chicken-grabbing, chism, choke the chicken, chones, chuck up, circle-jerk, clap, clit, cluster fuck, cob, cock, cock-cheese, cock ring, cocksucker, cock-teaser, cojones, come, cooch, coozey, coozie, cop a cherry, cop a feel, cornhole, cowshit, crabwalk, crack, cradle-custard, crap, crapola, crappy, crawl, cream, creamed, cream (in) one's pants, cream one's jeans, crotch-cheese, crotch-cobra, crotch rot, crud, crystals, cum, cum freak, cunt, cunt fart, cunt hair, cunt juice, cunt-rag, cunt-sucker, cunt-teaser, curse, cut a fart, cut one, cut the cheese, decunt, dick, dicked, dickhead, dick-sucker, dicky-licker, diddle, dildo, ding-dong, dingle, dingleberry, dingle-dangle, dingus, dingy, dink, dipstick, dirt-chute, dive a muff, diver, do, do a grind, do a number on something, dodads, dog-log, dog-fashion, dog-style, dog-ways, dohickies, dong, doodle, doo-doo, dork, do the story with someone, double-barreled slingshot, dry fuck, dry hump, duck-butt, duck-butter, dugs, dummy, dump, earp, eat, eat at the Y, Eat me!, Eat shit!, family jewels, fart, fast-fuck, father-fucker, F.B., feel hairy, feel someone up, F-ing, F-ing around, finger-fuck, fist-fuck, flash, flasher, flat-chested, flat-fuck, flopper-stopper, flute(r), flying-fuck, fomp, fork, Fork you!, free-fucking, French, Frencher, French-fried-fuck, fricking, friend, frig, frig oneself, fuck, fuckable, fuckathon, fuck-brained, fuck bunny, fucker, fuck-film, fuck-freak, fuck-hole, fucking machine, fucking-rubber, fuck like a bunny, fuck off, fuck one's fist, fur-pie, gang-bang, gang-shag, garbanzos, gash, george, get a hold of oneself, Get any?, get a piece of ass, get down, get horizontal, get in, get in(to) her pants, get it in, get it off, get it on, get it up, get one's ashes hauled, get one's knob polished, get one's nuts off, get one's rocks off, get one's shit together, get some action, get some ass, get some cunt, Getting any?, G.I. shits, gism, give head, gizzum, go, go all the way, go down on someone, golden shower, good in bed, goose, go to bed with someone, grind, group-grope, grunt, hair-pie, hammer, hand job, hard, hard-nosed, hard-on, have a bone on, have a hard-on, have hot pants (for someone), have it both ways, have lead in one's pencil, have the hots (for someone), have the rag on, head, head-cheese, head-job, headlights, hide the sausage, hole, honey fuck, honkers, hooters, hoover, horny, horseshit, hose, hose monster, hot-assed, hot to trot, How('re) they hanging?, hum job, hump, humpy, hung, hung like a bull, hustle, If you can't use it, abuse it!, jack off, jag off, jail-bait, jammy, jerk off, jism, jizz, jizzum, jock, jock itch, jockstrap, Johnson, joint, Jones, joy stick, jugs, jump, junk, kaka, kinky, knob-job, knockers, knock a woman up, kweef, laid, lard ass, lay, layed, leg, leg-man, lemons, let a fart, letch, letch after someone, letch for someone, let one, lickety-split, lift his leg, lift up, love sausage, lunger, make, make it with someone, man-eater, maracas, meat, melons, muff-diver, muffins, muncher-boy, munch the bearded clam, murphies, nads, N.D.B.F., needle dick, nips, nookie, nooky, nose-lunger, notch, nuggets, number one, number two, nuts, one-night stand, on the make, on the moon cycle, on the rag, O.T.R., oyster, P., pair, pansy, paps, paste, patoot, patootie, pecker, pecker-checker, peckerhead, pee, pee hole, peenie, peep, pee-pee, peter, peter-cheater, peter-eater, piccolo-player, piece of ass, piss, pisser, piss freak, piss hard-on, piss on someone or something, pity fuck, play doctor, play grab-ass, play hide the salami, play hide the sausage, play hide the weenie, play with oneself, pocket pool, pogie, pogostick swirl, poke, poker, poke through the whiskers, poo, poon tang, poop, poo-poo, pork, porked, porker, potatoes, pound one's meat, prick, prick-teaser, primed, pud, puke, pull a train, pull oneself off, pull one's pud, pull one's wire, pump, pump ship, pussy, pussy-bumping, pussy-fart, pussy-simple, pussy-struck, put it in, put it to someone, put lipstick on his dipstick, put (some) balls on something, put the blocks to someone, put the hard word on her, put the make on someone, putz, quick one, quickie, racked, rag, rag time, ram-job, ramrod, ream, ream-job, rear end, redeye, red sails in the sunset, ride the cotton bicycle, ride the porcelain train, ride the rag, ride the white horse, rim-job, rocks, rug, rug muncher, rump, runs, safety, San Quentin jail-bait, San Quentin quail, S.B.D., score, screw, screw around, screwed, scrog, scrump, scum, scumbag, scum-sucking, septic stick, serve head, shat, shit, shit-fuck, shit green, shit-hole, shit in one's pants, shit on someone, shit-scared, shits, shitstick, shitty, shmuck, shoot one's wad, short-arm, short-arm inspection, siff, sixty-nine, skeet, skeet-shooting, skin flick, skin flute, skirt, slash, sleep with someone, slime, slit, slop-chute, sloppy seconds, sloppy sex, slot, small-arm inspection, smell the place up, snatch, snot, snotty, split-tail, spread beaver, spud, squeeze the lemon, star-fucker, stiffy, stones, stroke, suck queen, suck someone off, sucky-fucky, swing, swing both ways, swinger, syff, tail, take a leak, take a piss, take a crap, take a dump, take a shit, take a squat, take oneself in hand, T. and A., target practice, tea, tee-tee, thing, third leg, tinkle, tip, tit hammock, tit job, tits, tits and ass, titty, tochis, toe jam, tokkis, tokus, tongue-fuck, tonsil hockey, tool, tool bag, tool-check, toolshed, toot, toss in the hay, toss off, transy, troller, trots, tuchis, tummy-fuck, turd, turk, turn a trick, tush, tushy, twanger, twat, twisted, twister, undy-grundy, unt-cay, upchuck, urp, V.D., vige, wack off, wad, walk-up fuck, wand-waver, wang, wank off, wazoo, weenie, wee-wee, well-hung, whacker, whacking material, whack off, wham-bam-thank-you-ma'am, whang, whanger, whanker, whanking material, whank, whank off, whank-pit, whip-off, whip one's wire, whip the dummy, whiskey dick, white meat, whiz, whore, whorehouse, wiener, winkie, winkle, woman-flesh, woody, wool, yank one's strap, yank someone's crank, ying-yang.*

Note 32.

The expressions in LIST EE below are forbidden because of the taboo words *used in expressing the meaning,* not necessarily because of what the listed expressions refer to. Compare to LIST DD in note 31.

LIST EE. *abso-fucking-lutely, apeshit, ass-fuck, asshole, ass-kisser, ass-licker, ass-wipe, bad-ass, bad shit, bag ass (out of some place), ball-face, balls, bigass, big shit, bird-shit, bird-turd, bitchen, (bitchen-)twitchen, bitchin', bullfuck, butthead, bust-ass, candy-ass, candy-ass(ed), chew someone's ass out, chicken shit, chick(en) shit habit, cocksucker, cocksucking, cover one's ass, cunt,*

cunt cap, cunt-hooks, cunt hound, cunt juice, cunt-rag, cunt-sucker, day the eagle shits, dead-ass, dick-sucker, diddly-shit, dipshit, doodly-shit, drag ass around, dumb-ass, dumbshit, fart, fart around, fart hole, farting-spell, fart off, farts, fart sack, fiddle-fart, flat-ass, flat on one's ass, flying-fuck, French-fried-fuck, Fuck!, Fuck a duck!, fuck around, fuck around with someone, fuck around with something, fuck-brained, fucked out, fucked up, fuck-head, fuckheaded, fucking, Fuck it!, Fuck it (all)!, Fuck me gently!, fuck off, fuck-shit, fuck someone around, fuck someone or something up, fuck someone over, fuck some-one's mind (up), fuck up, fuck-up, fuck with someone or something, Fuck you!, full of shit, ghost turd, give a fuck (about someone or something), give a shit (about some-one or something), go apeshit over someone or some-thing, Go fuck yourself!, good shit, gripe one's ass, gripes one's butt, half-pissed, have a shit-fit, have one's ass in a crack, have one's ass in a sling, have shit for brains, head-fucker, Hell's bells (and buckets of blood)!, Holy dog shit!, Holy fuck!, Holy shit!, horse's ass, I don't give a flying-fuck, I don't give a French-fried-fuck, If that don't fuck all!, im-fucking-possible, in deep shit, inde-goddamn-pendent, in shit order, in the shit, irre-fucking-sponsible, It's no skin off my ass., jack-shit, jive-ass, kick-ass, kick-ass on some-one, kick in the ass, kick in the butt, kick some ass (around), kiss-ass, knee deep in shit, know shit about something, Like fuck!, little shit, mind-fuck(er), mind-fuck someone, monkey-fart, mother(-fucker), mother-fucking, mungshit, My ass!, on one's ass, on the make, panther piss, penis breath, pimp someone over, pimp up, pimp walk, piss, piss and vinegar, pissant, pissant around, piss around, piss-ass, piss-cutter, pissed off about someone or something, pissed (off) (at someone or something), piss elegant, pisser, pisshead, pisshouse, pissing-match, pissing-spell, piss-mean, piss off, piss on someone or something, pisspiration, piss-poor, piss someone off, piss-ugly, piss-wizz, piss(y)-faced, pussy-whipped, put one's ass on the line, put one's balls on the line, put (some) balls on something, rich-bitch, royal screwing, save someone's ass, scared fartless, scared shitless, scare the shit out of someone, Screw you!, Shee-it!, shit, shit-ass, shit-ass luck, shit-bag, shitcan, shit-eating, shit-face, shit-faced, shit-fit, shit for the birds, shithead, shitheaded, shit-hooks, shit-hot, shit-house poet, shit-kicker, shit-kicking, shit-list, shitload of something, shit locker, shit on a shingle, shit on wheels, shit out of luck, shit parade, shit-scared, shitsky, shits, shitstick, shit-stomper, shit-stompers, Shitsure!, shitty, shitty end of the stick, shit-work, smart-ass, some-one's ass is grass, sorry-ass(ed), S.O.S., stupid-ass, suck-ass, suck someone's hind tit, tight-ass, tight-ass(ed), turd, turd face, un-fucking-conscious, un-fucking-sociable, up shit creek (without a paddle), up the creek (without a pad-dle), vagina juice, What (in) the fucking hell!, What the fuck!, Who the fuck!, Why (in) the fuck!, wild-ass(ed), wise-ass, wise-ass(ed), work one's ass off, work one's butt off.